WHAT GOES ON TOUR STAYS ON TOUR

WHAT GOES ON TOUR STAYS ON TOUR

BRIAN MOORE

WITH DEBBIE BECKERMAN

**SIMON &
SCHUSTER**

London · New York · Sydney · Toronto · New Delhi

A CBS COMPANY

First published in Great Britain by Simon & Schuster UK Ltd, 2014
A CBS COMPANY

1 3 5 7 9 10 8 6 4 2

Simon & Schuster UK Ltd
1st Floor
222 Gray's Inn Road
London WC1X 8HB

www.simonandschuster.co.uk

Simon & Schuster Australia, Sydney
Simon & Schuster India, New Delhi

A CIP catalogue record for this book is available
from the British Library

ISBN: 978-0-85720-254-3
Ebook ISBN: 978-0-85720-255-0

Typeset in the UK by M Rules
Printed and bound by CPI Group (UK) Ltd, Croydon, CR0 4YY

To my tremendous editor and equally tremendous friend, Debbie, without whom this book would, literally, not have been completed.

Contents

Preface

I'm often asked if I miss playing, and the truth is that I miss it more than is healthy for someone who has been retired for nearly seventeen years. The fact is that I cannot recreate the adrenalin-fuelled battles that took place on the pitch, whatever other pastime I take up, and I know I am simply too old and unfit to play at anything approaching a decent level again.

All that said, while the thrill of combat is the essence of what we do on the pitch, it is the camaraderie and the fun off it that I miss even more. I miss my friends; I miss the verbal jousting; I miss their warmth and their humour. Nowhere are all these elements more apparent than when a team tours or plays in a tournament, and that is one reason why I have written this book.

I wanted to recount some of the highs and lows of touring, the special way in which rugby approaches the challenges thereof, and in particular the experience of playing with some of the characters with whom I was lucky enough (or not) to tour. I think that I am one of only a few people left who played and experienced tours and tournaments at all levels of the game: Junior tours (with the Old Crossleyans), England Students and England Under 23 tours, a Penguin tour to Brazil, a Barbarian sevens tournament abroad, England tours and World Cup tournaments, and tours with the most famous touring team of all, the British Lions. I counted up the number of countries I have visited through rugby, and while not all of these visits involved full tours or tournaments, they did involve playing a game of some sort where a team travelled abroad and stayed to play that game. The total number of countries came to 29.

The early chapters set out what might be called 'coarse touring': the average junior club non-professional trips that annually take place in various parts of the country and globally. The descriptions will be instantly recognisable to players who have enjoyed such tours, and will, I hope, provide an insight to senior and modern players of what still happens at that level of the game. Tour Courts – those quasi-ubiquitous rugby tour institutions – entertainment committees, tour rules and songs, all feature heavily, illustrated by examples that I hope readers will find entertaining.

Inevitably, many of the stories involve tales of drinking, often to excess; when that happens, what comes next is hardly ever edifying. The bar games and songs might be seen by some as boorish, even stupid, and readers are entitled to their views. All I will say is that those who understand the team dynamic will attest to how these things help foster team spirit. In any event, they are harmless when all is said and done, and if others don't like them, who cares? They don't have to join in. I apprehend that some people will also seek to stigmatise and caricature the stories as macho and, worse, sexist and/or homophobic. It is almost impossible to prevent those determined to be vicariously offended from being so. What I would say is that these things pertain to both male and female rugby tours, and the number of women's tours has grown hugely in the last few years. Behaviour by male and female, gay and straight teams might still be riotous and bawdy, but given that they all go in for it, and in a similar way, if they are not offended, why are you?

Later in the book I detail the development of international

tours and how they evolved from being not much above that of an amateur level to a semi- and then fully professional one. This, I hope, will be of interest to junior players who will not experience touring at a higher level, as they will see not only the differences between the latter and their own more modest sojourns abroad, but also the similarities. Conversely, when today's international players consider what used to happen on earlier tours, they will understand what they have gained and lost as a result of the game going professional. They will look with envy at the relative freedom enjoyed by their predecessors in terms of what they could do off the field and the enjoyment that went with that. But they will probably not envy or perhaps even understand how international teams put up with the relatively primitive standards of preparation, travel and accommodation.

While the book tells many stories of happenings on and off the field, it also tries to explain the logistics of travelling and playing in large and disparate groups, issues the reader might not have thought about, but which were important, if only in a subtle way. I especially wanted to explain why tournaments are different from other forms of competition, and why experience of them is essential to success at later tournaments, something that some sports do not appear to have understood yet and/or accepted.

While writing the book, I had time to relive some of the challenging, funny and important moments of a long career. In doing so, I was constantly reminded how lucky I was to have played in an era that saw huge changes in rugby at most levels. I was also reminded of one of the great benefits of playing a team sport: I could not only derive enjoyment from my own experience of playing, but could also vicariously share in the enjoyment of others. When I meet former team-mates of mine years later, from whatever team, I almost instantly rediscover the rapport I had with them – and that is especially true if I toured with them.

Touring, above all else, creates a unique and ever-lasting bond. I hope that those involved in rugby will identify with the themes in the book, and that even readers who have neither played rugby nor toured will get an insight into why those who are fortunate enough to do both feel the experience is a special one.

1

The Art of Coarse Touring

The first tour I ever went on was an Old Crossleyans cricket tour. Well, it wasn't a tour, really, more of a long weekend – to Watford. As we were coming down from Halifax, I nonetheless viewed our trip 'south' with some excitement, given that I was seventeen at the time.

I attended Crossley & Porter grammar school, and had started playing senior rugby and cricket for the Old Crossleyans when I was seventeen. Although I played at hooker for their first XV, I also played in the centre for my school team, and would often turn out for both teams on Saturdays: I would play for the school in the morning and for the Old Crossleyans in the afternoon. You are not allowed to do this now under RFU rules, as they view it as a health and safety hazard, which it probably would be for many people.

The cricket tour to Watford turned out to be a complete riot, which of course is the sole point of a junior tour (i.e. a tour by a lower-league, amateur, club). The games – be they rugby, cricket, football or any other sport – are frankly incidental, because the purpose is to have fun. In fact, the games are often a distinct inconvenience, because everyone is exhausted from other activities that have nothing to do with the sport in question.

On this tour, we did actually play two games, but I have no re-collection of where or against whom. What I do remember are incidents that went on to become part of club folklore, recounted many times in subsequent years and indeed decades. That they linger, rather than the details of the games themselves, is signifi-cant because it is these moments that often bring the fondest memories when you retire. It isn't the minutiae of the battles, it is the havoc of the celebrations.

Although every playing detail escapes me, I do remember that we got thrown out of our hotel in Watford, the worryingly named Spider's Web Motel. On the first night, we decamped to the bar and, despite arriving late, made up for lost time by drinking until the early hours of the morning. As residents, we could do this, although the night porter appeared to view serving us as a nui-sance rather than an opportunity for a large increase in bar takings.

For some reason, the hotel had a huge fish tank in its lobby that contained several large trout. You could actually specify which one you wanted to eat for your dinner if you wanted to – an odd con-cept you might think, but not that unusual, at least in those days. At one stage that night, someone had the idea of catching one of the fish, but despite repeated attempts, they were all too fast. Even when he did actually get hold of one, they were too slippery. Having mocked his failure, a few other players decided to show him how it was done but suffered an equal lack of success. One of the disaffected catchers then decided that the job would be better done by a more natural predator, and the obvious one was the hotel cat who was promptly launched into the tank from several feet away. Instead of being excited at the prospect of being able to choose – rather like the other diners in the restaurant – which fish to have for its dinner, the cat was so shocked that it immediately started to flail around before mustering up a supercat-like effort, leaping out of the tank, and dashing off with a look of blind panic, leaving a trail of water, but sadly (or luckily, depending on whether you were the fish or the cat) no trout in its wake.

The hotel manager was eventually placated, and normal order restored – until the next night, when the 'traditional' kitchen raid took place. Kitchen raids are very common on tours. Men get hungry, they might have had a bit to drink, it's late at night, they want to quell those hunger pangs, and before long someone suggests a trip to check out the hotel kitchens.

Technically this is probably theft but it doesn't quite register at the time as an illegal act. As usual, on this occasion most of the kitchen cupboards were locked. But just when we were about to leave disappointed, one of the boys discovered that one of the fridges had been left unlocked. Expecting a savoury feast, we opened the door to find only a number of huge catering-sized cream gateaux, already in pre-cut portions. Not perfect, but at that time of night we would have eaten almost anything. Besides, we didn't even need a knife. Several of the cakes were duly taken up to one of the bedrooms, and about twenty of us followed, all tiptoeing along the corridor, giggling and loudly 'ssshh-ing' each other. Other than me, all were grown men, yet they must have looked like excited 12-year-olds fresh from a tuck-shop raid.

We all went into one player's room and sat down to enjoy the food. At first we did even eat some of it, but it was soon clear what everyone was thinking ... All it took was for one person to push his neighbour's slice into his face, then it all kicked off. People were just grabbing handfuls of cake and hurling it anywhere and at anyone. The walls, beds, TV, wardrobe and everybody's clothes were eventually all covered in gateau. In the cold light of day, it was juvenile behaviour, and that, not unreasonably, turned out to be the view of the hotel manager. Early the next morning, he made the entire tour party assemble in the room in question in order to give us the dressing down that was to precede our expulsion from the hotel. He just was getting into his stride, trying to shame us into acknowledging how reprehensible our actions had been. 'Look at this,' he raged, with a dramatic sweeping gesture towards the cake-spattered Standard Twin-bedded room, one of the Spider's Web's finest. 'This is disgusting! Who in their right mind would want to stay in this room after what you've done to it?' Slight pause. 'Charlie Cairoli?' – a well-known clown at the time – sniggered someone at the back. We all collapsed in gales of laughter. That was the last straw. We were made to pay for the clean-up costs of the room and told to 'get out' in no uncertain terms.

One of the great bonuses of these tours is that they are often made up of men from all walks of life, and of all ages (within reason, obviously). In most rugby clubs, there is real mixture of backgrounds and jobs, even in Wales where rugby tends to be a more working-class sport than in England. Although the Old Crossleyans name gives the impression that, as it is an Old Boys' club, it's full of public schoolboys, nothing could be further from the truth. The school was a grammar school and, being in Halifax, turned out pupils from all backgrounds. So people from the professions – doctors, accountants, lawyers, teachers – played week in, week out, with people whom they would not usually spend much time with, and they formed very firm bonds, not least when they went on mini tours. Many of these respectable members of society also happened to be great characters, but touring is an egalitarian affair where differences are most often used as a source of fun, and you would be hard pushed to tell who are the more educated when it comes to being irresponsible.

Junior club tours tend to take place over a long weekend, in order to minimise the impact on work commitments. Plus, to be honest, three or four days is usually just long enough to hold the body together to play two or three games. After that, it proves too much on the metabolism. After all, before each game, players inevitably go out the night before for a long, liquid evening, so once the actual game gets underway, it is usually a case of seeing how long it takes before the first person throws up. And there is no doubt that people routinely take to the field when they would still be legally over the limit – which is one advantage of travelling everywhere by coach.

The Old Boys' rugby tour I went on after the cricket tour was again over a long weekend, this time to the Isle of Man. While being granted full tourist status, I was in fact still underage and still at school, though that didn't spoil what was another memorable three-day trip. We all piled on to the coach in a car park somewhere in Halifax, some of us wearing the rather dazzlingly coloured gold and blue club blazers, others rather more informally attired.

These were the days before official tour kit, when any self-respecting tour has at the very least an official T-shirt proclaiming the date and place of the forthcoming trip. We drove over to Liverpool, boarded the ferry, and finally arrived at our rather basic hotel in Douglas later that evening. In true touring tradition, no thought was given to the game to be played the next day or to pacing ourselves for what would be an extended assault on our livers and a test of our ability to exist on minimal sleep. We convened for dinner, started with wine and then moved on to the local beer, Okkels Ale, which seemed to slip down quite easily.

Service at the hotel offered a Fawlty Towers-style of welcome and, unlike the Spider's Web Motel, we got no cooperation at all from the night porter when it came to extending our drinking session. On reflection, I suppose it was after hours. Not willing to accept what we deemed to be a poor welcome, and with several in the tour party having some knowledge of the law, we pointed out that their refusal to reopen the bar was out of order. 'We're residents,' we insisted. 'Plus, you've got a night porter, so we're entitled to be served,' we pointed out, using a last-ditch legal technicality argument. But the man in question refused to cave in, and after closing the shutters to the bar, he remained firmly behind the reception desk. No amount of arguing changed his mind, not even the offer to make it worth his while by slipping him a few quid, so our thirty-odd party was left high and dry.

What happened next is an example of how things get out of hand on tour, and how being a professional is no bar to being daft. Some of the players, including two lawyers, spotted that the bar shutters had quite large gaps in the grille through which they calculated that bottles of beer and spirits could pass if we could find a way to get them off the shelves. Using two pool cues and a couple of broom handles taken from a cleaner's cupboard, they tried to lift the bottles by putting a cue or broom handle on either side of a bottle. While this was theoretically possible, it required a huge amount of strength and precision to obtain enough sideways force to grip the bottle and carry it firmly and steadily through the gaps in the grille.

Despite impressively getting various bottles off their shelves and even off their optics, nobody managed to get one successfully all the way through and into our waiting hands. Instead, the bottles either bounced onto the bar or smashed all over the floor. Looking back, I don't think it helped that most of us were three sheets to the wind by this time. Needless to say, we had to pay for the damage and clean it all up the next morning.

Doubtless some people will say that this, and other similar behaviour, amounts to nothing more than criminal damage and hooliganism. And that tours such as this give rugby a bad name.

If the police do get involved then, yes, those on the tour have to be prepared to put their hands up and accept that what they did was wrong. But what I will say in the defence of rugby tours is that trouble hardly ever occurs in the majority of them, and even if it does, it is usually minor, whereas incidents of people getting stabbed in nightclubs or glassed outside a pub occur regularly on a Saturday night on many of Britain's High Streets.

I can't remember much about the two games that we played, although I do remember two players running behind the goal posts and vomiting after the first ten minutes of the second game. Although I was the youngest member on both tours, I was the best player of the rugby tour (and a decent wicket-keeper on the cricket one), and they didn't have to look after me on the field of play because I was already quite feisty and streetwise. Actually I was a bit of a lunatic at times and would fight with anybody, no matter what their size or position. In the second game, for example, after a massive set-to, the opposing captain confronted our captain and said, 'Listen, will you stop this hooker? Ours is only eighteen years old and just out of school,' to which ours replied, 'Well, ours is only seventeen and still *at* school.'

I loved both the tours I went on. As I was still a schoolboy, I had no money, but others in the party who were of working age looked after me and were generous enough to allow me to drink to my heart's content for nothing and despite being underage; no one cared about such things in those days. My parents, who were Methodist lay preachers, had hardly ever been into a pub in their lives, so they had little idea – indeed it simply did not occur to them – that alcohol was the *leitmotiv* of all such tours. Good job, really.

Also, mobile phones hadn't been invented, so it was a case of 'out of sight, out of mind'. You just couldn't check up on what your kids were doing, even if you had wanted to, unlike parents nowadays who often expect the reassurance of near-constant text messaging when their children are away somewhere. And conversely, the fine upstanding geography teacher couldn't be filmed on someone's phone with a flaming piece of toilet paper up his arse, there for all the pupils, parents and governors of his school to watch on YouTube.

Finally, importantly, the elf'n'safety brigade had not yet made an appearance, so on tours involving underage players, it was basically a case of *caveat emptor*. If you wanted to drink, that was up to you. If you courted danger, that too was your responsibility. Unless you got injured on the field. Even then, if you were unlucky enough to have an injury that required you to go to hospital, the chances are you would go to the nearest A&E department, while your team-mates would basically say, 'Tell you what, once you've finished, call the hotel. We'll let them know which pub we're in so you can make your own way there.' Simple as that.

These days, tour organisation is much more sophisticated, but back then the Tour Committee was basically made up of people who could be trusted to sort out the logistics that really mattered, like hiring a coach, getting on the ferry, or knowing where the hotels and the games actually were, given that Google maps and satnavs didn't exist.

Junior club tours are usually the highlight of the year, and a lot of work goes into planning them, hence the importance of the Tour Committee. When I played for the Old Crocs, Watford and the Isle of Man represented the limits of our furthest horizons. Nowadays, tours often go further afield, and I don't just mean to Wales or Scotland, but all over the world, and for weeks instead of days. Specialist travel companies have sprung up to do much of the organising; full tour regalia is now a given, whereas in the past, cheap screen printing was not available; but the Tour Committee remains in charge of arranging fixtures, tour clothing and travel. Nevertheless the same mix of ages and abilities go on tour, and at junior level it remains the case that playing is very much a secondary consideration.

If a tour is well organised, it will not only have a Tour Committee to cover the logistics, but also an effective Entertainment Committee to cover the after-hours element. Both bodies are unelected, and the Entertainment Committee is often more important than the Tour Committee because as much planning goes into what happens off the field as goes into the fixtures to be played and the hotels to be booked. A good Entertainment Committee finds out which bars and pubs are lively, for example, and which serve good food. Most importantly, they check and clear in advance with whichever night clubs the tour party wants to visit: nothing ends the revelry quicker than the 'No large groups of men' rule.

Rugby tours have tour rules. These can be prohibitive or prescriptive, reasonable or ridiculous. It depends on whether there is a formal Tour Court in place as to which body is responsible for making and disseminating these tour rules, but it is not uncommon for them to be printed up on headed notepaper. Common rules include those where people are forbidden to mention a particular subject or say a certain word or words. I am quite partial to the one stipulating that the whole tour party has to burst into song if anybody outside the party asks a particular question, such as 'Where are you from?'

Clubs that are touring regulars may have even more committees or defined positions like a Tour Taste Committee that makes arbitrary rulings on whether a comment or act is within the acceptable limits of taste – basically an excuse to get everyone drunk, as their choices are completely arbitrary and inconsistent. A Tour Fitness Officer might be assigned to ensure that each player's drinking is up to scratch, and to impose appropriate remedies if it is found to be deficient. One of the junior clubs near to where I now live in London, the Old Isleworthians RFC, appoints a Tour Jester for each trip whose job is to maintain morale by telling jokes, playing practical jokes and leading the singing. One year, on their trip to Amsterdam, the jester's first little wheeze was to cancel every room at the hotel at which they intended to stay, apart from his own. I bet they saw the funny side of that joke straight away.

Breaches of tour rules usually won't end up in the Tour Court as they are probably covered by a standard fine within the rules: usually a pint downed in one. However, egregious and repeated offending may still find the miscreant before the court. (It's a measure of the enjoyment that rugby tours derive from the judicial process that I devote an entire chapter to Tour Courts.) Sensible rules aside, the aim of tour rules is to act as a leveller, to make sure no one takes themselves too seriously and, unsurprisingly, to guarantee that large quantities of alcohol are consumed.

One of the most disastrous rules – because it gets people very drunk – is also one of the most well known. It involves switching from left-handed to right-handed drinking every hour or half-hour, depending on how evil one wants to be, and how fast one intends to get people drunk. Because if you drink with the wrong hand – and let's face it, unless you're checking your watch with OCD-like regularity, you will eventually get it wrong – you have to down what is in your glass. That rule is a very quick way for people to become completely hammered, because it doesn't matter what your capacity is: if you suddenly have to drink at a faster pace than you are used to, then you will get drunk. That tour rule is made to be broken, and is often instituted to last an entire day, or several days at a stretch. And before long, people are checking their watches in order to catch others out, and anarchy breaks out.

Although there are standard rules that are regularly instituted on tours, the most memorable are the quirky ones. They often arise out of nowhere, and no one can remember who thinks them up or why. On the above-mentioned cricket tour, it was decided that everyone had to speak in a Dame Edna Everage voice for an entire day. This included a mass visit to a pub in St Albans and having to order drinks from the bar. People were obviously staring at us, mentally going 'WTF?' or words to that effect, but we managed to get through our drinks without being set upon by the locals, which was an achievement in itself.

During that same tour, the idea emerged that we should also all have to speak in a sort of semi-falsetto operatic voice for half a day, which is obviously extremely stupid and pointless, but certainly means that it's very difficult to be pompous if you've got to speak in that sort of way. Still, at least on that occasion we didn't have to run the gauntlet of a pub-full of stares and the smirks of the bar staff.

What is great about tour rules, such as the last two examples, is that you often discover people with hidden talents. Sometimes, it's the quiet ones, the ones whom you never seemed to have much in common with or much time for – they are the ones who turn out to have surprising talents, who can sing incredibly well, or whatever. And suddenly they take centre stage for the evening, and the ice is broken. Tour rules are good for taking people out of their comfort zones, but in a good way. They make people bond, and in the end they add to tour morale.

Along with the standard tour clothing, people are often made to don particular items. A yellow jersey is often produced for the person to wear who has had the most success with the opposite sex. Conversely, other tours – and I know this is quite common – have a paper bag, to be worn by the one who has hooked up with ... well, I'm sure I don't need to spell it out. I know, it's not very sophisticated, but I know of many female tours where outrageous things go on that would never win a Good Taste Award either. For a particularly stupid act, the 'Dick of the Day' T-shirt or other suitably humiliating accoutrement is commonly worn for one day only. Indeed, one of the things that attracted criticism during England's disastrous 2011 Rugby World Cup campaign was the decision by Lewis Moody, the England flanker and captain, to resurrect this tradition. While in keeping with the best traditions of coarse rugby, it perhaps wasn't the best symbol of professional preparation. Moreover, as one press wag cruelly, and unjustifiably, commented, 'Why do you need a Dick of the Day Award when James Haskell is in the tour party?'

2

The Sexual Life of a Camel, and Spoofing

Tours are an opportunity for players to get together and sing. While junior club tours have a tradition of singing and playing games which is maintained to this day, sadly these have almost disappeared from senior rugby. By 'games', I do not mean fireside games of Monopoly, but rather drinking games, or games played on unsuspecting team-mates. Taken out of context, these can appear puerile, irresponsible and juvenile. They may reinforce some people's opinions of rugby players as boorish oafs. On the other hand, they are a lot of fun. The common denominators are alcohol and drinking and probably a lot of noise. If others disapprove, they might remember that all these things are a matter of taste, which is entirely subjective. I don't like The Smiths and find Morrissey offensive, but I don't berate people who put their music on pub music systems.

The great thing about singing is that because it is communal it encourages team-spirit and, as we all know from programmes like *The Choir*, it's just hugely uplifting. Great singers are sometimes revealed as a result of a sing-song, players whom you would never suspect of being able to sing a note. Others turn out to have an encyclopaedic knowledge of particular types of music. With that in mind, I'm reproducing at the end of the book a few of my favourite songs, in the hope that readers can enjoy learning and singing them.

The consumption of alcohol explains why these songs and games were much more common when I toured with England and the British Lions. Nowadays, the only drinking being done at senior level – whether at club or international level – involves, in the main, the imbibing of isotonic drinks. I'm not surprised the players sit during their down-time staring at iPads and laptops, playing on phones or listening to iPods in order to while away the hours; they're hardly going to start a sing-song or play games when they're stone cold sober.

Having served a long apprenticeship at various levels of rugby in my formative years, I could lead a singalong for literally three hours if I wanted or had to. With the Halifax Colts, Old Crossleyans, Nottingham University and Nottingham rugby teams, singing was a part of every match day. It wasn't compulsory, it didn't have to be; nobody wanted to abstain because, like drinking games, going through the club repertoire of songs was fun. The types of songs ranged from the traditional rugby songs, through medleys of songs, to songs which were specific to one club; basically anything that was fun to belt out in a group. And that was the point: a big sing-song is just bloody good fun. Everyone joins in; it doesn't matter if they can't sing. The singing can be done almost anywhere, on the coach, in bars, hotels and pubs.

The highpoint of my singing career was undoubtedly at

Nottingham RFC, where I played from 1981 to 1990. Nottingham was a 'singing club', but not in the manner of other senior clubs where after-match singing was also customary. At Nottingham we sang the typical medleys of rugby songs but never touched the bawdy songs at all. Unlike many clubs, where only a few players know the words to all the verses of songs and the rest join in the first couple and the choruses, all the players took the trouble to learn all the words. In fact, so seriously did players take this after-match part of the game that they learned and introduced a huge variety of songs from musicals, films and the pop charts. On top of that, it was terribly frowned upon to shout while singing or to start a song which you did not know in its entirety. I remember several players having to do drinking fines for shouting in the middle of the song 'You've Lost That Lovin' Feeling'.

When it was my turn to lead, I often used to do songs from *Oliver!* and *The Jungle Book* and I knew the words to all the songs from both. Personal favourites were 'Reviewing the Situation', 'Consider Yourself' and 'Oom-Pah-Pah' from *Oliver!* and 'The Bare Necessities' and 'I Wan'na Be Like You (The Monkey Song)' from *The Jungle Book*. So seriously did I take my duties that I went away and learned all the nonsense words sung by Baloo the bear after I heard the Loughborough students give a perfect rendition in one of their post-match singing sessions. Should you ever find yourself leading this song, you will get instant fame and adulation if you add this part of the song because nobody else will be able to match you. For your assistance on this walk to greatness the 'words' go like this (you can thank me later):

Hey, de-zop-ba-nonie
Hap-de-dee-ba-lat
Da-dat-dat-non
Hey a-baby-dot-doo

Zaba-doo-doo-day-doo-bop
Doo-boo-doo-day, ze-bonz
Za bop-bop-bobby
Za bah-doo-dee
Well, a-reh-bah-naza
He-beh-do-beh-doy
Well, a-lah-bah-zini
Wadahlabat-boodalabat
Seebahlalat-dodie
Oooh-ooh-ooh
Well, a ha-ha-ha.

Having now set out those words and looked at them again, I am forced to ask: what kind of person goes away and learns stuff like that? The answer: an addictive perfectionist with a mild personality disorder.

If you are unfamiliar with the genre of entertainment that is the traditional rugby song, the words of 'Four and Twenty Virgins' are at the end of this chapter. It is sung by male – and female, I should point out – rugby players up and down the country. There are, literally, hundreds of others in the same vein and at one time I knew the words to hundreds, although now that is probably down to about eighty or ninety. The truth is that while I know many traditional rugby songs and am happy to join in when they are sung, I find some of them a bit crass. We didn't sing them at Nottingham, other than to accompany any away team that sang them. Instead, we would often start with what I call 'tour medleys' of well-known songs. One medley began with players dipping their hands in their beers and flicking drops of it into the air to accompany the starting verse which was:

The Sexual Life of a Camel, and Spoofing

I'm singing in the rain, just singing in the rain
What a glorious feeling, I'm happy again
I walk down the lane, to the happy refrain
Just sing and dancing in the rain.

Then we went immediately into:

Pack up all your cares and woes, here I go, singing low
Bye bye blackbird
Where somebody waits for me, sugar sweet so is she
Bye bye blackbird
No one seems to love or understand me. Oh, what hard
    luck stories they all hand me
So, make my bed, light the light, I'll be home late tonight
Blackbird, bye bye.

Then:

Show me the way to go home, I'm tired and I want to go to
    bed
I had a little drink about an hour ago and it's gone right to
    my head
No matter where I roam, over land or sea or foam
You will always hear me singing this song
Show me the way to go home.

Followed by, if you knew it, this second lesser-known verse:

Indicate the way to my abode, I'm fatigued and I wish to
    retire
I had a small beverage sixty minutes ago and it's gone right
    to my cerebral cranium

No matter where I perambulate, over mass or water or
      atmospheric pressure
You can forever perceive me orating this melody
Indicate the way to my abode.

Without pausing for:

You are my sunshine, my only sunshine
You make me happy when skies are grey
You'll never notice how much I love you
Oh, please don't take my sunshine away.
The other night, dear, as I lay sleeping
I dreamt that you were by my side
When I awoke, dear, and found you gone, dear,
I just laid on my pillow and cried.

And then:

Shine on, shine on harvest moon up in the sky
I ain't had no living since January, February, June or July
Snow time, ain't no time to sit around and spoon
So shine on, shine on harvest moon for me and my gal.

And into:

The bells are ringing for me and my gal
The birds are singing for me and my gal
Everybody's been knowing, to a wedding they're going and
      for weeks they've been sewing
Every Susie and Sal – every Susie and Sal.
They're congregating, for me and my gal
The Parson's waiting for me and my gal

And someday soon we're gonna build a little house for two,
    or three or four or more
In Love-land, for me and my gal, for me and my gal.

And swiftly to:

Abie, Abie, Abie my boy, what are you waiting for now
You promised to marry me someday in June it's never too
    late and it's never too soon
All the family, they keep on asking me
Which way, what way, I'm in the family way,
Abie, Abie, Abie my boy.
What are you waiting for now?

Wait till the sun shines, Nellie,
As the clouds go drifting by
We'll be so happy, Nellie, don't you cry.
Down Lover's Lane we'll wander
Sweethearts you and I
Wait till the sun shines, Nellie,
By and by.

And so we would continue, song after song, for sometimes up to half an hour without stopping. Once the standard medleys had been sung, a player would pick one of his favourites from shows, films or anything else they wanted as long as it was a decent tune. 'There Is Nothing Like A Dame' from Rodgers and Hammerstein's *South Pacific*, would move seamlessly on to a *Guys And Dolls* number, maybe 'Luck Be A Lady'. The breadth of songs was wide, and provided it was a good song, nobody minded if it wasn't to their taste. Even Country Western music got a look in with 'Coward Of The County', 'Ring Of Fire' and 'Lucille' being regularly sung.

I miss doing this terribly; the singing that is, not the manner in which we performed.

Some of the more traditional rugby songs are actually quite inventive, though they probably are of their time, when rugby clubs were almost the sole province of men. They are egalitarian only in the sense that they are rude and insensitive about men, women, gays, straights and animals alike. In today's politically correct world where people are quick to take offence, they no doubt have the capacity to invite outrage. However, they are not sung with any intent to offend and, given that they are usually sung within the confines of a members' clubhouse, not really in public. So the following may offend you, but if you don't want to risk this, please don't read it; skip this chapter and go to the next one. If you don't heed this caveat, please don't feign offence thereafter!

Such songs might be sung elsewhere, but what is unique to rugby is that you could go into any clubhouse in England, plus many others around the world, and if you started singing any of these songs, you would find that most of the assembled company would join in, knowing the words and tunes. I can't think of a similar thing in any other sport. That is nothing startling but you should maybe ask yourself why it is that only this sport has that tradition, particularly as anyone can learn or invent a song. For those involved in rugby, these songs and the tradition of singing represent a much-valued addition to the atmosphere of communality that everyone wants to exist in their club, and one which does indeed exist in most.

The difference between this tradition and, say, the songs and chants sung in football is amply demonstrated by what happened when I went on a whirlwind 'tour' of three days to Japan to see the England football team play Brazil during the 2002 World Cup finals. We went to the game in Shizuoka by coach, and I was the only person on it with a rugby background. The rest of the passengers were solely football people, including many Arsenal fans. At one stage, two Gooners spotted me and eventually started pressing me to share a singalong with them. 'Come on then, you can sing rugby songs, and we'll sing football songs.' 'Okay, fine,' I replied, reluctantly, fearing this was not going to be as much fun as they imagined.

I started with a rendition of 'The Good Ship Venus', an extract of which goes like this:

CHORUS:
There's frigging on the rigging;
Wanking on the planking,
There was fuck all else to do.
   Chorus

T'was on the good ship Venus,
By God you should have seen us,
The figurehead was a whore in bed
And the mast the Captain's penis.
   Chorus

The captain of this lugger,
He was a dirty bugger,
He wasn't fit to shove shit
From one place to another.
   Chorus

The captain's wife was Mabel.
Whenever she was able,
She'd fornicate with the second mate
Upon the galley table.
   Chorus

The second mate's name was Andy,
His balls were long and bandy,
We filled his arse with molten brass
For wanking in the brandy.
  Chorus

The cabin boy was Kipper,
A dirty little nipper,
He stuffed his arse with broken glass
And circumcised the skipper.
  Chorus

And so on and so on.

Even if you don't find that entertaining, they did and, on finishing, I received a round of applause. In reply, they sang this ditty, sung to the tune of 'When The Saints Go Marching In':

We won the League,
We won the League,
We won the League in Manchester
We won the League at Old Trafford
We won the League in Manchester.

I joined in the fraternal spirit by reciprocating the round of applause, even though the song was a little limited in its ambition and content. I would have been considerably more entertained if I'd known that they would win so few trophies over the next ten years. Still, moving on ... 'Okay, that's your song, fine,' I went, and then sang 'The Vicar's Song', a well-known rugby ditty, which goes like this:

One evening after Evening Song
The curate said for fun
I bet I've had more women than you
And the Vicar said you're on.
We will stand at the door as the women go by
And this will be our sign
You Ding Dong for the women you've had
And I'll Bing Bong for mine.
There were Ding Dongs, there were Bing Bongs
There were more Ding Dongs than there were Bing Bongs
Until as certain lady walked by and the Curate said Bing Bong.
Just a minute said the Vicar there's a mistake there
That's my wife I do declare.
I don't give a bugger, I've been there,
Ringa-dinga-dinga, ding dong, ding dong.

Cue further clapping from the Gooners, followed by their extended rendition of the classic:

'One-nil to the Arsenal; one-nil to the Arsenal, one-nil to the Arsenal, one-nil to the Arsenal . . .'

I followed that with 'The Sexual Life of a Camel' (sung to the tune of the Eton Boating Song), whose first verse goes thus:

The sexual life of the camel,
Is stranger than anyone thinks,
At the height of the mating season,
He tries to bugger the Sphinx,
But the Sphinx's posterior orifice,
Is filled with the sands of the Nile,
Which accounts for the hump on the camel,
And the Sphinx's inscrutable smile . . .
[Further verses at the end of this book]

Their retort was to swing into 'There's only one Arsène Wenger', sung, unsurprisingly, to the tune of 'Walking in a Winter Wonderland':

> There's only one Arsène Wenger
> One Arsène Wenger
> Walking along, singing this song,
> Walking in a Wenger wonderland
> *Refrain*

I refrained from singing the alternative football version, which I knew, used by the fans of all other Premier League clubs, as that would have been uncivilised. This pattern continued for a good half hour and I thought throughout that it was a shame they didn't have better songs as they obviously also enjoyed the communal experience of singing.

Interestingly, when I filmed a piece for the BBC with the King's Cross Steelers, an openly gay rugby team based in London, they told me that they sang not only the above song, but the alternative version, details of which are at the end of this book. That visit to the Steelers also demonstrated what I knew already, having lived right in the middle of Soho for six years: gay people are far more cutting and explicit about each other than anyone else, and I'm sure they sang the song at their 'fixture of the year'. This, they proudly told me, was against the firemen's rugby team, and they loved it because the latter really camped it up: they turned up wearing all their uniform, they played up to the whole gay thing with lots of suggestiveness, and the fixture was played in the spirit of having a really good time and a good laugh.

Drinking games are also confined now to junior rugby, as they definitely rely on being fuelled by alcohol. They can follow on from

Court Sessions, but often just turn out to be stylised versions of them, with the same sort of hierarchy.

Before anything can begin, a good Chair must be appointed. The Chair must know the rules of every game, as they will be asked to rule on points arising during play, and they must be able to keep up the pace, because, as the saying goes, 'A fast game is a good game.'

I was often the Chair. Not just because my legal background and naturally 'combative' temperament gave me the edge in arguing the toss, but also because I simply knew the rules to the many games we played, thus limiting unnecessary interruptions while rules were challenged or mistakes made.

Plainly incidental to drinking games is the probability that the players will get drunk. Indeed, that is part of the fun of playing them. That said, as the Chair, unless you have an Armageddon approach it's probably better to temper the rate at which players lose their sobriety by trying to pace out the speed at which they are fined. Remember that, once a player starts making mistakes and incurring drinking fines, they make more and more mistakes. It's not good for players to become insensible within half an hour, and once you've seen a player vomiting all over the table, repeats aren't quite as hilarious. I have seen countless people just fall over, be sick or pass out, but I also recall someone once being sick and running off, only for the Chair to announce, on their return, 'First of all, you didn't ask for permission to leave; secondly, you didn't ask for permission to be sick; thirdly, you didn't ask to come back into the circle. So I think that's a pint down in one.' The player agreed, carried out the fine, only to throw it all straight back up again. He then just fell over.

Drunken players provide amusement, but in reality the novelty soon wears off for a number of reasons. Most people, within reasonable limits, are harmless drunks, but some are not. The purpose of the games is to have a laugh, not cause a fight. Nor is the aim to end up with alcohol poisoning and a trip to A&E to get someone's stomach pumped. Also, when players get drunk they start pointing, shouting and disregarding the rules. While this attracts fines, it disrupts the flow of the games, and in the end makes them difficult to continue. Not only are they interrupted by the drunk's actions, the fact is that drunken players invariably get things wrong. This means that the games always stop when it's their turn.

A good Chair understands all this and tries to manage games by trying to spread fines around the circle. One way of doing this is to make sure that different players start games. This means there is the possibility of mistakes being made before the turn reaches players who are starting to tip over the edge.

Another reason why you should have a Chair who knows all the games well is that they are less likely to make mistakes. This, at first glance, might seem unfair, but any perceived inequity is balanced by the fact that the Chair's fines are double those of other players. Furthermore, the last thing you want is a Chair who themselves gets drunk early on in the session. If this happens you won't get much further, as the games won't flow and you won't get any sense over rulings, fines and so on.

THE CHAIR

- Can be elected, imposed or chosen by any means you want, but only one person can be in charge. So make sure you get a good Chair.
- Rules on disputes, is responsible for keeping the action flowing and handing out fines.
- Cannot be addressed without putting your hand up and waiting to be recognised. Speaking without waiting for permission is an offence.

- Must be addressed as Mr or Ms Chair or any other title the Chair decrees. If the address is wrong, it is an offence.
- Decides on which games to play, and if necessary will explain the rules of that game and any conditions that pertain to it.
- Can impose any general rules they like – these are non-negotiable.
- Can issue an order, 'General drinking', which means all players, including the Chair, drink two fingers; this means two fingers' depth of the drink before them.
- May appoint any number of aides, including a Chief Sneak, Weights and Measures Enforcers, or none, at their discretion.
- May ask the players to vote on the guilt or innocence of a player alleged to have infringed. This is done by secret ballot, i.e. all players put their right thumb inside their left fist until the Chair calls 'vote'. Players then put their thumbs up for innocent and down for guilty (actually the reverse of what the Roman crowds did when voting on the life or death of gladiators or fighters in the arena).
- Regularly asks for votes, rather than simply issuing decrees, as this involves the whole group, lessens enmity towards the Chair, and players are usually adept at pleading their case, often with unexpected wit.
- If the Chair or the group vote acquits a player, his accuser is fined for making a false allegation. This does not apply to the Chair.
- The Chair's word is final and dissent therefrom is an offence which usually attracts a harsh fine.

Examples of general rules

The examples below are at the discretion of the Chair who decides which ones and how many to impose. For obvious reasons, some, such as the 'no pointing' or 'no open-mouthed laughing' rules, are very difficult to keep up, and lead to frequent and repeat fines.

A. Fines must be consumed or done immediately, and if not fully complied with must be repeated.

B. Fines for Court appointees are 1½ times those of ordinary players.

C. Fines when the Chair errs are double those of ordinary players.

D. No pointing: players may only use their elbow to indicate someone or thing.

E. No talking: save for comments that relate to the game at hand. This sounds draconian but it is actually the best way to play games, as otherwise you get players not concentrating and messing about.

F. Each player, apart from the Chair, is given the name of an animal. During the session a person must be referred to as Mr or Ms —— and not by their real or nickname and not as he or her. This rule is unusually useful for attracting fines.

G. Specific words may be banned: 'he', 'him' and 'her' are particularly effective.

H. Right- or left-handed drinking may be imposed. It is usual for this to change every half hour. Drinking with the wrong hand attracts a fine and if a fine is done with the wrong hand it has to be repeated with the correct one. This rule can also be used as a general tour rule when it will apply to any drinking at any time of the day. For example, during all even hours it is right-handed drinking and left-handed during odd hours.

I. No open-mouthed laughing is a rule that is sometimes imposed; it is funny at first seeing people trying to guffaw, but it can become a bit of a pain.

J. Players can be given a particular accent in which they have to say anything during the game. Failure to do so is an offence. If you are really sadistic you can fine players for the quality of their accent. It is very difficult to keep a flawless accent that you are not used to, and if you punish every slip you will get players drunk very quickly.

Tactics

These suggestions are no guarantee that you will not get slaughtered but they may somewhat delay the moment.

1. Pay attention. It is amazing how many players do not.
2. Scrutinise the turn of every player to make sure they have done things exactly right. If they get fined, it delays your own possible fine. However, be careful not to be pedantic as the Chair may call 'Pedant' and fine you.
3. If the game involves passing the turn around the circle (see games below), but you do not have to pass to the player next to you, identify players – for example, prop forwards – who are likely to err. Remember, once a player is fined a few times they are likely to make more mistakes. Also, the game will start again.
4. Far be it from me to advocate collusion, but it is not unknown for players to have informal pacts not to pass a turn to each other, or conversely to pass to a specific person/people. Sometimes this happens without subterfuge, as players see a vulnerable player, or on the contrary pick on a relatively unfined player to even out the group.
5. If you do collude, do not get caught. If the Chair suspects there is pre-planning, they can – and usually do – issue very heavy fines. Even in cases of instant collusion the Chair can call 'Bullying', and fine those they deem responsible.

6. Don't be a dick. Games should be fun for all players and not dominated by a few. Remember, being smart is fine; being a smart-arse is not.

Shotgunning

Special mention should be made of this particular fine which, for some reason, seems to get people drunk more quickly than just drinking the same amount by normal means:

1. Take a can of beer, and hold it horizontally with the tab at the top.
2. Make a small hole in the bottom of the can with a pen knife, key, or other sharp instrument. Be careful to keep the can steady and level.
3. Get your thumb under the tab, ready to open the can.
4. Bend forward and put your mouth over the hole at the bottom.
5. In one smooth action, stand up so that the can is vertical and, while standing, pull the tab to open the can.
6. The air pressure will force the liquid out of the hole and into your mouth. Fast. Be ready to drink (gulp) quickly if you don't want spillage and then be made to repeat the entire fine.

A Chair will sometimes issue, for a particular fine, an order to shotgun something, rather than simply drinking a pint in one go from a glass. It's much more difficult to do because you're not drinking at your own pace, as the liquid is being shot out under pressure from the can. That said, I've seen people doing it standing on their heads, drinking upside down. The beer still came out, because someone was standing next to them, holding the can just above their mouth, so they were in effect drinking upwards.

The yard of ale

This well-known measure of immeasured drinking requires a certain technique in order to complete successfully. A yard of ale contains (depending on the container) about 2.4 pints of ale (or about 1.4 litres). The long stem of the container typically ends in a round bubble shape. As you drink, the liquid comes down the stem, but, if you are not prepared, at some stage an air bubble from the end of the container builds up and suddenly forces the liquid to shoot out and splash all over you. To avoid this, you should either start to turn the stem quickly, or swing it in a gentle, circular motion to stop the build-up of air, and keep the liquid flowing smoothly down the stem to the aperture.

I perfected the technique to the extent that, with practice, I was once able to drink three yards of ale in a row; though I have to admit that the last one came straight back up. I know it's nothing to be proud of, but as a student my stomach was sufficiently used to being abused that it somehow coped with that volume of liquid.

I should, at this point, state that I am fully aware that today's binge-drinking culture, aided and abetted by the internet, can sometimes cause vulnerable people to go too far. Drinking games can involve drinking a lot but usually over a period of several hours, reducing the overall risk to the individual. Stupid fines, like downing large quantities of spirits in one go, should never be given. They aren't funny; they are dangerous. As you usually play with friends or team-mates, the last thing you want is for anyone to come to serious harm. The purpose is to have fun, not prove you can drink until you are unconscious or put someone else in that state.

As for the actual drinking games, there are so many in rugby that it would be impossible to list them all. Listed below, however, are all ones that I have regularly played, on tour, on training camps, during tournaments, or elsewhere. They were played by me and my friends at university at least twice a week, and both males and females were welcome.

Spoof

This is a game close to rugby's drinking heart and I played it worldwide. In Hong Kong, they host the world spoofing championships around the Hong Kong Sevens, with the unofficial champion being named as the winner, or at least the one who managed to stagger out of bed for the final.

- You probably need at least five players for this but any more than ten makes the game too long.
- Each player has three coins and puts both hands behind their back. When called upon, they have to put their right fist in the air with as many coins as they want to hold – it can be zero, 1, 2 or 3. The remaining coins stay in their left hand behind their back.
- The Chair or the last winner starts, and says a number which he thinks is the total number of coins in the hands that are held out. Each player in turn then guesses but they cannot call a number that has previously been called. When all have guessed, the hands are opened and the coins totalled. The person who guessed correctly is out of the game and doesn't take part in the next round.
- The process is repeated until there are two players left – the loser knowing they will have to down a pint in one.
- There are disputes as to whether you are allowed to call an impossible number: for example, if you are down to the last three players and you have no coins in the hand you are

holding out, can you call 7 or above, knowing that this number is impossible (the maximum being 6)? Or, if you are in the last two and are holding one coin, can you call zero? Some groups allow this; some don't. When I play, it is usually forbidden to call this way, but it's up to you.

There are two general rules that apply to Spoof:

First, no gloating. When a person guesses correctly they are not allowed to shout, 'Yes', pump their fist or even grin. Any hint of triumphalism of any sort means the player stays in the game.

Second, when the player guesses correctly, he has to withdraw by saying, 'Thank you, Gentlemen, for a very nice game of Spoof,' and without sounding smug or exhibiting any of the things above.

It is surprisingly difficult to adhere to these rules.

Fizz Buzz

- Players generally sit in a circle.
- The player designated to go first says the number '1', and each player thenceforth counts one number in turn.
- Any number divisible by three is replaced by the word 'fizz' and any divisible by five by the word 'buzz'. Numbers divisible by both become 'fizz buzz'.
- A player who hesitates or makes a mistake is eliminated from the game.

For example, a typical round of Fizz Buzz would start as follows: 1, 2, Fizz, 4, Buzz, Fizz, 7, 8, Fizz, Buzz, 11, Fizz, 13, 14, Fizz Buzz, 16, 17, Fizz, 19, Buzz, Fizz, 22, 23, Fizz, Buzz, 26, Fizz, 28, 29, Fizz Buzz, 31, 32, Fizz, 34, Buzz, Fizz . . .

Numbers

- You need at least eight or so people for this, and although you can play it with a large group, anything up to about 15 works well. Beyond that, the game can get unwieldy, and not everyone gets to join in. It is very simple – in theory.
- Once the Chair signals 'go', and starting with the number 1 (obviously), players (a different one each time) call out whatever number is next in the sequence by standing up and saying that number. Once a player has successfully stood up and called a number, they do not have to call again in that round. Simple.
- If two or more players stand and say the number at the same time, they have to drink four fingers' worth of their drink and the count starts gain. So there is a tactical element to timing your 'call' because you have to decide that no one else is going to stand up at the same time as you. However, you don't want to leave it too late because the loser is the person who hasn't shouted out a number by the time the count gets to the last number: he has to down a pint in one go.

You will be surprised at how long it takes to actually complete a whole count, because the pressure to call increases as you get to the final few numbers, and people sit there thinking 'shall I, shan't I', or dummying, i.e. pretending they're about to get up and call out a number.

Bunnies

- The Chair calls a 'general hover', which means all players put their thumbs on either side of their head and waggle their fingers like bunny ears.

- To pass the turn on, a player, starting with the Chair, has to point to someone by taking his hands off his head and pointing with both hands to a specific player – it can be any player.
- The player pointed to keeps both hands on his head, and still waves his fingers, while the players either side of him have to drop their outside hand but keep the hand nearest to that player on their head still waving. The pointed-to player then points to another player, and so on.
- If a player points to the person next to them, they must remember to immediately put back on their head the hand which is next to the player pointed to.
- Players are allowed to dummy call by feigning to point to someone. But in so doing, they are not allowed to have their hands leave their head. If they do, it is an illegal feign and they have to drink two fingers.
- Equally, players who wrongly put their hands up due to a dummy feign have to drink two fingers. Any player who does not put his hand up quickly enough when pointed to has to drink, and any player next to a pointed-to player who does not put up the correct right or left hand also has to drink.

It sounds much more complicated than it is, and when you have had a few rounds it will become a very fast game. In experienced circles, the time given for players to react can be shortened to almost immediate.

Names of . . .

Another simple game. The Chair can either start or nominate another player. Usually, the player who fails and has to drink starts the next round.

- On the initial call, all players slap both palms on the table, clap and then click the fingers of first the right and then left hand in a 1-2-3-4 rhythm.
- After a few sequences the person choosing the topic will say, 'To my left/right' *click, click*, 'Give me' (this is timed on the clicks) 'names of' (again in time to the clicks) 'types of' ... he then names the topic. For example it might be 'motor cars'. So the sequence will be *Slap, Clap*, 'Give me' (said in time to the two clicks), *Slap, Clap*, 'names of' (again, said in time to the two clicks), *Slap, Clap*, 'motor cars' (in time to the two clicks), *Slap, Clap*, 'Ford Mondeo' (in time to the two clicks).
- Each player in sequence then has to name a different example within the topic in time with the two clicks, and after doing the *Slap, Clap*. If they fail, or say one that has previously been said, they drink and the game starts again with another topic.

Just to make sure the Chair doesn't choose ridiculously abstruse topics, if challenged, they have to be able to name as many examples from their chosen subject as there are players. This prevents someone choosing a topic that has no chance of going at least once round the circle. If they can't, they get fined.

Fuzzy Duck

This is another game where the 'onus' is passed around the circle until someone makes a mistake.

- The Chair or the person last making a mistake starts any new game by looking to the person to his left or right and saying, 'Fuzzy Duck'.
- The next player to the left or right passes the onus on by looking in the same direction and says, 'Fuzzy Duck', and so

on, as the game moves around the circle. This carries on and can go right round the circle until a player says, 'Does he?'

- This reverses the direction and the player who last said, 'Fuzzy Duck' has to face the opposite way and pass the onus on but he then has to say, 'Ducky Fuzz.' The onus passes from each player in that direction, each saying, 'Ducky Fuzz' until a player says, 'Does he?'
- This again reverses the direction but now the next player has to change the call back to 'Fuzzy Duck', and so on.
- Any player who hesitates has to drink and also anyone who gets the call wrong.

The usual mistakes include saying 'Does he fuck' and 'Fuck he does!' The faster the game goes, the faster the mistakes arise, and the more gets drunk.

The following are not really games, unless you call 'Hunt the Gullible' a game.

The Three-man or Fireman's Lift

You need three people who know what they are doing and one who doesn't know what is going on. One of the three approaches the innocent bystander and says, pointing to another of the three, something along the lines of, 'My mate here reckons he's so strong that he can pick three people up at once. And I've told him, it's bollocks. We've got two people – do you mind being the third?' If he agrees, two conspirators stand either side of him, binding like prop forwards round his waist and ask him to bind round their shoulders like a hooker. The alleged 'strongest man' then tries to lift them off the ground, which is obviously impossible. 'Tell you what,' he says, 'I need leverage off the floor so that I can lean back.

So lie on the floor so that I can pick you up. And you need to be really tight up against each other.' The unsuspecting man is always made to lie in the middle, between the two in the know. The three are still bound like in the front row of a scrum. So he's locked in on his top half. They are lying on the floor, and Mr Strongman will come up and make an attempt to pick them up. Which is, of course, impossible. You can't pick up three big blokes lying on the floor. So he goes, 'No, no, you're still not holding tight enough.' The three grip each other even tighter. The second attempt fails – of course. Mr Strongman opines, 'The problem is, it's the legs.' So the two outside guys wrap their inside leg around one leg of the middle man, who now literally cannot move at all. And that's when Mr Strongman comes up, undoes the middle man's trousers and everyone just pours beer down his pants.

Sometimes this gets out of hand: I've seen Ketchup, Tabasco sauce, the contents of ashtrays, peanuts, mushy peas and other unspeakable things go down a hapless volunteer's pants. Like I said, it helps to have drunk a bit . . .

Spoons

Another popular tour game with which many readers will be familiar. Take one gullible person, mix with at least two seasoned campaigners, add three tablespoons, and stage in a public place such as a bar. Beware, this can cause serious amusement and serious damage if you have a particularly stubborn player on the other side.

You get two people to sit face to face, each with a spoon in their mouth. They take it turns to bow their head and allow one player to raise his head and strike the other on the back of the head with the spoon. Both players make out that each blow hurts and each tries to use increasing force with each blow. In reality it is nothing more than a mild knock that doesn't really hurt. Eventually, after growing demonstrations of pain and injury, one of the players finally gives in and the other is declared the winner.

You then call for a challenger, someone tough enough to beat what you say is the unbeaten Spoon Champion of the Year. A prop or someone similarly thick usually leaps forward to challenge.

The combatants sit down as before and you let the challenger go first. You make great play of telling the so-called Champion that he cannot cheat and look upwards at all as he might gain an advantage by being able to anticipate the blow. When the challenger delivers the blow, the Champion makes out that it hurt. You can encourage gasps of 'Ouch' and so on.

It is then the Champion's turn, and again you make sure the challenger is not looking up and you stress that he must look straight down at the floor. The Champion then lifts his spoon and feigns the strike but doesn't deliver a blow. Instead a person standing behind the challenger uses his own spoon to whack the challenger's head – this will hurt, so you shouldn't hit him too hard at first.

The challenger then thinks that although it hurt, his opponent must have felt the same degree of pain when he was hit, not realising of course that it doesn't actually hurt much. This scenario continues, with the challenger receiving increasingly painful blows until he gives in or you show mercy and reveal what is going on.

This can get out of hand. When we played this on the 1989 Lions tour, an Aussie chef was so stubborn and so determined not to be beaten by the Poms that it was only when he was finally hit with a ladle that he called 'enough'. He then went berserk when he found out what had been going on.

Blow Football

Here, two people who know the score get a beer tray and fill it with water. Two small goals are made at either end, and, using straws, the players try to blow a piece of rolled-up paper, or better still, a little plastic ball, into each other's goal. First one to score ten, wins.

From the onlookers, you then call for a challenger, someone who doesn't know what is going on. You must insist that both players get their heads right down at tray level before the ball is put into the middle. Then, the person who seems about to place the ball down instead slams his hand into the water, and the 'knowing' player anticipates this by leaping out of the way, leaving the dullard at the other end to get drenched. I thought every rugby player of any seniority knew this one but not Ieuan Evans, the Welsh winger, who got conned on the 1989 Lions tour of Australia. Oh, how we laughed.

To finish on a somewhat more elevated note, I am amused to have now become part of a drinking game myself, the 'Six Nations Drinking Game'. Invented by a certain Dai Lama, the self-styled Welsh Dalai Lama (or perhaps a certain member of the Wales squad), it features a number of phrases to look out for during the BBC coverage of the Six Nations tournament, and how much should be drunk when the viewer hears these things being said by the assorted members of the commentary and studio team.

The 2014 version of the game is reproduced below, by kind permission of the Exalted One himself, and I confess to attempting to include, in every broadcast, unusual words or Shakespeare quotes that might tick the elements in my category. (There is no need to attempt to include complaints about the scrum, because it is a given that I will be doing that anyway.) Thus, in the 2014 England v France game, for example, I had fully intended to use the word 'batracophagy' which means the eating of frogs. If the emotions of the day hadn't got the better of me, it would have been simple. All I needed to say was something like 'The England fans will be hoping that the England back row will be in their batracophagic mood.' I did manage a *Coriolanus* quote, however (flagged up by me for the many viewers who would otherwise not have known), and a couple of other bastardised *Hamlet* quotes: 'To kick or not to kick', and 'To thine own self be true', which I managed to mix in seamlessly when describing how England were sticking to their expansive game plan. Sadly, I'm not sure how many of those partaking in the drinking game got those references. I will obviously have to try harder.

The Dai Lama's Six Nations Drinking Game

2014 SIX NATIONS DRINKING GAME

Presented by Dai Lama 🅑 @WelshDalaiLama

KEY

1 DRINK — *Or a glug, a swig, a gulp, a finger, etc...*
2 DRINKS
3 DRINKS
! DOWN YOUR DRINK

THE MATCH

1 DRINK FOR EACH POINT SCORED
1 Penalty
2 Penalty try
3 Yellow card
! Red card

KICKOFF

1 Each starting player whose club is in France
1 Each player not singing his anthem
3 Each player gaining his first cap

COMMENTARY

2 Any reference to Gatland dropping O'Driscoll...
3 ...if it's Keith Wood
! A pundit needs to be replaced during a match *Imodium*
2 Discussion of Welsh rugby "politics"
3 Reference to England beating NZ
! Phillip Matthews disagrees with a decision that favours Ireland
3 Eddie Butler voiceover
2 Dodgy scarf
1 Mention that it is Brian O'Driscoll's last 6N
2 "Which France will turn up"
2 Reference to France tending to win the 6N after a Lions tour

INCIDENTS

2 Steve Walsh admires himself on the big screen
1 A ref says "yes nine"
! Roger Lewis booing his own team, Vincent Tan style
1 Drink for each angle used during a TMO referral...
3 ...and the TMO still gets it wrong
2 Handbags
3 Someone actually lands a punch
! Someone shaves off Kelly Brown's eyebrows

1 Uses a word you don't know the meaning of
2 Complains about the scrum
3 Quotes Shakespeare

INTERVIEWS

1 Each of the following:
"Point to prove" "Get a result" "Y'know"
"Physicality" "To be fair"
"The boys" "Obviously"
"Front up" "To be honest"

! "It's all the ref's fault"

@WelshDalaiLama

! North lifts a player over his shoulder
2 Farrell has a tantrum
3 Alun Wyn Jones smiles
3 Scott Williams scores at Twickenham

1 "Numbers"
1 "Stop it there"
1 "Run it on"
! Goes one half without saying any of the above

Follow @WelshDalaiLama on Twitter for more words of wisdom and a blessing for your hangover

3

'Here Come the Judge'

Many rugby tours have Tour Courts, but in their fullest finery they are an English institution, though copied to a lesser degree by other countries. I don't know if they exist in other team sports, but they are as integral to rugby tours as the option for French players not to bother playing on any given day. They cover some of the most infamous stories that take place on tours, the ones that usually don't make it into books because they involve the things players have been caught doing that, on mature reflection, they ought not to have done.

Tour Courts have a dual function: on the one hand, they are used to hand out fines and punishments for genuine infringements of tour rules, or for antisocial behaviour, such as having an especially annoying habit; and they help everyone to air small, genuine, grievances without resorting to confrontation. That way, such things can be dealt with while providing entertainment at the same time. Courts are a lot of fun and also give the chance for players to stitch each other up with sometimes spurious accusations and allegedly heinous crimes. All are brought before what can often amount to a kangaroo court led by a judge who then hands out punishments to miscreants, the range and severity of which can vary from the slightly suspect to the unashamedly cruel.

Courts vary in the way they address errant behaviour, depending on the level of rugby played. As many of the fines involve drinking, it means that courts on junior tours are often the ones that inflict the most extreme fines; whereas those on, for example, a Lions tour have to be a bit more inventive, as it's not advisable to tip pint after pint into players.

Court sittings usually take place after each game, so this would amount to once or twice a week on an England or Lions tour. Sometimes they took place on coaches during a long trip somewhere, but more often than not they took place in a makeshift courtroom. With England, we would try and make the setting as formal as possible within the boundaries of our circumstances. Ideally, we had a proper bench (i.e. a table) and if possible it would be on a raised platform to add solemnity. On it sat the Judge, flanked by the Court Clerk, while the prosecutor would stand on one side. The defendant – and his counsel, if he had one – would stand on the other side of the Judge, preferably at a lower level, in order to feel suitably inferior. Other actors in the courtroom drama would come and go as requested by the Judge, wherever possible with suitable flourish. In the last few years of my England duties, the Judge actually got a wig, gown and gavel, and his entrance was formally announced by the Clerk as follows: 'Order, order, pray silence for His Honour Judge Rendall' (or whoever had ascended to that lofty height). The assembled would then clap slowly as the Judge entered, while chanting, 'Here come the Judge, Here come the Judge; everybody know that here come the Judge.'

We didn't always have the formality of a courtroom, so courts were sometimes hastily convened in places like an airport lounge. On the England Students tour of Japan in 1982, where uniquely a court sat every day, they were held on the bus. As an aside, on that tour I was fined every day for masquerading as a local!

The Tour Court's main protagonists are usually – but not always – made up of senior players. First of all there is the Judge. During my years of touring, I served under several judges, but Paul Rendall, the Wasps and England prop, was universally known as 'Judge', not only because he fulfilled this role for many years, but also because he had a reputation for meting out tough but fair punishments and fines. Rendall's sobriquet became so commonly used that a young Jason Leonard was once overheard asking him, ''Ere, Judge, why don't you have a nickname?'

In 1990, during England's ill-advised tour of Argentina, a new Judge had to be appointed, as Rendall didn't tour, so an appropriately judgemental replacement had to be found. The ideal candidate turned out to be another prop, Mark Linnett of Moseley, who also happened to be a policeman, so eminently suited to the job, if you think someone dubbed a pervert – and he won't mind me calling him that because he actually volunteered the description – from the West Midlands is the right man to preside over a court and hand out justice. If that description sounds a tad harsh, readers should take into account that Linnett claimed that two of his earliest childhood memories involved rolling around in a tray of ball-bearings and the heavy-duty hand cleanser Swarfega, and an encounter with a dog and a furry glove; the details of both incidents are too disturbing to print.

It will come as no surprise to readers to discover that I was always the prosecuting counsel: not simply because I am a qualified lawyer but also because I had the sort of deviously inventive nature needed in that position. Nor will it surprise readers to know that I took my role extremely seriously.

Court enforcers are also appointed. It is their job to enforce the fines and punishments, extract them, or simply inflict them on people if they are not carried out willingly. Court enforcers are invariably – and again unsurprisingly – big men from the second row, and when I played they also had the happy coincidence of being members of various constabularies; men such as Wade Dooley, Dean Richards and Martin Bayfield, in the face of whom resistance was futile.

As in real courts, the Court Clerk is responsible for taking in the complaints, and reading out all the charges, ideally in a Crown Court-esque manner that makes the defendants fear the worst. As the prosecuting counsel, I used to enjoy working with the clerk to dress the charges up into something that sounded as serious as possible. This often meant having to be creative with the offences. So, for example, a charge of 'corrupting public morals' would apply to a player caught wanking in bed by his room-mate, a regular occurrence on month-long tours. A count of 'offending public decency' might apply if a player was seen heading off with a particularly average-looking woman. There was always the ubiquitous charge of 'damaging tour morale' which, if framed in the right way, could cover anything from mistakes in games to, well, almost anything we wanted.

It was always interesting to see how certain players assumed natural roles in the court process. Some were found to be very effective conduits of knowledge and became known as the right people to go to in order to get an incident highlighted. Often the quieter members of a tour party are the most useful because, by not talking, they listen and pick up all sorts of gossip.

So many things happen on a tour that they cannot all be brought up, so there was often a competitive element (surprise surprise) between players to have their reported events heard. In fact, some players got really hacked off if they reported something that didn't then get in, to which I'd just say, 'Sorry, we can't put every-thing in – and anyway, yours isn't funny.' Because if the alleged charge didn't relate to an actual discipline issue, the first consider-ation was always, 'Can we make it funny?'

In order to have one direct line only to the court, a tour sneak is appointed, to which players, particularly the 'conduits' referred to above, grass up their colleagues. With the England team, he was universally known as Mr X. In court, he sat wearing dark glasses and a hat to protect his anonymity. Mr X also had an active interest in the errant behaviour of players. Not content merely to wait for reports, he searched for cases, questioning players to extract infor-mation. He gave the results of his investigations as evidence in court, and his testimony could not be questioned because he was deemed to be inviolable. There was usually no shortage of volunteers for this position because it was huge fun and meant that the player got to know everything that went on. But of all the men to have filled the role of Mr X, John Olver, my fellow hooker, was the most naturally gifted. This was partly due to his undisputable sense of humour and popularity, and partly due to his enthusiasm; but mainly, it was because (as he was the first to joke) he was the sort of horrible little man who delighted in the downfall of his contemporaries. It is therefore no coincidence that his nickname was 'Vermin'.

That nomenclature came about during a court session out in France when Olver and Peter Winterbottom were caught talking while the Judge was addressing the court. When asked by His Honour what they were saying, Olver, who was never slow to fab-ricate anything that would drop his fellow players in it to save his own skin, replied, 'Mr Winterbottom just said that he wished he could shove that pineapple [which was part of a bowlful of fruit on the dinner table] up your arse.'

Winterbottom, taking the view that to dispute this invention would only make things worse for him, admitted uttering the subversive remark and was duly punished. As he returned to his table he shook his head and said to Olver, 'You really are vermin.' Thus was born was a life-long nickname and one which Olver has never raised serious objection to or been able to refute.

Certain players specialised in giving character references, and one in particular, the winger Mark Bailey, now the High Master of St Paul's School in London and a former academic from Cambridge University, was particularly brilliant at this: because he is very clever, his reference would start off sounding very complimentary, but in a very oblique way; then, gradually, he would turn things round, until by the end, he would go in for the kill and just end with a withering 'and it's just the sort of thing this fucker would do'. And bring the house down.

The defence counsel was usually the thickest person on tour, or the newest person, on the basis that they were still really shy – in either case, they would be useless at defending their man. Defendants usually had the choice of whether to settle (and thereby plead guilty), or use the court-appointed defence counsel. If they chose to defend themselves – because quite rightly they had no faith in their counsel – and they were subsequently found guilty, they were then fined double. So invariably they were fined double.

When witnesses were brought before the court to give evidence, they swore a suitable oath, such as, 'I swear by the balls of the mighty "Judge" to tell the truth, the whole truth and nothing like the truth.' (Note the final phrase.) Some players found that even speaking in the public (actually the semi-private) confines of the court was a bit of an ordeal, while others used it as a platform from which to show off. The latter group invariably threw up a few surprises, as hitherto quiet players were sometimes unexpectedly entertaining and witty. However, any nervousness they might have experienced might also have been explained by the fact that witnesses were liable at any moment to find themselves up on an instant charge of being utterly incompetent if they stumbled, stuttered or got things wrong. Dewi Morris, always reliable when it came to foot-in-mouth moments, once memorably began his evidence with the immortal words, 'Right, er, to tell this story properly, I have to take you back to next Thursday!' Instant merriment; instant fine.

Evidence-gathering is a key part of proceedings, and people regularly seized (stole) evidence in order to produce it later before the court: magazines, videos of questionable taste, clothing, almost anything that was relevant or incriminating. On one Lions tour, in the case of one of the backroom staff, a piece of evidence was introduced thus: 'I produce before the Court, M'Lud, exhibit A: a video entitled *1001 Cum Shots*.' Nothing was off-limits.

The 1990 England tour to Argentina was a shambles, and I should not have gone on it, but so many stories emerged from it that it became memorable, at least for me, for reasons other than rugby. As mentioned above, the Tour Court had a new Judge, Mark Linnett, who proved to be a more than adequate substitute for Rendall. He effortlessly maintained the tradition of hideous unfairness and savage sentencing that is required to do this most important of jobs. It was a good thing that Linnett was up to it because on that tour the court was kept busy.

However, when it came to being late, the Geordie flanker Mickey Skinner was a serial offender, to the extent that Tour Court fines and His Honour Judge Linnett's punishments were insufficient to keep him on the straight and narrow, and the management fined him on a regular basis. One morning, he and three others had yet again been late, so their punishment this time was simply to run all the way back from training, which meant running about four miles. Coach Roger Uttley led by example and set off. 'Follow me,' he announced before pounding off down the road. The rest of us got on the team bus which afforded us the best seats from which to enjoy the scene. The problem for the miscreants was that Roger was super fit, so although the others tried to keep up, they were soon left trailing in his wake, huffing and puffing along the hard shoulder of the dual carriageway we were on. Skinner had other ideas. He simply jumped into a passing taxi. Our bus duly got stuck in a bumper-to-bumper traffic jam. 'Rog, Rog!' we cried out, waving our arms to try and attract Roger's attention, to no avail, as he had already sprinted on ahead.

Meanwhile Skinner, in his taxi, was also waving to everybody as it slowly inched alongside our coach, while on the hard shoulder, the other three so-called runners continued to lumber slowly towards the team hotel. Uttley duly got to the hotel first and stood there waiting outside for everyone slowly to arrive, on foot or by coach. Just as we neared the hotel, the taxi overtook us and we watched as it crept slowly up the ramp that led up to the entrance . . . then crept equally slowly back down, before finally disappearing round the corner, never to be seen again. Mysteriously, no one got out, and no one was sitting in the back any more. In fact, Skinner, having found out from the taxi driver that a tall, Mr Potato-Head lookalike – i.e. Uttley – was standing outside the hotel, had promptly lain down on the floor of the taxi and ordered the driver to keep going and not to stop. Two minutes later, just as our coach finally reached the entrance and we were getting off, who should come walking back to the front of the hotel from around the corner, but Mickey Skinner, looking remarkably unfazed. 'Have you got any money, Rog? I need to pay for the taxi.'

Needless to say, the events were retold by various witnesses, each from their own standpoint, at the subsequent court case, and Skinner was forced to drink an unholy cocktail of substances that were so awful they should have come with a health warning.

For most people, that experience would have served as a note to self: 'Do not be late again.' But for Skinner, it was the launchpad for yet another outrageous attempt at avoiding a punishment. By then, he was on a final warning. 'If you are late again, there will be serious consequences, because it's not funny any more. It's not a game.' A few mornings later, it was not so much a case of 'Where's Wally?' but 'Where's Skinner?' Half an hour later, he finally appeared, with the tour liaison officer, a guy called Fafa, at his side – who must have been about 4ft 10in when standing really straight. And Fafa was saying, in his best garbled English, 'Oh Skinner, he foil burglary, robbery, he chase man down, very brave …' Skinner was nodding enthusiastically: 'Yeah, I saw this guy in one of the rooms, trying to rifle stuff; so I went, "Oi, mate!" and he scarpered, so I had to chase him, the police comes along and what have you …'

Though initially accepted, this of course turned out to be a complete and utter fabrication. But Skinner, as we later found out, had woken up late – again – and realised, very accurately as it happened, that 'I'm really in trouble this time, so I'm going to have to make something up that's so extreme that people won't question it – at least initially. And by the time they do find out the truth, they will have half forgotten what actually happened and they'll forgive me.' So he had basically threatened poor Fafa, who had had little choice but to go along with the cunning plan, given the height differential. The artifice lasted a couple of days; but, as so often happens, the truth finally emerged, not least because Skinner couldn't help telling people about the wheeze – and he got seriously whacked in court. Nonetheless, he stayed on tour, so his end justified his means.

Punishments could be highly original and reveal the warped mind of the Judge and others in charge of thinking them up. This was especially so on some of the earlier international tours I went on. I remember Dean Richards on an England tour of Australia coming up with a historic cocktail that had to be drunk from a full-to-the-brim pint glass. Should you want to try this one at home, the ingredients were:

- Brandy
- Lager
- Beer
- Half a cigar
- A pilchard
- Salt and pepper
- About four other things which nobody could properly identify (suitable licence to be added to personalise the cocktail).

In Argentina, Bob Kimmins, the 6ft 10in Orrell second row, was given as a fine to down a bottle of champagne in one go. 'No problem,' he shrugged, 'I once downed a bottle of brown sauce in one go, so this is easy.' 'Okay,' we said, part sceptical, part surprised. In the end, because he had to drink from the actual bottle, he downed it in two goes, pausing to catch his breath halfway through because of all the bubbles. He was lucky the court showed leniency for the tremendous effort as, technically, he should have downed it in one. But the belch he let out at the end remains memorable to this day. Still, Kimmins's efforts pale in comparison with those of a complete lunatic on a Nottingham University weekend tour, who, for a bet, got two-thirds of the way through a bottle of Tabasco sauce before vomiting copiously.

Obviously, punishments often meant drinking a seriously large volume of alcohol in one go: an entire glass of whisky, a pint of beer or sometimes two or three in a row. However, there is little point in detailing specific instances here, as once someone has heard one story about a player downing a drink in one, they have heard them all. Suffice to say that there was a strict rule that if you didn't drink everything in one go, you had to repeat the fine, no matter how much you had been ordered to drink in the first place. There is, again, little point in recounting the numerous times this meant a player spontaneously vomiting after the repeat drink, only to find himself having to drink a third fine for not keeping the original or second drink down.

On occasion, though, in accordance with the saying that 'the punishment has to fit the crime', different types of punishments were handed out. If two people had been a bit cliquey, for example, and had been hanging out a bit too much together, a pair of handcuffs would be found, and the guys would have to spend the night handcuffed to each other. During an England tour to Fiji (and Australia) in 1988, John Bentley, the Yorkshire winger, got tied to a tree, for reasons I now can't even recall, and made to sing '*Chanson d'amour*' every five minutes. He was happy to do this until John Orwin, who was tour captain, went out and pissed on him, for no apparent reason at all. After that he wasn't very happy at all. 'It was funny until then!' he complained.

The power and pleasure that court officials derive from running the Tour Courts are, however, double-edged because at the end of the tour, a People's Revolutionary Court is appointed and another set of players takes over the positions of the existing officials. And in the best tradition of revolutions, when the People take over, they wreak terrible revenge on their former oppressors. So, if you are an official from the original court, you have to decide how you are going to play it: are you prepared to be sadistic during the tour, knowing that you are bound to get it in the neck at the end? Although, in practice, it doesn't actually matter how you conduct yourself as a Judge: you get it anyway. In essence, you've got to be able to dish it out as well as take it.

Even for the mildest offences tried by the Revolutionary Court, any drinking fines were at least double, often treble, the amounts issued by the Tour Court as standard. Furthermore, if one of the officials hadn't actually done anything that could be made the subject of a specific behavioural-based charge in the Revolutionary Court, they could be charged with treating the ordinary members of the tour party with contempt by the manner in which they had discharged their duties while acting in an official capacity. On the 1994 tour of South Africa I was made to wear a red dress for the evening, on the spurious grounds that I had got off with a local girl who, on the evening of the alleged offence, had herself been wearing a red dress. I tried to protest by telling the truth, namely that she was the friend of a friend and actually I had gone out to dinner with her and her boyfriend. Truth didn't matter to these people and I was duly found guilty; which is as it should have been.

They weren't above dragging in matters that had not even happened on a tour: I was once convicted of the equally spurious charge of propositioning one of the girls in the health spa of the hotel at which we had stayed between the semi-final and final of the 1991 World Cup. This was not brought up then but two years later at a Revolutionary Court on an England New Year training camp in Lanzarote. I was accused of having said to her, 'Have you ever seen a body like this?' What I had actually said was, 'Do you see many battered bodies like this?' At the time, I had rake marks all over my back and my sides from the previous game against the Scots. My fine was announced: on the shout of a particular word (I can't recall what), I had to strip to my underwear and do a body-builder's posing routine – merciless.

Perhaps the most memorable example of retribution was that visited on Mark Linnett. He had been spotted ogling a girl round the hotel pool who was wearing an unfeasibly small polka dot bikini, and it was this that formed the basis for the charge of perversion that was brought against him in the Revolutionary Court. He was quite happy to plead guilty to the charge and, when his sentence was read out, showed little of the embarrassment that usually went with an extreme sentence. It was ordered that on the journey back to England, Linnett had to wear a similar bikini to the one worn by the girl – believe me, it didn't even cover his modesty. Thereafter, upon the calling of a trigger word, he had to perform a striptease down to said bikini, whenever and wherever he/we happened to be. In order to prevent players calling out the word continuously, as they would have done if allowed, it was held that this could not occur more than a certain number of times on the journey home.

The first call happened almost straight away as we assembled to board the coach back to the airport, and Linnett duly stripped in the hotel lobby, raucously encouraged by the squad and under the bemused looks of other hotel guests. On completion, he received a huge round of applause, after which he then donned his number one travel clothes over the top of the bikini and clambered onto the coach. The second call came in the departures area of Buenos Aires airport where, once again, Linnett performed the striptease to pretty much the same reception from players and onlookers as had accompanied his first effort. However, the second time, Linnett added many more flourishes to his routine, smiling throughout and betraying absolutely no sense of self-consciousness whatsoever. It was therefore decreed that his punishment be withdrawn, on the grounds that it was no punishment at all as, plainly, he was enjoying it far too much.

Tour Courts are an integral part of any rugby tour, although not all countries go about organising them in the same way, and from my own experience it is clear that the concept is far more developed in English rugby than elsewhere. The Tour Courts even on Lions tours were a pale imitation of the ones held on England tours. When with the 1989 Lions, Donal Lenihan assumed supreme authority as the Judge, with me, again, providing legal expertise as Prosecutor. The popular but not particularly effusive Welsh prop, Mike Griffiths, was given the thankless task of being Defence Counsel and was often reduced to ending his submissions with, 'Well see, it's like this – the bastard probably done it.'

The Scots had sporadic courts where John Jeffrey played a role, as did the Irish where Keith Wood was prominent – indeed I think Wood was made Judge on the 1997 Lions tour of South Africa. I don't think the Welsh had anything other than the odd court session, and the French never had them. Our Gallic friends are probably far too cool for such levity.

The All Blacks' Tour Courts reflected the dominant role of the senior players. Other than the captain, who for obvious reasons could not be part of the mock judicial process, it was the senior players who filled all the official tour positions and who dealt out justice as they saw fit. It seems that Richard Loe, the formidable if slightly unhinged Waikato prop, featured in many guises.

Unlike the England courts, they didn't have a Revolutionary Court at the end of the tour, as this would have contravened their idea of the importance of hierarchy. The Kiwis, being more focused on performance than fun, eschewed spirits in any of the fines meted out, sticking to beer instead. For those who didn't drink, like Michael Jones, their legendary flanker, the drink for fines would be orange juice, which is actually a lot more unpleasant to drink in large quantities than beer.

In stark contrast, the Australians had a relatively egalitarian and democratic approach to all matters on tour, and Tour Courts were no exception. They rotated court positions. 'Yeah,' I was told, 'that way, everyone gets a go, and it makes younger players feel involved.' To which my response was, 'What the hell for? Surely that's a lot less fun?' Very strange people, the Australians.

All this might sound incomprehensible to non-rugby people and, in truth, I have to say that the practice is a little odd. However, Tour Courts were hugely entertaining and players looked forward to the sittings as they knew they would have a laugh and, more importantly, see someone else getting into hot water – *schadenfreude* is an ignoble but powerful sentiment. Of all the memories I have of touring, the courts will remain one of the most powerful because they were fun, and showed players at their best – and worst. Plus, I got to indulge my advocacy fantasies.

The Ideal Tour Court

If you haven't been on tour where a court has sat and want to have one on your next tour, here are a few recommendations to help you:

A. The Judge – he is obviously the main figure in a Tour Court, so make sure you get the right person in order to get the most out of what should be a tour highlight. He should be a senior figure who is universally popular, but should not be the captain, as it's important to demonstrate that nobody is above the law. He should be someone who is used to speaking, can think quickly and is inventive; while you do not need an academic, you cannot have a dullard. An inventive Judge will come up with more varied punishments, and this will add to the entertainment; dull Judges who only hand out larger and larger drinking fines soon try everyone's patience.

B. Prosecuting Counsel – it isn't mandatory to have someone with legal experience, but if he does, from whatever area of life, he can usually frame charges in a quasi-legal manner which makes them funnier. Although it is traditional that the accused is almost invariably found guilty, on occasion this won't happen if a quick-witted defendant or his counsel is able to run rings round a prosecutor. This should not become the norm.

C. Court Clerk – not necessary if you are short of people, but someone who can actually organise the proceedings is a help.

D. Chief Sneak – another crucial role, and one for which there is usually no shortage of volunteers. However, take care to choose someone who is able to work in the background. This

56

usually means someone who is not necessarily a star player. Informers get more information if they work quietly, taking players to one side to elicit information. Also you don't want someone who is unable to keep information to themselves or from court officials, as this spoils the surprise. People will then be reluctant to go to them to report potential cases.

E. Enforcers – this means what it says. They have to be able to keep order and ensure strict compliance with court orders and sentences; strangely enough, policemen tend to be quite good at this.

F. Defence Counsel – you don't actually need a defence counsel, and if you can't find a suitable one it's best to let defendants defend themselves. However, if you can get someone who is either very witty or, paradoxically, very dull, it's worth appointing them. The former will provide some jousting between the two counsels and can make cases even funnier, though the premise that defendants are not supposed to be found innocent should at all times be kept firmly in mind. With the latter, it's worth offering the defendant a choice: he can use appointed counsel or defend himself. However, if he defends himself, any fine that might be imposed is doubled.

G. Court rules – these can be as fulsome or as spartan as you like, but it's worth at least agreeing on the basics, such as how to address the bench; not talking during cases; which hand to drink fines with, and so on.

H. Miscellaneous – anything can be added to your courts if you think it will help, but remember this: courts are for entertainment, not the pursuit of personal vendettas; they should not to be unduly embarrassing, and any sentences passed should not be dangerous.

4

Masquerading as a Local

The first time I played representative rugby abroad was with England Universities in 1981. We played against the French Universities in – of all places – Dunkirk. I had travelled down to Dover with Dylan Davies, a terrifying Welsh prop who was technically studying at Loughborough but seemed strangely available to freelance for Nottingham on a regular basis. We had been told to book in to a bed & breakfast in Dover as we would be catching a very early ferry the next morning to Dunkirk. While some players got an Athletic Union subsidy for this, I had to pay my own way. Clearly the game in France was to be played on a no-expense-spared basis.

It turned out to be a memorable affair as we played against a strong and brutal French side that contained the soon-to-be French international fly-half Didier Camberabero. We lost the game, but the after-match function made up for the loss.

The pre-dinner reception was sponsored by Ricard and their

Pastis 51 was the only drink available, along with tiny jugs of water for use as a mixer for the spirit. By the time the dinner started, both teams had consumed about a pint of pastis. To aggravate matters, for some unknown reason the French handed out a box containing not only novelty hats and party streamers but also a number of tubes and polystyréne balls. These were meant as harmless kids' toys. In the hands and mouths of rugby players, they were transformed into weapons capable of firing the balls nearly fifteen metres.

Fuelled by wine, beer and more pastis, both teams got louder and wilder, to the point that complete anarchy broke out. The British consul refused to speak after being pelted with balls and fruit and his French counterpart tried but was prevented by the French team standing up and singing each time he opened his mouth. They don't do dinners like that any more.

When the time came to go through Customs on the way back, Davies realised he couldn't find his passport. This being pre-9/11 days, he immediately came up with a cunning plan: he simply shuffled through passport control on his knees, surrounded by a group of teenage schoolchildren. The fact that he was sporting a rather large moustache did not seem to alert the customs officers that anything was amiss and he safely made it back without a hitch.

My first proper overseas tour was the England Students tour to Japan and Hong Kong the following year, 1982. The squad was picked from students at all English tertiary education establishments, as opposed to the English Universities squad which comprised only students from actual universities, although not from Oxbridge (for reasons that I never quite established, but which probably had something to do with them not considering themselves to be just any old university).

Junior tours are usually memorable because of the non-playing elements, notably the drinking and the fun and games. The results of the actual matches are completely incidental – in fact, sometimes it's actually an inconvenience to have to play. Senior tours, on the other hand, whether at club or representative level, tend to stand or fall according to how successful the results are. The England Students tour remains my favourite of all the tours I went on, but not just because it was a successful one. There was something special about the group of players that made it hugely memorable for me, which might be surprising, given I went on some very successful England and Lions tours.

In part it was because we were all of a reasonably similar age; in part it was because, being students, despite all our many faults, we were perhaps of a more homogenous mind-set and intelligence bracket than was the case on other tours, which were invariably made up of some very dissimilar people. That's not to say I didn't enjoy being with people who were very different from me, simply that so many of us on the students' tour were on the same wavelength. In particular, and this is a very important part of a tour, the humour was of the same clever and cutting quality.

Though I might be influenced by the fact that this was my first representative tour, I believe it was special because it contained so many talented players who went on to gain international honours. The backs, in particular, were extremely good. Simon Halliday, Mark Bailey, Barry Evans, Chris Martin, Steve Bates and Simon Smith were all subsequently capped for England. Andy Dun, Francis Emurewa and I gained caps as England forwards and most of the others went on to play at least at senior club level. When I recently took the time to track down many of the tour squad, it was notable how many had gone on to have outstanding success in wide-ranging fields. To give just a few examples and without embarrassing them by name, here is a selection of their later careers: director of a specialist Neurosciences Trust; Honorary Professor of Interventional Radiology; High Master of St Paul's

School; international advertising guru; senior director of UBS and author. I could go on – suffice to say, they were a genuinely exceptional group of people.

Not only was it the first major tour for many of us, it was to a part of the world that, to my knowledge, none of us had ever visited before, and that made it feel even more special.

All these factors meant that we developed a bond between us on this tour that felt totally unique, and the fact is, I still think back to it regularly because it represents the ultimate touring experience for me, as I know it also does for several of my then team-mates.

The tour itself had been organised on a shoestring. Everyone had been asked to pay a £200 contribution towards the costs of the tour, which was quite a lot of money for students in 1982. Like the Dunkirk trip above, some had applied to their university or college Athletics Union for funding, and in some cases, this amount had been approved. But in my case and that of others, the trip had to be financed by extending an overdraft.

A solitary training shirt and playing kit were provided, as was some sort of tour bag, plus a tour blazer, slacks, tie and one polo shirt. It was a far cry from today's tours, even representative student tours, where players are given vast amounts of sponsored kit, luggage and clothes. We did have a bit of sponsorship and help from a few individuals who supported the tour financially, although again, by today's levels, the sums were paltry. Interestingly, it is not widely known that a certain Denis Thatcher – who was a qualified rugby referee, and a passionate rugby fan – helped the tour get off the ground. I believe the fact that Castrol also participated financially may have been down to him, as I think he had worked for them in the past. When I look back, the lack of funding and provision actually provided a kind of unity in adversity in the party. 'We're all in it together,' as David Cameron would say, although on that occasion we really were all in it together.

On the coaching side, we had a tour manager, and an assistant manager, John Robbins, who doubled as the coach. Robbins was an intense and thoughtful man who, despite a conspicuous lack of top-level coaching experience, was nevertheless impressive, and I liked him a lot. We took with us Brian Anderson of Scotland, who I also got to know well and liked, even though he was a referee. And that was it. No forwards or backs coach; no defence coach; no fitness analyst; no nutrition adviser; no statistician; no PR people. And no lawyer.

When it came to the medical side – and I had to check this because I couldn't believe it was so – we had neither doctor nor physiotherapist. Today it is scarcely believable but, again, it created a determination to get on with the job. All very English.

The effect of this lack of qualified medical advice had a few consequences. Five of the party were medical students at varying stages of their studies and, though not yet qualified, they were endlessly pestered over various injuries and ailments about which they knew a limited amount and could do nothing anyway. At one point, I remember going for acupuncture for a back strain I was suffering from. It didn't work, but at least I can now say I tried it, although the fact that it was recommended by a medical student might explain its lack of effectiveness. It is astonishing that, despite having no medical back-up, we managed to stay reasonably fit and had a full squad to pick from for nearly every game.

The lack of a qualified specialist in sexually transmitted diseases wasn't so inconsequential for one player though. 'Will you have a look at this?' he asked one of his medical student team-mates. Advised that he had indeed caught an STD as a result of a brief fling, the player was cornered by his girlfriend on his return when she demanded to know why he refused to consummate their reunion. Judging that he had no alternative, he confessed to the dalliance, only for the girlfriend to end the relationship there and then. He later found out that his symptoms had been caused by some dodgy penicillin he had been given to treat what turned out to be the non-existent disease – unlucky. The medical student was luckier: he went on to qualify and to treat many patients much more successfully.

Very quickly, some unofficial one-upmanship took place regarding where people were studying, but it's a measure of how well we got on from the start that this was taken in good humour. The Oxbridge contingent included Simon Halliday, Peter Enevoldson and Tony Watkinson, and many others were at what were considered 'proper' universities, as opposed to those where you had to ask, 'Where is it you're at? Which Poly?' On the other hand, no one got the piss taken out of them for reading a book, whereas on other tours I have regularly had to fend off the predictable 'Huh, you reading again?' with a resigned, 'Yes. Because I *can*!' Here, there was diverse taste in reading, music and general interests, but no one felt they had to tone down who they were.

Even the Tour Courts and their fines were inventive and unusual. In fact, we so enjoyed the courts that we made sure we held a session every day, during coach journeys if necessary. I was given – already – the role of Chief Prosecutor because I was studying law. Others found similar vocations. Mark Bailey, who was a PhD student at Cambridge at the time, went on to be an England winger and, later, headmaster at a top public school, established his reputation as an expert witness. Players would go to significant lengths to try to think up charges to bring before the court, regularly reporting people, coming up with ideas and accusations, along the lines of, 'You know so and so did this.' They would also try to devise original fines with which to punish offenders, so that, for once, fines were not the usual drinking fines. For example, it was on this tour that I saw how amusing it was to make people act in a manner totally opposite to their normal self. Whether it was their accent, look or demeanour, making them act in such a contrary way usually produced huge fun. It could be as simple as making someone who was quite posh talk in a yokel accent; but it was made much funnier if it had to be one for a whole day until the next court session because the player would have to call moves during training in the accent, and the same in team meetings.

The fact that we were in Japan meant that the extent to which alcohol played a starring role on the tour was limited. As a student I drank a lot and almost every night, even though I was still very fit. It was the same for most of the other players but, as alcohol was very expensive in Japan, we simply couldn't afford to. We had a very small daily allowance which just about covered incidental things but didn't enable us to hit the town in search of bars in the evenings. After each game, though, there would be a reception and formal dinner, and because our hosts, the Japanese, on the whole spoke very little English – or none at all – they were very insistent, as part of their impeccable hospitality and politeness, on toasting us a lot, and on us toasting with them. Sign language was invariably used to indicate 'just drink', which we duly did.

Most dinners went by with no more than a bit of high-spirited fun and lots of singing, but the final farewell dinner ended in ignominy for one player. The Japan RFU hosted us and the New Zealand Universities team in the beautiful setting of the Imperial Hotel, Tokyo. Speeches were made by the President of the Japanese RFU and the managers of the two touring teams, and the menu, described in flawless French, included '*Cocktail de crevettes*' (prawn cocktail for those in doubt), '*Sole bonne femme*' (nothing to do with a good single woman, simply sole in a cream and white wine sauce) and '*Filet de bœuf poëlé à la mode*' (pan-fried fashionable beef . . . or whatever). It was all supposed to be a dignified, classy evening.

Though it didn't get off to the maniacal start of the English Universities game against France, the fact that the mini-tournament had finished enabled us to mix freely with the Kiwis and the Japanese. As usual with rugby, the on-field battles were forgotten and the serious socialising began, with a lot of drink consumed. Towards the end of the dinner, we had a toast to the Queen and the Emperor, after which Simon Halliday issued a general toast to those of us sitting on an adjacent table. This is a rugby tradition and means that, when toasted, you have to drink down in one go whatever is in front of you. If you like, you can pass the toast on to another table or back to the person who has toasted you.

I wish I could claim to have thought up our response, but in truth I can't remember who had the idea.

Anyhow, we decided to keep toasting Halliday by return, but instead of the *sake* that we could see he was drinking, we swapped ours for water. Both being clear liquids, Halliday did not spot this, probably because we were pouring our water from a *sake* bottle. So, not only was Halliday drinking to the official toasts, of which there were many, given the formalities, he was also toasting to our invitations. Halliday refused to eschew the challenge of multiple toasts, showing the sort of pluck that one would expect from an Oxford gentleman. Eventually, the alcohol hit him and he began singing and shouting, and generally flailing around until, finally, he had to be carried out, a gibbering wreck. I can only imagine what his headmaster or university tutor would have said about it all – his utterances weren't even grammatically correct.

In contrast, Halliday did show his cultured side when the two of us and a small group of players went to dinner with the Chief Executive of Honda and his stunningly beautiful wife. We were just having a few drinks in a hotel bar, when at one point she just got up, went over to the piano in the corner, and started serenading us for a good half hour. She played extraordinarily well, and we sat there with total admiration for her talent, marvelling at the beauty of the classical music she played for us.

Everywhere we went in Japan we were stared at. Not in a rude or intrusive way, because the Japanese are the politest of people, but in a way which betrayed the fact they had never seen specimens quite like us. This was especially true of players such as our flanker Andy Dun, who was not only 6ft 3in tall, but also had a shock of blond hair. Anyone who is either tall or has blond hair stands out in Japan, so those who combined both features, like several in our group, were objects of total fascination and were practically mobbed. Girls would gather together and giggle and point, in their typically demure way, because they had literally never seen quite so many extraordinary-looking men. However, when it came to Francis Emurewa, our other 6ft 3in flanker, he was black, and physically very imposing, so rather than giggle and point, the girls would simply stand back and gawp. It was all very strange and amusing.

It has to be said, on the subject of Japanese women, that there were very few public morals charges brought up in the Tour Courts, which may have something to do, firstly, with the decorousness of the women we encountered, and secondly that nobody spoke Japanese. The hotels we stayed in were on the whole standard and Westernised, so the food was generally the sort we would have been used to back home. We did get the opportunity to try out sushi, though, which in 1982 was not yet the commonplace food it now is in England. Although I like most things, I decided during that tour that sushi and I don't really go together. I can cram it down if I need to, but if I'm honest, I don't actually like it. Fortunately, it's not typical food for a rugby player.

The absolute non-playing highlight of the tour wasn't a drink-fuelled night out or some of the tremendous scenery; it was the three nights we spent at a monastery in Tenri before our game against the full Japan side in Osaka. The monastery itself was quite isolated and as a result was completely self-sufficient. On a mundane, practical level this meant that it had – and it sounds ridiculous because nowadays laundry is always taken care of by the host union – its own, free, washing machines. Once that became known, everyone went rushing around in a state of high excitement because up until then we had either had to pay for extortionate hotel laundry services, do it ourselves in hotel laundry rooms, or not do it at all. Here it was free, so everyone put everything in, down to the last sock.

Staying at the monastery gave us a small insight into traditional Japanese life. We slept on low futon-style beds, we took off our shoes indoors and ate at low Japanese-style tables; screens separated out the various public areas of the main building, and an air of total peace and serenity pervaded the entire place. The monks themselves lived in another building, so we were not able to meet them, but the three days we spent there were very simple, and completely different from the normal hotel-style life on tour. In addition, we had a Japanese liaison person who explained the fascinating history of the monastery to us. Though this is a pejorative claim, I doubt that any other party I toured with would not have had at least a few players scoffing at the simplicity of life there or who would have found it boring. As students, we were interested and wanted to learn; the atmosphere of the place permeated through to us all. I remember a lot of discussions taking place among us about different philosophies and religions; some people even did some meditation. Complete calmness and spirituality descended on the party, and with it the special bond between the players was strengthened. Often the chat among players on tour stays at a superficial level, but there players talked about personal things in a way that does not usually happen in a group of relative strangers. Many of us, myself included, subsequently said that our stay in the monastery was by far the best part of the tour. As an experience it was unlike that of any other rugby tour, and it will stay with me for ever.

The tour itself lasted three weeks and took in six games, of which the last was in Hong Kong. The first two games were in the cities of Fukuoka and Neagari against representative regional sides. We were pleased that we won both games easily, because the Japanese teams were fielding grown men, unlike us students, most of whom were either still in, or barely out of, our teens. Age difference is important in rugby, where a young man's physical maturity continues to progress throughout his twenties. In addition, the Japanese by and large played for the corporations they worked for and, although technically amateur, they were nonetheless given afternoons off to train. They were almost semi-professional, and were certainly better prepared than we were. The fact that we were racking up big scores against them, and that our backs in particular were proving very effective, was really encouraging.

After these first two games, we moved on to Osaka to play Japan, and while they were not a major rugby-playing power, they were nonetheless a full national team. The promise of the warm-up games was spectacularly fulfilled in a game in which we thoroughly outplayed the Japanese. With our backs in spectacular form, we ran in eight tries and won 43-0, and for many years were the only team to whitewash Japan. They were not a poor side and confirmed this by beating New Zealand Universities 31-15 in Tokyo the following week. Our win put us in good spirits for the tripartite tournament in Tokyo between us, New Zealand Universities and Japan Universities. While we had been working our way up to Tokyo from the south, the Kiwis had been doing the same from the north. Although we had faced Japan, the game against the Kiwis was the one which everyone thought would be the toughest test. In retrospect, they were no better than Japan; but then, and to a certain extent even now, any New Zealand side had an aura of indomitability about it. The English rugby public, us included, got their reports of New Zealand games from newspapers which often contained the poetic licence favoured by journalists trying to write floridly. These were the pre-YouTube, pre-internet days (hard to remember), and pre-televising of games from the other side of the world. So the reality was that, because we had never seen them play, and knowing nothing about them, their training methods, their fitness, their tactics or indeed any other element, there was a definite sense of expectation and tension among us as the game approached.

This mood was heightened by the decision by the Japan RFU to put up both teams in the same hotel for the duration of the tournament. Breakfast and dinner were in the same hotel, in the same dining room. The two teams contrived to sit as far away as they could from each other, though inevitably still within eyesight. We had seen their tour brochure, so each of us had identified our opposite number. As the player in question went about his business in the dining room, we each eyed him up, trying to get an impression of what he was like. No doubt they were doing the same with us and the tension increased day by day.

We also shared the same training ground, so we took it in turns to do our training: one team would do the earlier session in the morning, and the other would do the later one. The earlier team would get on the bus back to the hotel just as the later team got off theirs. Being aware as we were that we could be playing against future All Blacks meant that it was a very strange two days; probably for them as well.

The pre-match mood in the changing room was particularly fevered and I remember saying to the team just before we went onto the pitch, 'Nobody gets left on the floor.' We had all talked about New Zealand rucking which, as a result of the All Blacks, had rightly become famous for being both efficient and unforgiving. The stated aim of our forwards was not to lose that battle.

They performed their Haka before the kick-off but it was a long way from the aggressive, stylised event it has now become. As such, though we watched in a focused way, we did not perform the now seemingly obligatory manic stares in response. Nonetheless, by the time the game kicked off, it's fair to say we were fairly wound up. The fact that we beat them – not a trouncing, but a good win nonetheless – was extremely satisfying for us all. Our forwards, who were not as good as the backs as a set, were very physical and out-rucked them for large parts of the game. We were very, very pleased not only to have beaten them but to win that battle.

No sooner had we won than we were off to Hong Kong for the final game. We arrived exhausted, and had very little time to adjust to the energy-sapping heat and extreme humidity before playing the game against Hong Kong. The evening game took place when it was still very hot and, more tellingly, very humid. The British and Irish Lions of 2013 found out that playing with this combi-nation of factors is difficult. I remember distinctly that, despite being young and very fit, after about 20 minutes, I tried to pick up the pace and just wasn't able to do it. My legs wouldn't cooperate. It wasn't necessarily the running I had done on the pitch that had sapped me of any energy, it was all the scrummaging, rucking and mauling, the sheer physical nature of the game. It was like taking body blows in boxing: gradually they take their toll until suddenly you can't function properly any more. It was a very odd feeling, and I spent the remainder of the game just slogging around, feel-ing slow, heavy, drained and basically shattered.

One interesting thing that did emerge from that tour, right at the end, was my relationship with Paul Sidi, the other hooker in the squad. And it highlighted the rivalries that go on between the two players competing for each position on a tour. In my case, Paul was technically the senior player: he was a year older than me and had kept me out of the Yorkshire Schools team when I was younger. In fact, while he had been their chosen hooker, I had spent an entire season sitting on the bench, thinking, 'It should have been me.' He'd then gone down to play for Harlequins and, as a result, had had a final England trial match, which had hacked me off at the time, because I was up in Nottingham, and had not been given the opportunity. My extreme competitiveness therefore meant that I was ready to battle for the first-team place on this students' tour, and was delighted when he was the one who basically sat on the bench, while I was selected as the first-choice hooker.

However, just like John Olver in later years, Paul Sidi is a very affable bloke. So at the end of the tour, when we were in Hong Kong, Paul and I were chatting about an incident that had happened in the New Zealand game when there had been a flare-up and, taking no nonsense, I had just smacked the nearest Kiwi to me without thinking. It was then that Paul admitted to me, 'You've been the first choice on this tour, and it's really hacked me off, because I was first choice over you in the past. But you know what, in that last game, when all that started, I probably wouldn't have reacted like that. And maybe that's the reason you were selected and I wasn't.' Maybe it was. I admired his honesty and his generosity because, had I been in his position, I would not have been able to display either quality. It was a measure of how impressive he was as a man that he was able to say that to me.

The next step on the representative ladder for me was the England Under 23s, and I was selected to tour with them on three separate occasions, to Romania in 1982, to Italy in 1983 and to Spain in 1984. I was still a student on all three tours, but they were very different from the England Students tour. There were in effect two demographic groups: the students and the non-students. Those of us who were still at university used to get the piss taken out of us from the others about being lazy tax-scroungers; our retort was that at least we could read and write.

The cutting, clever court sessions largely disappeared but the ones we did have were still amusing and served their purpose. It was, however, a little trying to explain to one of the defendants that eyewitness evidence was, in fact, evidence, when he protested that nobody had produced the item he was seen spiriting away from the local restaurant as a souvenir.

Undoubtedly, one of the factors that limited our enjoyment was the realisation that although this was still an age-limited international tour it was a step closer to the next representative stage, the England B team, and the real goal – a full England cap. The possibility of getting a full cap was reinforced for all of us when we were addressed on assembly at Bisham Abbey before leaving for Romania. We were given the standard information about what was expected of us as England representatives, how we were to train and other logistical details. However, the final sentence of the address was the one which ignited my determination to do whatever it took to achieve a full cap. We were told that, statistically, 40 per cent of players who played for the England Under 23 team went on to be capped. 'Look around; four out of ten of you will probably get the honour of playing for the full England team. Will you be one of that four?' There was no need to say anything else.

The tour to Romania was the first one under the coaching of Dick Greenwood, an intelligent and intense northerner who had played for England as flanker and was to coach the national team from 1983 to 1985. He was the first to try to instil a work ethic into an England representative team, though his methods were questionable when first attempted.

Greenwood's intentions were good and he was one of the first people to realise that our fitness, diet and general approach were a world away from what they could and should be, particularly if we were compared to other athletes. However, in his desire to inculcate the necessary mindset, he failed to take into account that, given he only had ten days and the tour came at the end of the season, there was virtually nothing he could do that would be beneficial. His way of working us until we were absolutely exhausted was, if anything, counter-productive. While his sessions proved beyond doubt how deficient was our preparation, they were hellish. Looking back, I think he actually realised that his approach would be ineffective as far as this tour was concerned but that the overall message was more important.

A taste of what was to come was given at the first training session at Bisham Abbey where we were worked ferociously and for a long time then, as a warm down, we were told to do a four-mile run to Marlow and back. Although I didn't, a few of the boys hid in the bushes outside the Abbey and waited for the rest of us to return.

To make matters worse, when we got out to Romania, we discovered that, in summer, it is a very hot place. One session took place in a vast, baked, bare and airless concrete stadium that absorbed then generated even more heat. With the temperature over 100 degrees, we did a series of timed 400-metre runs that left everybody gasping for breath. The following day, in the same heat, we did a normal rugby session but were given the prospect of being able to play a five-a-side later. However, not until we had completed a continuous 20-minute drill where we had to sprint the diagonals of the pitch and jog along the goal-lines to recover. When we finished, a football was thrown to us but no one had the energy to even kick it.

At that time, Romania was a decent rugby-playing nation. Their full national team regularly played against a French representative team and on occasion managed to win. Many of their players were in the armed forces and, like other Eastern European athletes, they were given a lot of time to train and play. It was the same with their younger players, and we knew the tour games would be hard. What we hadn't realised was that the country itself was to pose its own problems for us.

In 1982, Romania was a country few Westerners went to, and President Ceauşescu was approaching the height of his megalo-maniac dictatorship. The consequences of his rule and the communist economy were all too apparent everywhere you looked. Between the two world wars, the city's elegant architecture and the sophistication of its elite had earned Bucharest the nickname of 'Little Paris'. Under a mad scheme to urbanise large swathes of the rural population, Ceauşescu tore down buildings and violated public open spaces, building thousands of shoddy flats. The unhappy residents were forced from their village homes into these unhappy blocks that were grey, soulless and in many cases only par-tially completed. To make matters worse, the regular shortages of power made the blocks dark and dangerous at night. When you live, as I do now, in a major city, you take for granted the presence of neon and fluorescent lights but these were isolated features in an otherwise dimly lit city centre. It was depressing to visit; God knows what it must have been like to live there.

As with every other centrally planned economy, Romania's didn't work, producing huge shortages of staple food products and every-day necessities but large surpluses of non-essential things. The latter were displayed in a vain attempt to cajole people into buying them, while items that we would consider very minor luxuries were either too expensive for ordinary people or simply absent.

One afternoon I went into Bucharest's biggest department store, which was about the same size as Harrods. But that's where any similarity ended, because although all five floors were filled with some form of goods, there was not a single thing I wanted to buy.

On one floor, there were rows of jars filled with pickled cab-bage, each row probably 40 metres long. The sight was so alien that I stood and stared for nearly ten minutes trying to take in what I was seeing. On another floor, there were racks and racks of shabby items of clothing; further along, a counter full of small, individual watch parts, as if individual watches had been taken apart and strewn about; another counter would contain parts for a specific piece of machinery. All these were displayed in department-store fashion, and the contrast between what was there and what would normally be sold in most similar stores was so acute that it made the whole episode bewildering.

To compound the effect, there were conspicuous 'dollar-shops' nearby, which were intended for tourists or Party members, where you could see that all the normal things you would expect to buy in a shop were still available. The currency, the lei, was of such little value that their notes were worth less than 1p, and I remember some of the smokers among my team-mates setting fire to them in order to light up. At the time, we all thought that was very funny indeed, until it was pointed out to me, on a subsequent tour, that perhaps the locals hadn't thought it so hilarious to see a load of young Westerners setting fire to their hard-earned cash. Crass, ignorant behaviour, I now realise, which makes me squirm when I recall it.

We stayed in hotels that were, on the outside, large and modern but again shortages of power, food and goods meant that they were not much more than budget hotels in the Western sense. Meals consisted largely of questionable meat, chips and Coke, and at one point we found out the bottled water was being filled from an outside tap. It's a measure of how pampered we are in the West that, after a few days, some of our party started to moan that the food was really boring and please could we be given something else. One of the management team had to bring in a bit of a reality-check: 'I know you're not happy with these arrangements, boys, and I know they're not first class, but to be honest, this is all the Romanian Union have got.' I was well aware of the politics and history of Romania and the way its population was brutalised first by the Nazis and then by the Soviets, so I tried to be stoic about any difficulties we had. I seem to remember telling others using slightly less diplomatic words that I was also getting pretty tired of the moaning and could everyone just get on with the task in hand. It was a sobering reminder of life behind the Iron Curtain and it was not a pleasant experience.

We were not actually prevented from going anywhere, so we did venture out of our hotels to go wandering around Bucharest, but we did notice that we were followed everywhere by men from their secret service, the Securitate. That was made obvious one day when a group of guys went out and got chatting to a group of girls. No sooner had they left them and walked off down the street than they looked back and saw that the girls were being interrogated in a doorway by some Securitate men who were pointing in the players' direction and shouting at the now terrified girls. It was clear from the body language that they were being interrogated, no doubt because it was well known that on national sports tours things were couriered through customs which the host country was not happy about. After that incident, we realised that we only risked getting girls or indeed any locals into trouble if we tried to approach them and that even talking to them was out of the question. It would be wrong to say that we did not have some fun but it was unity-in-adversity fun with largely black humour.

To get from one side of the country to the other we had to fly, as the alternative road journeys would have taken a whole day given the state of the roads and the small fact that the large Carpathian mountains had to be circumnavigated. We flew with their national airline, TAROM, on old propeller planes that sounded and looked barely serviceable. I am very glad that I did not find out until after the tour that that particular year TAROM had the fourth worst safety record in the world.

The host union decided to entertain us one evening in a way which was memorable, but not in the way they had intended. We were taken to an imposing-looking theatre and I thought that we might be seeing a classical concert, which I would have enjoyed, even if most of the party would not. Instead, we attended a performance by Romania's top comedienne, and so popular was she that the theatre was full to the rafters. Quite what our hosts had been thinking when booking up this evening for us is beyond me, because, while the entire audience spent the show howling with laughter, our group spent it staring at the stage, bemused and unable to understand a word of what was going on. The comedienne was doubtless one of the big names on Romania's comedy circuit but I'm afraid I failed to see the funny side – or indeed the point – of the evening.

The tour to Italy the following year, again coached by Dick Greenwood, provided a big contrast, not surprisingly, to the Romania trip. It was largely confined to the Veneto region of northern Italy where rugby has at least gained some measure of recognition in an otherwise football-obsessed country.

By this time, the England Under 23s were starting to look a bit more like a tour party. That was the first tour I remember being supplied with at least some semblance of tour kit. We were all given a huge holdall (with no straps or wheels, mind, so really impractical). Blue with a big red rose on it. In retrospect it was garish but at the time I thought that was marvellous, and I still have it somewhere. We had a full set of number ones – a tour blazer, shirt, tie and trousers – and number twos which was casual wear. The only problem was that none of it fitted properly. In fact this was to be a consistent theme of nearly every subsequent tour until the end of the 1980s and it became a running joke. Whatever was produced looked shoddy and, certainly in Italy, we were never in any danger of being mistaken for the locals.

Nonetheless, gone were the privations of Romania, and the food was spectacular, not that this stopped some of the players displaying the worst sort of Brits Abroad attitude.

After a very pleasant morning's sightseeing in Venice, we were taken to a traditional restaurant where our Italian liaison officer announced we were to be served a typical Venetian meal. This featured wonderful fresh local fish, plus some salad, but this didn't find favour with at least half of the party.

'I don't like this, Dick,' cried one, as he spied the fish coming his way. The penny had just dropped that we weren't being served fish in batter. 'Can we have some chips?'

'No, they don't have any,' answered Greenwood, who had played in Italy for a number of years, spoke fluent Italian and was familiar with what a typical Venetian meal was.

''Ave they got any salad cream?' asked another of the players, a Gloucester boy, in his best West Country accent.

'Er, no,' Dick replied, 'that doesn't exist here.' Cue a panicked look in the player's eyes and a mouthed 'Fucking hell'. Meanwhile, I was busy mixing myself some vinaigrette, putting mustard in, olive oil, vinegar, a bit of black pepper . . . the usual, in other words.

''Ere, you really like that stuff, don't you?' said the same player who had asked for salad cream, genuinely perplexed.

'What stuff?' I replied, equally so.

'Well . . . that stuff,' indicating my concoction.

'Er, it's just vinaigrette,' I pursued, actually wondering if he was serious; which I think he was.

The thing is that Gloucester boys are just different. There were four on that tour who, while remaining close, soon mixed with the rest of us but emerged as the dominant personalities. One in particular became the unlikely tour leader off the field. Steve Ashmead, a Gloucester prop, was a gnome-like figure who was popular and funny and became known as the Tour Pope after donning a white headrest cover on the coach and looking just like the Pontiff blessing his errant flock. One afternoon, I was invited by three of the Gloucester boys to play cards, and to this day I don't know if what happened was a colossal joke on me or on them. We sat down and I asked if they wanted to play bridge and when they agreed settled down to play a few rubbers. The cards were dealt out and they played them each in turn until two matched and one of them shouted, 'Bridge!'

The following year's tour to Spain regressed in terms of professionalism but because of that produced some memorable touring moments off the field. This time the coach was Alan Black, the then RFU Development Officer and former Wasps stalwart. Black's approach mixed old school with some of the new but the balance didn't quite work as the boys, given a bit more latitude, regressed quickly into a more junior club approach. Perhaps this was due to the fact that the opposition was not that strong but more probably because that is what boys do if they are not given strict boundaries at that age. I can't remember any of the results though I know we didn't lose a game and beat the Spanish national side comfortably.

What I do remember is the different characters that we had on the tour and the now notorious Dead Ants calls that caused trouble on several occasions. The tour party also consisted of more students than the previous two and that also might explain why the social side of things took greater prominence than before. While none of the players took the training or games less than seriously, it was clear that there were some players, like me, who were by now very focused on using the Under 23s as a means to further their representative careers; others were less ambitious.

It is interesting which characters come to mind when you look back on tours because they are not always the most talented or the ones that went on to achieve great things later on. Alex Woodhouse was a scrum-half for Harlequins and from a wealthy background, so wealthy in fact that he didn't have to have a job unless he particularly wanted to. When one of the boys accused him of being a lucky bastard, his effortlessly patrician reply made me guffaw. 'Yes, dear boy, but you see you probably never have the time to sit around and worry about whether your passing off your left hand is sufficiently good.' His eccentricity was matched by that of the then Moseley winger John Goodwin, a being who was on a different planet from most of the human race. As an example of the way his mind worked, he used to think nothing of lying under people's beds in their hotel room for hours just so that he could jump out from underneath as soon as they walked in, and scare the living daylights out of them.

Though I was more serious than most of the party, I still had a couple of epic nights out and after one of them swayed back to my room feeling much the worse for wear. I was sharing with a young Cambridge University centre called Kevin Simms, who was not only very wholesome but also a devout Christian. Just as I realised I was about to throw up, I displayed great presence of mind and team spirit and managed to avoid being sick not only all over him but also all over his daily prayer guide which he kept beside his bed. To this day, I remain proud of that achievement.

What about the Dead Ants? Well, this was started by Alan Black and, much though he might want to deny it, he must bear some of the blame for introducing this juvenile option, popular though it may have been. It is quite simple: on the call of 'Dead Ants', every player had to dive to the ground on his back with his arms and legs in the air waving them around like a dying ant. It could only be called by a senior member of a tour party and only at certain times of the day and with a certain frequency. The first couple of calls didn't cause much bother, as they were done in the team room, but when they were called elsewhere, the reactions of onlookers ranged from bewilderment to something more.

The Spain tour consisted of three games, the last of which was played in Seville against a *de facto* Spanish A team. The first game, however, was played against a regional side in San Sebastián, in the heart of the Basque country. One morning, Peter Buckton, our flanker, called a Dead Ants in the breakfast room of our hotel, and our entire 30-strong tour party dropped to the ground. All the other hotel guests assumed the Basque separatist group ETA were launching an attack. Total mayhem broke out as people either dived for cover or ran out of the dining room as fast as they could, leaving broken crockery, food and belongings in their wake.

The Spanish liaison officer proceeded to explain as diplomatically as possible the political situation and why a repeat incident would not be advisable. Nor indeed would our intention of wearing black Basque berets when alighting from the plane taking us to Barcelona, in Catalonia, the venue for our next game.

My only Dead Ants call also caused trouble as I called it just after our second game on tour as the players walked off the pitch. The tour manager, Mike Weston, was incandescent with rage as he marched from the stand and tore into me there and then, telling me that this was completely out of order and that if anything like it happened again there would be serious trouble. I didn't tell him at the time that I thought he was lucky, as I had intended to call it after one of the conversion kicks at goal; it didn't seem the right time to bring it up.

Mind you, Weston's own judgement proved not to be entirely sound when he made the decision that, as an England representative party, we should not only go and support the England Under 21 football team in their game against their Spanish counterparts, but should do so wearing full number one dress.

We filed off the coach at the stadium and found our seats, conspicuous in our tour blazer, complete with identifying badge, tie and flannel trousers. So far so good. When England scored, however, we all leapt up, cheering madly, until we realised that the entire stadium had gone silent and was now watching that corner of the stadium that was forever England (with apologies to Rupert Brooke). We could not have stood out more if we had been wearing ball gowns. Suddenly the mood in the stadium changed; it became menacing; the locals started closing in on us, muttering, spitting and threatening, throwing lighted matches, waving Spanish flags, and making it so uncomfortable for us that with about ten minutes to go, we decided to beat a hasty retreat and try to find our coach. With the more hard-core opposition supporters following hot on our heels, it was all we could do not to actually break into a run, and once outside the stadium, with no sign of our driver anywhere, we soon found ourselves surrounded. We then had a very unpleasant stand-off, with us forming a tight group in the middle, and facing outwards towards our potential attackers, desperately hoping they would not suddenly decide to charge, like mad Spanish bulls, towards us. This carried on until the driver finally arrived, after which we bolted into the safety of the coach and ensured a fast getaway. It was a triumph for the stiff upper lip and the English penchant for formality over practicality – it's lucky that nobody got knifed.

The last of my non-senior international tours involved a trip to Brazil in 1984, when I was still a student. The Penguins was a unique tour party that was led and put together by a lovely old chap called Tony Mason, whose wife, Doris, often accompanied the tours. He told me that his selection philosophy was to combine a range of players that ordinarily would not go on tour together, because it usually meant a highly entertaining and capable squad. Along with some promising new talent, he would include a couple of established players nearing retirement, and was very keen to reward players whom he thought had been unlucky and overlooked in their representative careers. It was an eclectic mix of people from all four Home Unions, a bit like a fun version of a Lions tour, and somehow it worked really well. Another feature of Penguins tours was that players were billeted with local and expat families, so when I went on the Brazil tour, it meant I was able to experience life from the locals' point of view, in a way which I was never able to do on other tours.

Derek Wyatt, the former Bath winger, was one of the organisers of the tour. He was a larger-than-life character, famed for his over-the-top speeches, a fact that may have accounted for him subsequently becoming an MP. I remember one particularly dithyrambic speech he made, during which he extolled the virtues of two Welsh players, Stuart Evans and Geraint John, and how they were destined for great things with the Lions ('Hang on a minute!' I distinctly remember thinking). Sadly, although both went on to play for their country, neither became a Lion, for a variety of reasons, whereas I was the only one of that tour party to do so.

Equally memorable was Mick Quinn, the former Ireland and Lansdowne fly-half, who unusually for an Irishman did not drink. Whether this was from choice or necessity I don't know, but whatever the reason, it is a good job he didn't. A hyperactive man who seemed to live at full speed whenever he was awake, Quinny was the best sort of tourist: serious on the field but a witty and engaging man off it. He had actually mastered the art of appearing to be pissed when all around him actually were, ensuring he had a good time and could remember what happened during evenings out – unlike everyone else.

Interestingly, another teetotaller was Marcus Rose, the future England full-back, and he too was one of the more extrovert personalities of the tour. Marcus was simply different from most people. His view of the world was never dull and he had a penchant for mischief that was barely restrained at times. He once told me that when he and Huw Davies played for Coventry, they struck a bet to see which of them would be first to attempt an own drop-goal. I would not have believed him had it not been for the fact that both Davies and the then Coventry coach, Martin Green, confirmed the story. To this day I don't know what would have happened had their plan succeeded.

Brazil was and is a fascinating country. Its glorious scenery is vast and varied and it has an indigenous population that, unlike some other countries I have visited, has no homogenous look. Brazilians are as likely to be dark-skinned and -haired as light-skinned and blond. We played in Rio and São Paulo and saw the extremes of poverty and immense wealth that co-exist, often in close proximity. The cardboard cities that ran alongside and underneath the freeways contrasted with our games in elite clubs such as the São Paulo Atlético Club, a beautiful, gated oasis for rich, professional Brazilians and expats.

Though very different from any European or English-speaking country, my experience of Brazilian rugby was no different from that of any other rugby around the globe. The people had common values of teamwork and fun. I cannot judge other sports because I haven't toured in the same way, but it is to rugby's credit that whatever country you play in you can be assured of a friendly reception and to meet decent people who will go out of their way to make your stay enjoyable.

The families I stayed with were delightful. In the first one, in São Paulo, the young guy whose parents were putting me up also had an older sister. I don't remember him very much, but I do remember her. She was older than me, and very keen. Though not partially sighted, she had less than good taste, because one evening she said to me, 'I'm far more attracted to you than I should be.' I realise it's hard to believe, but this didn't/doesn't happen to me all that often, and given she was my host, I felt duty bound to submit; it would have been rude not to.

The Rio family was equally welcoming, though in a very different way. Here, I got on really well with Case, the young local player whose family were putting me up. In fact, the entire family took me to their hearts, so much so that I stayed on for a week at the end of the tour, along with another player, Steve Burnhill. Case's mother was a lovely woman who looked after me like her own family. Though I stayed but briefly we got on so well that when it was time for me to leave, she was genuinely upset. As we waved each other goodbye, she kept saying, 'Please don't go, come back!' Strangely, I didn't seem to attract that sort of sentiment elsewhere.

The Penguins tour was huge fun, but the training, while serious when done, was hampered by the Brazilians' eccentric view of time-keeping. Several times, I would be fretting about the fact that we had set off for the training ground ten minutes before a session was due to start, knowing the journey was at least half an hour. I stopped pointing this out to my hosts, as the invariable reply was '*Amanhã*' (tomorrow); and anyway, even if I was late, several other players would arrive even later. Each one would run over, apologising profusely, explaining, 'There's nothing I could do – they just kept saying, "*Amanhã*".'

There were other cultural differences we learnt about. After one training session with a Rio rugby club, we went to the bar to have a few drinks, but after a while were puzzled that the local players didn't seem to be joining us, only the officials. It emerged that most of them preferred to stand out behind the stands smoking joints as their chosen method of winding down after a hard session out training. Fair enough, I suppose.

Rio was also the place where I witnessed the most unsuccessful and dull 'runner' of all time. The Corcovado Mountain, atop which sits the statue of Christ the Redeemer, is an iconic landmark but to get to the top of it involved a long walk up a winding road. We all trekked to the top and when we finished looking at the magnificent edifice and equally fantastic views we decided to have a coffee in the small mountain-top café. Four of the Welsh players thought it would be a wheeze to take advantage of the somewhat chaotic service and leave without paying. They sped out of the café, and the staff, who noticed almost straight away, nevertheless seemed less concerned than you would normally expect. Rather than chase the boys for payment, one of them went over to the counter and made a very short phone call.

What I hadn't noticed on the way up, but did on the way down, was that there was a checkpoint about halfway up the climb in which were local security men. As the miscreants gaily tripped their way towards the guards, they were confronted by one of the uniformed officers who took out a gun at them and told them to go back and pay. Thus, they not only had to trudge all the way back to the café, they also had to endure our gleeful mocking at their unsuccessful escapade.

That tour may also have helped nudge me towards the next step in my international rugby career, selection for the England B team, not that I knew it at the time. Some years later, I came across Neil Martin, the Bedford second row and Cambridge University coach, who had also been on the tour as a player. 'When I came back from the tour,' he told me, 'I told people I knew at Twickenham, "You must look at this boy, because he's so quick. If you don't pick him, you'll be missing a trick."' I was very touched by that, but it's true that, whatever else people might say about me, at that time I was certainly fast.

5

The Best a Man Can Get

By the time I was in my early twenties, I had been on an England Students tour and three successive tours with the England Under 23s. As a result, I had gained invaluable experience in how to manage time abroad, get on with team-mates and adapt to different playing styles. Aged 23, and fresh out of university, I had captained the England B team against Italy at Twickenham; the next stage would be to graduate to my first full England cap.

One evening in 1986, when I was down in London to play Rosslyn Park with my club Nottingham, the England management somehow – given this was pre-mobile phones – got a message to me while I was enjoying dinner in a Putney curry-house with team-mates: could I go straight over to the Petersham Hotel in Richmond to join the England squad for a training session the next morning? I just had time to grab some shorts, socks and boots, but had no other kit with me when I finally made it to the hotel late that night. The players were still in the bar, chatting away. They all knew each other. It was pretty intimidating, especially as many of them turned round when I came in, surprise written all over their faces, and the thought 'What the hell is he doing here?' clearly in the forefront of their mind, with some probably even thinking 'Who the hell is he?' To the few who openly queried my sudden arrival, I had to answer, apologetically, 'Oh, Steve Brain's gone down with an injury so I just got a call.' The problem was, I had little kit, so after failing to get any offers in the bar, I had to go up to Steve's room and ask him to lend me some, which was embarrassing, to say the least, as he seemed to be unscrewing a standard lamp at the time, apparently with the purpose of taking it home. He just tossed me a tracksuit top and bottoms – and a pretty clear sign to 'get on with it, and leave me alone', adding 'I'd better them back!' The next day, I acquitted myself well enough to be asked back, and that was how I came to be a fully fledged member of the England squad.

My first actual cap came in the final game of the following year's Five Nations campaign, against Scotland. I had had to accept, with enormous difficulty, that Graham Dawe, the Bath hooker, had been preferred to me for the campaign thus far. The first three games of that year's Five Nations had not gone well; England lost them all. To add insult to injury (or perhaps the other way round), the game in Wales had involved several fights, during one of which Phil Davies, the Welsh No.8, had had his jaw broken. The third game against France at Twickenham was a similarly ill-tempered affair, after which the RFU Committee demanded that four England players be dropped. Today it seems incredible that a committee had the power to force team selection but at that time they did. It's true that the issues were unsavoury, but the decision should have come from the manager and selectors and not an unaccountable non-playing body. Richard Hill, Gareth Chilcott, Wade Dooley and Graham Dawe were all dropped, and with that came my chance for a starting place. To be fair to Dawe, the case against him was the weakest of the four, but that didn't bother me – I had not made the decision. When I received the call out of the blue from Mike Weston, the manager, I had to make a huge effort to keep calm over the phone when told I was selected. As soon as I put the receiver down, though, I erupted into shouts of 'Yessss!' Most sporting careers require a bit of luck somewhere along the way, and this was mine. That said, you still have to take your chance when it comes and I was determined to do so.

Despite fearing, as I did at every new stage of my representative career, that this time I really would get found out, on my international debut I saw England win the Calcutta Cup at Twickenham. I was on my way in the big time. The England selectors were then sufficiently impressed to pick me for the squad to go to the inaugural Rugby World Cup taking place in Australia later that year. Hard as it is to believe nowadays, given the ubiquitous media presence at all big sporting occasions, but this first World Cup really did fall under the radar, and certainly in Britain. Even among the England players and the management, no one had any idea about the seriousness of the tournament – in fact, the RFU had voted against it even being held. That's how much they were planning for a successful campaign.

The fact that Dean Richards and I were sporting Gorbachev and Reagan masks on the flight over also gives an indication of the fact that, although in our minds we thought we were treating the tournament seriously, in effect, there was still some way to go. It felt more like an end-of-season finale than the career-defining event it has now become. On the other hand, one has to remember that, whether we were on England or Lions tours or at World Cups, we were not playing rugby for a living. We all had jobs and careers back home. At least I had a salary and had been granted leave by my employers; others like Paul Rendall were self-employed, and our daily allowance of roughly £23 didn't go far in compensating them for loss of earnings when abroad for several weeks. This is why, when the opportunities to have a bit of fun abroad arose, we didn't always look the other way.

There are very big differences in how players manage their time, depending on whether they are on a tour or playing in a tournament, and, this being the first ever tournament, neither the management nor the players had yet understood this. Furthermore, an England tour has a very different feel to it compared to a Lions tour, for reasons which will be explained later. So all three types of foreign trips have differences but also share certain common features. Nowadays, this is better understood and planned for, but when I first played for England, rugby was still an amateur sport, with a laid-back approach to tours of whatever nature.

This meant that the inaugural Rugby World Cup in 1987 was a revelation: to me, because it was my first ever time away with England; and to most players, because it was the first time England had actually toured since the infamously excessive tour of 1984. That tour had been to South Africa, and had been one of such excess and so little success that a lot of players were never seen again in an England jersey. Those who did survive the tour, such as Peter Winterbottom, Paul Rendall and Mike Teague, were still dining out on the stories three years later. Which is one reason why, in 1987, many of us did not realise that some of the issues that arise on tours are either more important or less important during World Cups.

First and foremost, when you play a tournament, you are based in one place, at least during the group games. With a tour, you change venue every few days, and therefore have to travel every few days. Although it's a relief not to have to pack up and waste a lot of time and energy travelling, the reality is that a tournament therefore provides a lot more spare time than a tour. In addition, players will probably have a week off between games, which is a long time to have to pass away from home, in the unnatural environment of a team hotel.

Often, the spare time equates to only two or three hours off, which is actually an awkward amount of time: it's not enough to go off and do some sightseeing or even play a round of golf, but more than enough to get very bored if you don't know how to use your time. These were, of course, the days before the advent of iPads et al. So it is really important during a tournament to ensure that the hotel the team is based in is suitable. It doesn't have to be ridiculously luxurious, but it needs to have enough space and facilities for everyone. In 1991, when the World Cup hosts were the countries of the Five Nations championships, England were based at the Petersham Hotel in Richmond for the duration of the group games. Now, the Petersham is a very comfortable hotel, and it did all it could to make life easy for us. But it's a relatively small hotel, in a built-up part of Greater London. And we had a games room that was little bigger than most people's kitchen. This was not ideal, when the stresses and strains of the tournament started to kick in.

A tournament also means that you are pitting yourself against several countries, whereas with a tour, you will only play the same national team, along with various other regional or representative teams. In addition, in tournaments, you more or less know who will be in the opposition's team, because it will be their best team, so you can – and must – do much of your preparation work before you even leave. Equally, you can have a reasonable idea of who, on your team, will be playing against the stronger nations in the pool games, and who can be fielded for the 'easier' (often midweek) games. On a tour, on the other hand, you don't really know who is going to figure in the line-up for the various midweek games you will be playing, so it is harder to prepare for them in advance.

Tournaments, unlike tours, are single entities, and what a team achieves in a tournament will be remembered at the next tournament, and the next, and the next. Players of today don't always understand this, yet England's results in previous World Cups are always analysed and remembered at the start of each new tournament, so past results matter, more so than England's performance on past tours. Lions tours are similar to tournaments in that respect, again because they occur every four years, and only every twelve years in the country where the tour takes place (New Zealand, Australia or South Africa). So what happens during that tour can get cast in stone in people's memories. To this day, every time the Lions go down to Australia, for example, David Campese gets reminded of the try he gave away to lose the third Test in '89 – it is shown again and again on TV, stadium big screens, you name it. 'All the good things I did,' he rails, 'and all anyone brings up is that one fucking moment from twenty-five years ago!'

The other crucial element of a tournament that is absent from a tour is the uncertainty about how long you will be there. You might go home after the group stage, you might make it to the knock-out stages, during which you might – or might not – need to travel to a new venue. This can all be quite destabilising. So you are perpetually thinking not only of winning your group matches, but also of where you are in the table – and you have to avoid wondering where your possible future opponents are in their tables as well.

A Rugby World Cup played at home, however, presents problems all of its own. We were completely taken aback by the explosion of interest that occurred when England hosted the 1991 tournament (along with the other Five Nations countries), especially once it looked like we might actually win. The non-sporting press and media were despatched to dig up all sorts of irrelevant information on the players, speaking to past schoolteachers, childhood friends – basically anyone who could provide anything like a useable quote. We had approached the tournament in much the same way as we did Five Nations championships, meeting up at the Petersham Hotel on the Wednesday before a Saturday game; because there were a few more games, we simply met up a bit more often. Otherwise, nothing changed. The game was still amateur, so we still had day jobs. It simply never occurred to us how much scrutiny of our playing and personal lives would take place. That was the first time it began to dawn on us that we were no longer part-time, amateur rugby players, but were now fully formed 'personalities', as well as sportsmen.

At first, it felt quite fun, being the subject of newspaper profiles, or having our photos on the front, rather than the back, pages of the papers. However, that tournament marked the point at which media attention on rugby reached heights that were totally disproportionate to the level of participation as a national sport. It also showed us that tours do not generate the same amount of column inches as tournaments, which always seem to exacerbate the media's hunger for news. When England or the Lions go abroad, it costs money to send a tabloid gossip-journalist out to fish for stories, so only a limited number are sent. Home World Cups, like home Olympic Games or other big international sporting events, are an altogether different matter, as it is open season for all areas of the media. Yet what happened to us back in 1991 was as nothing compared to what players have subsequently had to deal with, and what the 2015 World Cup will generate in terms of media attention. And as that tournament takes place in Britain, I just hope the squad – and all those who are peripheral to it, however near or far – are well prepared.

Selection for tournaments is more important than for tours – even Lions tours – for one key reason: if you get it wrong, you cannot summon more players without the consent of the organisers, and that could make the difference between you going through to the next round or getting the next flight home. As the stakes are much higher, you want as much competition for each place as possible, even though, if there are two players who are close in terms of selection, the reality is that they are both likely to play, because so many substitutions now take place.

This was less so when I was playing, so the fight for the number one spot was more keenly felt, and never more so than during that first World Cup in 1987 when Graham Dawe and I were both vying for that place in the starting XV. He had started the Five Nations campaign, then been dropped in favour of me. I had had only one cap but was predictably desperate to impose myself as the first-choice hooker. 'Let the battle commence,' was his opening gambit at the beginning of the trip, which summed up not only his own mindset but, to be fair, my own as well. A warm-up session in the gym soon after turned into a bizarre head-to-head duel. Instead of simply jogging round the gym, like everyone else, we each began to raise our pace, in order to show the other one up. Faster and faster we went, until we were in effect running at full pace round the gym, unaware that everyone else had long stopped jogging, and had started cheering and clapping, while we continued to sprint round like two dogs at the tracks. It needed coach Martin Green to physically intercept us and stop us from running ourselves into the ground. So far, so mature – but an indication of what could happen when competition for a place was acute. Nowadays, players' physical performances are judged much more scientifically and objectively, so there would be no need for such scenes. A shame, really, because I always enjoyed the fight.

Planned entertainment is vital during World Cups when there is so much spare time compared to a tour. In both cases, however, there will be a Social Committee (as with junior rugby tours). Their job used to be to find where the girls and the best bars were, but between my first time away with England in 1987 and my last, in 1995, there was a very definite progression towards a more professional approach to touring, even if we were still not officially professional sportsmen. Whenever he was in the party, Rory Underwood was usually our resident one-man social secretary, even though (or perhaps because) he didn't drink. Yes, we still went out, but the remit of the Social Committee definitely underwent a sea-change.

One of the best forms of evening entertainment was and is to have a quiz. Get a bunch of competitive guys together, split them into teams, and you're guaranteed an explosive evening, whether alcohol is in the mix or not. It's something the England football team could have done with at the World Cup in South Africa when the players complained of boredom. Many players subsequently said that the one quiz night arranged for them had been a highlight of the trip, but instead of repeating it, the idea was limply dropped. We used to have regular quizzes on general knowledge, sport and entertainment. They were always raucous fun and great for team bonding. On each occasion, some normally quite quiet people would reveal themselves to be Masterminds on unlikely subjects; some had a fantastic knowledge of films or music; for others it was sport and its statistics. This allowed them to outshine the alleged wise-cracking smart-arses who were duly brought down a peg or two.

Martin Johnson, for example, turned out to have a freakishly Statto-like knowledge of all sports facts and figures, so he came into his own during many of these quizzes. As an aside, I'm told Jamie Carragher, the Liverpool defender, is a walking music encyclopaedia, according to those who can understand what he is saying. Although perhaps that should be taken in the context of a sport that calls a player 'The Professor' if he has so much as an 'A' level, or thinks he might be gay if he reads the *Guardian*. In any event, there were lots of cultured, knowledgeable people on the various teams I toured with. I couldn't really claim to have an encyclopaedic knowledge of any particular genre but I do have a lot of general knowledge. Films, literature and history were my best topics, though when asked to go on *Celebrity Mastermind* (and win by the way, not that I'm competitive), I chose Genesis – the rock band, that is, not the first chapter of the Old Testament.

That said, we didn't always get it right. In 1987, between the end of the group games and our quarter-final against Wales, the RFU decided that it would be a good idea if the England squad spent three days letting off steam at a fantastic resort on Hamilton Island, north of Brisbane. Oh yes, we had a great time, spending hours dive-bombing and playing games in the swimming pool, playing rounds of golf, and generally messing around in blazing sunshine. Drinking was also part of the equation, of course, because it was the start of the week, so we all reasoned that we still had a few days to recover before the quarter-final on the Saturday. After all, that's what we'd always done in the past and we'd been fine. No one thought anything of it. You don't have to be a sports scientist to know that that is completely the wrong sort of preparation for an important game. Instead of resting – and for sportsmen nowadays, that literally means feet up, no walking, and preferably lying in bed or sleeping – we were jumping around having fun. We then lost to Wales. No great surprise in hindsight.

Tournaments and tours develop, for better or for worse, depending on the results. If they go well, attitude remains good; if not, attitude can badly degenerate and the tour can fast become a very negative experience for everyone. Nowhere is this more the case than on British Lions tours.

The dynamic of a Lions tour is unique to rugby and, though I stand to be corrected, I think it's the only team game in which four countries' teams combine to play – and tour – as one. From the outside, it is often assumed that this must result in a team that is stronger than any of the individual contributing teams. In reality, nobody can predict with any confidence that the sum of the squad will be better than its four parts. Consequently, a Lions tour is a tantalising prospect for players and fans alike. If it succeeds, it can be one of the most rewarding things in rugby. Failure leaves disappointment and sometimes bitterness in its wake. There are a number of factors which influence the outcome of a Lions tour and the degree to which they do so is never the same from tour to tour. Each of the following factors can be a strength or a weakness, depending on how the Lions team, management and players, deal with them.

The blindingly obvious point is the fact that you have players and management from four countries. When the manager and head coach are chosen, great care is taken to appoint two men who will be able to work through any clashes in temperament and differences in their methods of preparation. The head coach has the choice of assistants, and again they must be able to work together even though they might have very different ideas about how to approach training and playing. A coach does not want a team of assistants that is supine and simply agrees with anything that is said. They have to be independent-minded but able to cooperate and compromise when necessary. The coach could appoint his national backroom staff in their entirety if he wanted to, but that does not happen because the coaching talent available across the four countries has to be taken into account. Further, if the coach were to do that, he would invite accusations of bias in selection and criticism for the way the team plays, should it not succeed. You might think this should not matter, but it does; it matters a lot.

Players from the respective countries are used to their own team's methods and set-up. They have routines that accommodate them, and familiarity is a comforting factor. There can also be a natural reluctance to share information with players from the other Home Nations, even though, in order to produce the strongest team possible, it is vital to set aside such misgivings. This is a less relevant problem nowadays, because in their various clubs, players have team-mates from a whole range of countries. But in the past, there was far less knowledge of what other countries got up to in training. The communication methods didn't exist, and YouTube hadn't been thought up, so the first we might get to know about what they did, the way they trained, won the ball or jumped was when we met up with them on the tour. So we had to avoid thinking, 'We've got some really good tactics, they're really secret. I don't want to divulge them because I'm playing against you next year and then you'll know what we do.'

We would also have to stop ourselves from saying, 'We do it this way, and it's the best way.' Otherwise, there can be clashes in playing style or tactics, as happened in Australia in 1989. Scotland played a very definitive rucking game, whereas England were a much bigger, stronger, mauling side. The Scottish contingent, together with Lions coach Ian McGeechan, were insistent on playing their way against the Australians, while the English were equally insistent in saying that it wouldn't work, because the Aussies were so adept at getting back into formation. But where McGeechan showed himself to be a brilliant coach was that, after we had lost the first Test, he shelved the Scottish-style tactics. Without saying as such, he accepted that he had got it wrong, and switched to a more mauling style of play, which reaped the desired results. In effect, he could see that a pooling of knowledge for the greater good – even if not everyone is in agreement – was the only way to achieve success.

Players are also shaped by attitudes to many things on and off the field in their country, and often in ways they are not aware of.

Sense of humour, general outlook, social mores, all these differ, as the following examples will attest which, at first glance, would appear to have no relevance at all to a rugby tour. When I played, the Troubles still raged, and we had players from Northern Ireland and the Republic, while, of course, the rest of us were Brits. Although we did not have instant news via social media, we still had the TV, radio and newspapers, and we had people of strong opinions in the squad who did not back away from discussing anything they wanted to. Similarly, when I toured with the Lions, apartheid still existed in one of rugby's historical super-powers, South Africa, one of the three countries toured by the squad. Opposition to apartheid had steadily grown, and by the late 1980s it was impossible to be neutral when discussing the possible ways to defeat it. Although no player condoned apartheid, their attitudes to how the problem should be approached varied markedly. Indeed, it did become a direct issue on the 1989 tour when we had to debate whether we would accept an invitation from a representative of sponsors First National Bank to tour en masse. Given it was at the height of the anti-apartheid era, this was a decision that could have seen all of us banned from international rugby for life. In the end, although we did speak to their representatives, the issue was taken away when the SARFU, amazingly, went through our individual Unions.

The management tried to reduce the impact of nationalities on Lions tours by mixing us all up and splitting us into little units, or mini-teams, which would play each other, not only during practice, but also during quizzes, or other out-of-hours activities. Those smaller units would also sit together at meals, and room-sharing would be carefully arranged so that national cliques could not form.

The biggest difference between a Lions team and a national team is that on the latter, if there is competition for a place, it will be between the incumbent and one challenger. Often the challenger is very much the junior, and both players know that, barring the first-choice player playing badly or being injured, the selection order is likely to stay the same. Equally, nowadays, there are some positions, like hooker, prop, second row and scrum-half where it is standard for both players to play in every game; the only point of contention might be which one starts first and how long it will be before the other comes on as a replacement. As such, the room for ill-feeling within the squad when the starting XV and bench is chosen is reduced, and Test selections are more straightforward. There are always a few places in the team where the competition is very acute, and that can give rise to a certain tension between the players in question. When you are not selected, and you and others feel that the selection was marginal or even wrong, it is difficult to keep your feelings to yourself and stay positive and supportive of the team and the player selected ahead of you. That you do so is vital for team unity and morale, as nothing breaks up a squad quicker than backbiting and rancour.

This situation is not the case with a British and Irish Lions tour. Nearly every player selected to tour with the Lions will be first choice in that position for their country or, failing that, will be one of those few players who is genuinely on a par with the player presently first choice. That creates a unique situation where every player has an expectation, legitimate or otherwise, that he will be or should be in the Test team. There are very few starting Lions positions where you can say in advance that one player is certain to be picked. This means that the initial selections, and whether a player finds himself in the Saturday or midweek team, are important. On the one hand, the coach has to give all the players game time to press their claim for a Test place; on the other, he has to settle his starting XV as early as he can, so that it goes into the first Test with the selected players having had time to function in their units and as a team. If they get this wrong and players feel they are not being given a chance, it causes resentment, and the seeds of discord are planted.

What the coach will try to do is play units together in games but not in the same game, so that this keeps players incentivised while giving those units the chance to develop. So a prospective Test front row might play with a second row that is destined to play midweek games, and so on. One of the central tenets of the Lions is that all players have the chance to play their way into a Test team. On nearly every tour, a player initially unfancied to start has come through and forced his way into the Test team by his efforts in those pre-Test games. However, this aim is getting harder to achieve as tours become shorter, leaving coaches with fewer games in which to experiment and making them play the actual Test team, or as close to it as possible.

On my first Lions tour to Australia, in 1989, there were two examples of unfancied players forcing their way into the Test team. I was one of those players. The other hooker chosen, Steve Smith, from Ballymena, Northern Ireland, was about four stone heavier than me, and everyone assumed he would have the honour of wearing the Test jersey. Australia's hooker was the even bigger Tommy Lawton whose weight during his career was anywhere between 18 and 22 stone. It was reasoned that Smith had to be chosen to counteract Lawton's bulk, even though I had played against him four times in the previous two years and had had no problems at all in the scrum.

From the moment the squad was announced publicly and the articles appeared speculating on the likely Test XV, I resolved to fight my way into that team. I trained harder and longer than anyone else, and harder and longer than I had ever done. The result was that I got the call-up for all three Tests. It was not until almost the end of the tour that I acknowledged Smith with anything more than a barely discernible nod. That's how serious our rivalry had been.

The other unheralded player who played a crucial role in winning the second and third Tests was the England fly-half Rob Andrew. He wasn't even selected originally and had been called up as a replacement when the Irish number ten, Paul Dean, was injured. At the time, some of the Scottish players openly asked why he was the replacement and made it plain they did not rate him. 'What the fuck is he coming out for?' was John Jeffrey's contemptuous response. Andrew's first game was in the midweek side and he made several clean breaks and looked very sharp; he actually surprised some of his English colleagues too, as we hadn't seen that side of his game much. After we were heavily beaten in the first Test, Andrew replaced Scotland's Craig Chalmers, his reputation was made, and his doubters silenced.

Up until the first Test, we had played well and won all our games. However, we had not just lost the first Test, we had been hammered. When something major goes wrong, as was the case then, people tend to retreat towards the team-mates from their own country with whom they feel most comfortable. It is human nature, and the changes for the second Test saw several English players replace Celts. This did not go down well. In particular, the replacement of Welsh second row Bob Norster by Wade Dooley, made the Welsh players angry, and they were keen to point out that Norster had always got the better of Dooley in the Five Nations.

As a result of the various selection changes, some of the players who had played in the first Test had to play in the following midweek game against ACT (now the Brumbies), just a few days later. It would have been understandable if the dropped players who played in the ACT game had been physically tired and mentally not at the right level due to their disappointment at being dropped. It certainly looked that way in the first half when ACT led the Lions by some margin. It is at moments like this that a tour's fate is decided. Had we lost that game, the morale in the camp, which was low, would have hit rock bottom. What happened rescued the tour. Scotland's John Jeffrey, who had been dropped from the Test team, and Ireland's Donal Lenihan motivated the players in spectacular fashion, and they went on to trounce ACT and gave us, in the Test team, the crucial boost we needed to win the second Test.

The importance of the midweek team is not just that it gives players a chance to challenge for a Test jersey; it is still a Lions team and the results affect how the tour is perceived internally and in the host country, by fans and media alike. This situation is very different from a national tour, where everyone knows the midweek team is basically the B team. It is slightly different again with a tournament midweek team, because if you lose or have a bad midweek game, that can affect your position in the qualifying group. But a Lions midweek team is still a Lions team.

On the next tour, to New Zealand, in 1993, my rival this time was the Scot Kenny Milne. Inexplicably, as far as I was concerned, he was named as hooker in the first Test, while I sat resentfully on the bench for the entire game. That goaded me into action: I did everything I could over the course of the following week to get noticed in the rapidly disintegrating midweek side in order to be picked for the second Test. My tactics paid off, which was just as well, because, had I not been picked, I had seriously been contemplating feigning injury in order to fly home early.

In the past, when players did not move clubs very much, and tended to play in their own countries, they were much less familiar with other players from the Home Nations. When a tour went well, differences tended to be shelved for the greater good, because players were competitive and wanted to win. But national differences, rivalries and allegiances could and did get in the way of team harmony if results started to suffer, after which things could unravel. This is in effect what happened in 1993, when in my opinion the midweek team pretty much gave up, which poisoned the atmosphere of the entire tour. Five of the forwards from that midweek team were Scottish – though it would not have mattered what nationality they were – and lacked experience, which I accept was not their fault. But when the pressure came, they and various other players from the Celtic nations, shall we say, just seemed to give up, went drinking, messed around and generally turned into some sort of latter-day junior club tour. The fact that the 'offenders' were primarily from Scotland and Ireland, with a few Welsh thrown in, is simply a factual observation on my part. In criticising them, I was and am not criticising their countries. Nor were all the players from those countries to blame. And if the disruptive players had been English, I would have said exactly the same. Their attitude was poor, but they just happened to come from countries other than England.

At one stage, the views of the mini-team players were canvassed by Geoff Cooke, the manager, to see what could be done about the situation. Most, including Gavin Hastings, the captain, went for the softly, softly approach of letting the troublesome players know that the management were unhappy about things, and that they needed to stop.

I went for the full-on, nuclear option: 'Name every single one of the players, make them stand out in front of everybody, point to them, and say, "If you don't stop, you're fucking going home. And, by the way, do I really have to send you home, on a Lions tour, for you to understand your responsibilities?"'

Geoff Cooke just laughed. 'Yeah, I thought you'd say that.'

'Yes, because I'm right.' The tactful approach was chosen, of course, and nothing changed.

Thank God that I had managed to extricate myself from that team by the second Test, but I felt really sorry for some of my fellow England players, such as Peter Winterbottom and Stuart Barnes, who were all still trying, and were furious at what was happening.

'Have you spoken to any of them?' I asked Wints one day, halfway through the tour.

'No, not once. There's no point.'

As for Barnes, he was in despair, and as close as I had been to flying home with a feigned injury. 'I'm trying as hard as I can, but I'm not being given a chance, and it's making me look bad. Some people, they're not even going to bed – what can I do?'

Nothing, was the answer. But it killed off Stuart's chance of ever reclaiming the fly-half jersey from Rob Andrew. The net result of all this was that it became a tour of two halves: the midweek team in one half, many of whom frankly didn't give a damn, and the Test team in the other. Very sad.

That dynamic is much less likely to happen nowadays because so much attention to detail and to selection is given. But twenty years ago, the Five Nations Championships were *de facto* trials for Lions tours. Those who did well – and inevitably, they often came from the nations that did well that year – tended to be selected. End of story. The preponderance of Scottish forwards on the 1993 tour – their entire front five was chosen – was as a direct result of them doing better than us in that year's Championships, and left outstanding players such as Jeff Probyn behind in England to watch from afar. This was incomprehensible to many of the England players who did get picked. But in those days, the selection methods were crude: there was not mass televising of every single game, at both international and club level, nor was video analysis available. This meant that selectors could not say – as they do now – player A beat player B in the Five (now Six) Nations, but in the Heineken

Cup, or in two club games, player B demonstrably beat player A. It was a case of 'Five Nations good performance = selection for Lions tour'.

The situation now is completely different. The planning starts about 18 months ahead, and about a year before the tour the selectors will have a fairly good idea of who they would like to include. After that – although he won't actually know this – a player will either be playing himself out, or will be a fringe player who is on the reserve list. There are many such lists, and players are moving up and down them the whole time. And although selectors look at form, they also need to make sure players are good *team* players, as summed up prosaically by former Lions assistant coach and forwards coach Graham Rowntree, who memorably said: 'We've got one rule: no cunts! If they don't pass that test, it doesn't matter who they are, they're not going.' Quite right.

Generally, players do want to be part of the Lions ethos, they want to support the 'Four for one, and one for all' cause that ignores national interests. But if a selection is made for a position that others don't understand, especially if that player is playing out of position, then the other number one choices from the other three nations will be saying, 'Hang on, I'm the first pick for my country, but I'm not considered good enough to be picked compared to someone who isn't even a blind-side [or whatever]. What have I done? How can I get back in? All these years, with everything I've done, and that guy has got picked.'

So a selection of this sort is done with the greatest caution, and is unique to Lions tours. If, on an England tour, a player is omitted whom others think should be picked, there will be some complaining back home, by sections of the media or supporters from his club. But if that happens on a Lions tour, there is the potential for an entire country to object, and often loudly, as happened when Brian O'Driscoll was left out of the 2013 tour. The furore was absurdly polarising and, frankly, should have been stamped out much faster.

The essential thing to remember is this, especially if you are part of the touring team: you support the Lions, and you are all in it together, no matter who you are or what country you are from, otherwise don't bother going. We can fall out afterwards, but during the tour, you don't question who is there or who is not. If it happens that there are 13 Welshmen, then so be it.

The difficulty with a Lions tour is that it comes around only once every four years, unlike national sides which are built up over a period of years, with older players gradually giving way to younger players who are brought in and developed. With the Lions, a group of players are brought together for a very specific eight-week period and then all go back to their respective countries. The success and failure of a tour depend on the ability to plan and select the right players, to have the right coaching staff, and to react to what happens during the tour. There is always a high injury rate, not least because every game, whether midweek or Saturday, Test or non-Test, is a full-on match. For the opposition, they only play a Lions team every 12 years, so they are going to give it their all. When touring players get injured, the dilemma is always whether they can recover quickly enough to feature later on in the tour, or whether to send for a replacement, with the difficulties that that presents in terms of selection. Often, when a player flies out as a replacement, there are lots of cries, among supporters and the media, of 'What? Why hasn't so-and-so been picked? He should have been picked *first* time round, and now he's not even first replacement. That's an even bigger insult.' And the arguments rage on. And I can guarantee that if the supporters and the media are saying that, certain players are also thinking along the lines of 'This is bollocks – why is *he* coming out?'

I remember just such a situation, when Wade Dooley had to fly back from New Zealand in 1993 because his father had died, and the Home Unions would not allow him to rejoin the tour, even though the NZ RFU were prepared to waive the rule that says that you can't do so once you have left. To say that the dressing room was disappointed is as much of an understatement as saying that the Pope sometimes goes to Mass. But the ruling stood, and Martin Johnson flew out as his replacement. At the time, Martin only had a couple of caps, and was not the great player he was later to become. 'The England Development squad', some non-England players wryly observed regarding (English) manager Geoff Cooke's decision.

In the end, that is key: managing the mix of personalities and talents that are inevitably present. This is obviously essential on a Lions tour, but is also true on all tours, at whatever level of rugby. You can't only have live-wires, or leaders, important though both types are. You also need the quiet ones who just get on with it, and the ones who are responsible and organised.

John Bentley, a Yorkshire winger who was on the England tour to Australia in 1988, was firmly in the live-wire camp. He was a policeman by profession but a complete nutcase by character. John had two modes of operation: on; off. When he was off, he was in bed, you never saw him. But when he was on, he was a maniac and totally wired, as everyone who came into his presence would attest. If there was a lull in proceedings and Bentos was there, it wouldn't remain quiet for long, as he would start a game, conversation or anything that entered his mind that very second. The leaders did not have to be captains: people like Bob Norster, John Jeffrey and Dean Richards had an aura that made people listen and follow.

Brendan Mullin and Anthony Clement would be among the quiet players I have toured with, while Rory Underwood was one of the stand-out responsible and organised players. Unlike some players who were busy running around having fun, Rory would quietly get on with organising things, preferring to spend his time arranging outings for us, for example, to theme parks or local sights of interest.

Crucially, tours need players who are going to show team spirit, even if not selected to play. In my career, both Graham Dawe and Jon Olver were on the bench nearly thirty times each, and in those days no replacements were allowed unless a player was certified by the team's doctor as being medically unfit to continue. That they managed to remain integral members of the England squad and contributed without bitterness was very important to the success of our team. How they managed it I do not know, nor do I know whether I would have been able to do the same had the roles been reversed. Steve Bates, Dewi Morris and David Pears suffered a similar fate, yet never let that affect their attitude towards maintaining team spirit. In the case of the last two, they had to put up with being the only members of the 1991 World Cup squad not to play in any game, even though we went all the way to the final. I cannot imagine what that must have felt like, or how I would have coped.

England tours, Rugby World Cups or Lions tours each have their own particular characteristics, their easy and difficult personalities, and their positive and negative situations. They can enrage and enrich; they can be fascinating, fun and challenging in equal measure. But whatever their outcome, all three types of tour provided me and my fellow players with experiences that are unique and unforgettable, and anyone who nowadays goes on such tours is immensely privileged to do so.

6

'You're Sitting In My Seat'

Anyone who has ever travelled for work will know that the glamour soon wears off. I came to realise this as soon as I began to travel with the England team. Most people, when I told them I was going to foreign climes, would mutter something about going on another jolly and how lucky I was. Actually, I rarely saw very much of the places I went to but I did see a lot of foreign airports, foreign training grounds, foreign coaches, foreign car parks and a lot of very average foreign hotels. Glamorous it was not.

In addition, the *leitmotiv* for all foreign trips was basically: thou shalt hang around. Not only that, but we had to hang around *before* the planned hanging around. In contrast, not long before I joined the England team, in the days when amateurism still reigned, there appeared to be a rather more cavalier attitude to any enforced hanging around. Indeed, on the England tour to South Africa in 1984, Steve Brain, my predecessor as hooker, had been sufficiently unwilling to wait for anyone or anything that he'd simply missed a flight. Back then, nobody seemed to think this was a sending-home offence.

By the time I went on my first England trip abroad, to Australia, for the first World Cup in 1987, hanging around was the new order of the day though; missed flights were a thing of the past. Indeed, no effort had been spared in building in spare time during actual travel. This was the polar opposite to what happens on an Old Boys' tour, where there's much less waiting: everyone just rocks up to the car park where you are meeting; shortly after, you board the coach; off you go. Those who are late just get left behind to make their own way there. Now, large chunks of time are taken up by waiting, although with World Cups, you are at least based in the same place for the group games, which cuts down considerably on travelling time. The time-wasting really comes into its own on a tour, what with the packing and unpacking, and the travelling every few days to a new hotel, all of which swallow up vast swathes of a day. The requirement to be two hours early for international flights and an hour for domestic ones was extended in our case because of the large amounts of personal luggage and the various team paraphernalia that also had to be taken with us.

One consequence of all this moving around and waiting is that you get to know people. Being stuck in airport terminals, in hotel team rooms, waiting for the waiting to begin, it gives you a chance to chat about whatever comes to mind. And, though this sounds unremarkable, it is actually where team bonding takes place; it's just a pity it happens in dull circumstances. During my years with England and the Lions, we didn't often get to meet our team-mates, because we didn't have the extended training camps that players now have, nor did we move clubs in the way that happens now. This meant that new squad players probably had a club-mate or two whom they knew, but that was about it as far as acquaintances were concerned, so it could be a daunting set-up for some. Furthermore, the get-togethers before any home international took place three days before departure and for tours often only the day before, which did not afford much time to settle in and get to know the rest of the squad. However, the extensive amount of travelling and waiting we would be doing on the tour would put that right. Enforced hanging about helped us get to know another side of our team-mates from the one we saw on the field.

As I said earlier, England get-togethers for all tours or trips away (including Five Nations games) invariably took place at the Petersham Hotel, Richmond. For tours, we received a general itinerary in the post which would list hotels and contact numbers; but the tour kit and detailed schedules would only be handed out the day before departure in a fairly cursory manner. Information appeared to be given out on a 'need-to-know' basis by those in charge, probably on the basis that too much information would confuse the forwards anyway. On my earliest tours, it was assumed each player was fit enough to travel and play, otherwise he would have said so, and while we might have a training session the day before departure as a means of proving this, it was not exactly scientific. For later tours, the tests were more specific, but they were nowhere near the thorough assessments that now take place before any player is allowed to get on the plane.

Today, it is not just that preparations are more advanced; there now exists an element that was unheard of when I played: a player's contract insurance. We were not medically insured beyond having a standard group medical policy, though I'm not even certain that existed. The insurance today's players have for their careers is, as you would expect, very specific and often involves potentially large sums of money. It is even quite likely that a different insurer will cover a player for his club duties and his international duties, and there will in all likelihood be a third insurer when it comes to the British and Irish Lions. Not unnaturally, each insurer will, in the event of a claim, want to be satisfied that the injury or event actually took place while their policy was on cover and not when the risk was being carried by another company. This means being precise about the physical state of the player at the point the player moves from cover under one policy to that of another. As a result, the tests that are conducted do not involve a bit of cursory running around, as they did in the past. They are comprehensive and time-consuming, which is part of the reason why players gather together about a week before departure. When the British and Irish Lions returned from their successful tour of Australia in 2013, it took them fully two days to complete the necessary medical examinations, and they did not finally get home until three or four days after the last Test.

When we stayed at the Petersham Hotel, we would train at the Harlequins ground in nearby Twickenham, which, although close as the crow flies, requires crossing Richmond Bridge to get there. If we hit that at the wrong time of day, we could walk there faster than it took to get there by coach. Similarly, when we trained in later years at the Metropolitan Police ground out at Imber Court, in East Molesey, we could waste hours of our day crawling through rush-hour traffic and sampling the delights of the A308 at its gridlocked finest. Nowadays, players meet and train at Pennyhill Park in Surrey, where a full-sized pitch awaits them a short stroll away, together with full gym and physiotherapy facilities. Gone are the days of spending two hours travelling to and from training sessions, and probably rightly so. And yet, it is strange that, even as I write about what was unnecessary, arguably wasted, travelling time, it is worth noting that some of my fondest memories with England are of the savage and relentless banter that took place on the coach; more of which later.

When it came to our kit, it was handed out on the same day as the fitness tests were done, usually the day before leaving. For years it was a standing joke that when it came to our formal tour outfits or indeed that season's Five Nations' dress – blazer, slacks and so on – it made not one jot of difference who were the suppliers nor whether it was bought or sponsored. Whether it was RFU-sourced from the high street or provided by an official clothing sponsor, it just never fitted. Anyone. Part of the problem was that rugby players do not generally come in off-the-peg sizes; but even when the measurements were correct, somehow they got lost in translation, with the result that the cut of the clothes never seemed to match the player. Sometimes, the clothes were simply the wrong size altogether. This didn't only happen with the formal dress: the shorts provided by the kit sponsor for the 1991 Rugby World Cup, Cotton Traders, were so ill-fitting that we ended up, on the eve of the World Cup final, having to go to a local sports shop in Richmond and buy replacements, onto which then had to be sewn the necessary logos.

We were resigned to this, and took the view that as long as we could physically get into the clothes, then they would just have to do, irrespective of how bad we looked. If a player couldn't actually fit into what he'd been given, the management would probably try and find him something that he could squeeze into, but that was as far as it went. Close inspection of official squad photographs will reveal where the trousers or jacket sleeves are too long/short or where a player has tried to adjust a hem temporarily so that they don't look too ridiculous. Mind you, it also became a standing joke that for one player, Dean Richards, his particular shape produced measurements that were so absurd that, unless clothes had been meticulously tailor-made, they would simply end up resembling those worn by a scarecrow. Indeed, it was another standing joke that suppliers would pay Deano *not* to wear their clothing in order to avoid the bad publicity.

Those formal clothes constituted what are called our number ones. The number two outfits would be the smart-casual (whatever that means) clothes: the T-shirts, collared shirts and casual trousers (what used to be called 'slacks'). It meant that if we were told to wear number ones for a particular reception, or number twos, we knew what to wear and wouldn't have players turning up in shorts and trainers. This system, which still operates today, sounds a bit restrictive and formal, but in reality it works well because a squad looks, or should look, uniform and smart. Still, at least we didn't have the problem of a clash between official and personal kit sponsors. Players today have had to become well versed in ensuring they appear at the right times and, more importantly, in the right photographs in the correct sponsors' kit or clothing.

As for training kit, the amount and quality supplied to players changed massively over the eight years I played for England. When I first came into the squad, the only item provided was a tracksuit. I still have a hankering for the imperial purple tracksuit that was the RFU colour at the time, not least because I subsequently found out the Scots hated it with a passion. The rest of our kit was whatever we brought with us, which meant players on the same team ran around in an assortment of shirts; that made the training session look like the school football match in the film *Kes*. The opposition in training was only distinguished by the wearing of bibs. This not only looked shabby but was also impractical, as they often got ripped or torn off during sessions. A couple of years into my England tenure they started to give out a full set of training kit: tracksuit, shirt, shorts and socks. At first, only one shirt was provided, and it was reversible, so that sides could be distinguished; also, call me a cynic, but this was cheaper than providing two different-coloured shirts. They did, finally, extend their largesse to include two shirts; one small step for the RFU, one giant leap forwards in terms of preparation.

This kit was then the personal responsibility of the player, including getting it laundered and endeavouring not to lose it during the multiple stops made on tour. Both these elements sound straightforward but it would have been much better simply to have taken someone on tour to look after it all, as is now standard practice. When it came down to it, kit caused an unnecessary amount of difficulty. And no, I'm not being precious.

When it came to match kit, tradition dictated that it was handed out on the morning of the games, and it was always a notable moment. To go into a room and be given his England strip was a proud moment for a player, no matter how often he did it. It went far beyond the simple provision of the clothing, yet, unless it has been experienced, such an act may seem trivial. It was not; it was a recognition of achievement and responsibility, and I am sure that every international player would concur. To look at the beautifully embroidered national emblem, be it a rose, thistle, fern or whatever, sparks all kinds of personal emotions but mainly that of pride.

Even though all these different on- and off-field outfits were kept to a minimum, it still meant that, together with all our own clothes, there was a lot to squeeze into the tour bags. As with the kit and clothing, the tour luggage varied in amount and standard from tour to tour. The norm was a suit bag, plus a massive kit bag, plus another for everything else. For the first World Cup, in 1987, however, we were given a proper suitcase, and this burgundy-coloured, near bullet-proof item has continued to be used in the Moore household ever since then. All the bags were identical, with only each player's tour number on the bag to differentiate it from the others. Our tour number was allocated alphabetically which, in theory, made it easy because we only ever had the one number to remember.

In charge of this vast pile of luggage were the Duty Boys. They were, and still are, a standard feature of tours or any away trip, though their responsibilities have changed over the years. The job of Duty Boys was rotated daily among the squad, with the exception of the captain, and there were two or three Duty Boys for each day of the tour. When you looked at the rota, you prayed that you didn't get a travel day because the duties were far more onerous.

On a non-match, non-travelling day, Duty Boys had to go to the team manager, get the day's itinerary and post it on a chalkboard or flip-chart in the team room so that everyone knew exactly what the team was doing and when. Details might include what dress was required if a function had to be attended and where various rendezvous points were throughout the day. They also had to carry and load kit or equipment needed at training, such as tackle bags and balls.

On match days, the same practical information had to be disseminated; in addition, the tackle bags, pads and balls had to be taken by the Duty Boys for use in the pre-match warm-up. They also had to help carry the physiotherapy apparatus to the ground. This wasn't done on training days because players were expected to fit in any physio sessions before or after meetings and training. Duty Boys were also responsible for carrying anything required by the management for the game and for any ensuing reception, a concept that might surprise many nowadays.

If a player was unsure about some logistical detail, the Duty Boys were expected to have the answer, though the extent of any particular Duty Boy's knowledge varied enormously, from omniscience to total ignorance. The latter would usually find the ignoramus up on a charge of incompetence in the next Tour Court. Some particularly nefarious Duty Boys deliberately misinformed other players about the time of meetings and so on, in the hope that they would be late and then get fined. John Olver was a particular master at this, and I soon learned never to believe anything he said.

Nobody wanted to be a Duty Boy on travel days because it meant a lot of extra work. First of all, you had to make sure all your own luggage was securely packed and put on the transfer coach. If, like me, you are constantly forgetting odd items, this isn't as straightforward as it sounds. Moreover, you had to pack while your room-mate, if he wasn't also a Duty Boy, was probably still in bed. The reason why you had to start packing a good hour, if not two, before him was that you had to help transfer all the non-player luggage to the bus . If you roomed with someone like Jason Leonard, who was unbelievably messy, you would have to sort through piles of stuff all over the room to make sure something of yours hadn't been buried amid the debris, because you couldn't trust him to bring it along when he left.

Once you had made sure your own luggage was safely stowed, you had to transfer everything else the team carried on tour. This included, but was not limited to, the physio's bench and treatment machines; the tackle bags and pads, cones, flags and balls; the doctor's equipment, and anything used by management. When I first played, all this amounted to a small mountain; by the end, it had become a very large one. It wasn't that the job itself was inordinately difficult; yes, there was a lot to carry, but it wasn't heavy. What was annoying was that you had to do the job while your team-mates swanned about giving 'helpful' instructions and making plain their delight at not having to do skivvy-work.

When all the players had loaded their own luggage and the Duty Boys had loaded the team paraphernalia, the coach would finally set off. If we weren't flying, the reverse operation would take place when we reached the next hotel. However, if we were flying, what happened on arrival at the airport varied according to that airline's or airport's rules. If we were able to check in before arrival, the Duty Boys simply handed out the boarding passes, and grabbed a number of trolleys onto which they piled all the personal and team luggage, before taking it to the group check-in if there was one. It was reasoned that players could at least be trusted to bother to make sure their own luggage had been put on the coach; and that if they hadn't, then it was their own fault. If advance check-in was not possible and passengers had to do so individually, the procedure inevitably took longer, as each player had to identify his luggage, which was distinguishable only by a small number printed on each item. So far, so good.

It was when the flight arrived that problems really could occur. During numerous, seemingly interminable, waits for luggage, players got bored and, being juvenile at heart, found ways to amuse themselves. One particular prank was to purloin another player's bag without him noticing, open it and then deposit individual items on the carousel at regular intervals. Suddenly, a shoe would appear; then a T-shirt; followed a bit later by a sock; then a toothbrush; and so on – very much like a downmarket version of *The Generation Game*. This used to cause much hilarity. 'Why is everyone staring at me?' would say the unwitting person whose belongings they were. Suddenly, the penny would drop, and everyone would burst out laughing, 'You fucking . . .! Who's done this?' that person would exclaim, while rushing around trying to retrieve his bits and pieces still going round on the carousel. 'No, no, it's not me,' we would each protest when accused.

With luck, everyone would eventually retrieve their luggage and put it on the coach, and the Duty Boys would do the same with all the team luggage. However, anyone who has ever been away in a large group will know that, while they cannot leave the airport until the last party member has retrieved all their luggage, they get a bit hacked off at waiting for the one or two unfortunate travellers who are still waiting for their last bags to appear. It also isn't much fun being that last person waiting, because you don't want to be delayed, and you're well aware that your team-mates' sympathy, if there had been any to start with, is limited, especially if the flight has been a long one. In our case, we knew that, as well as settling into our hotel, we would soon have necessary meetings, training or an official function to attend.

As a result, on three of my tours, one of the Duty Boys came up with a cunning plan, in an effort to minimise the hanging around. Irrespective of who the Duty Boys were, the plan would always be the same, and they were always adamant that it would work. 'Tell you what, guys,' we would be told, once in the baggage reclaim area, 'in order to save time, you all get on the coach, and me and [insert fellow misguided Duty Boy's name], we'll just stand there with a load of trolleys and we'll put everything onto them, pack it onto the coach, then we can go.' The first time, I stood there, resignedly shaking my head, and saying to them, 'It won't work,' but they insisted to the contrary. 'Yes, it will, Brian, it'll be fine.' The second and third times I didn't even bother voicing my doubts; I would just quietly think, 'It won't work, but okay, make your own mistakes then.' Sure enough, all the bags would get hurled into the coach, whereupon someone would inevitably pipe up, 'Is my suit carrier on?' or 'Is my kit bag on?' or whatever. 'I don't know,' would come the equally inevitable reply. 'Well, I'm not leaving if that's not on board; it's got all my stuff in there,' or words to that effect.

There was no option but to remove all the luggage from the coach while we all piled off as well. We would then have to spread all the luggage out in the car park in a neat fashion so that we could each identify our luggage from its identification number, during which audible mutters of 'You stupid cunts!' came from many a player, and 'I fucking told you that would happen' from me. Eventually, about an hour later, if everyone had actually identified their luggage, it would be put back on the coach and we would finally be ready to set off.

Of course, on paper, the plan should work. Everyone could indeed be relaxing on the coach while all the luggage was being sorted by the two or three hapless members of the squad, saving everyone a lot of hanging around. The problem was, this cunning plan had at least one drawback that was obvious enough, at least to me, to render it unworkable: how would the Duty Boys know when our luggage had finished arriving? It's not as if they were ticking off each numbered England bag as it came off the carousel. They just waited, randomly, until all the bags appeared to have stopped coming through, with no real idea if there was anything still to follow. They would then just head off, more in the hope than expectation that nothing had been left behind or lost. In the end, I was philosophical about each of these predictably farcical episodes, because the worse it was, the more fun would be the court case in the next Tour Court – and the better the ensuing fine.

In contrast to how it was when I toured, a good example of the way major tours are now organised, and in particular how the team of support staff has expanded, is the 2013 British and Irish Lions tour of Australia. In addition to the eventual total of 45 featured players, the back-room staff included the following: Head Coach; four Assistant Coaches; Head of Strength & Conditioning; Fitness Coach; Sports Scientist; Head of Performance Analysis; two Video Analysts; Tour Manager; Chief Executive; Director of Sales & Marketing; Head Doctor; Assistant Doctor; Masseur; three Physiotherapists; Operations Director; Logistics Officer; Baggage Master; Lawyer; Head of Security; Head of Media & Communications; Media Manager; and Communications Manager.

It would take pages to detail all the equipment used by the support staff; suffice to say it was as extensive as the above list suggests. Moreover, it was supplemented not only by all the usual training aids but also by a huge amount of sponsors' signage and advertising. The sponsorship agreements for the main sponsors dictated that places such as the training ground, press conferences and other areas which would attract media coverage had to be appropriately decked out with an agreed backdrop. Moving around what amounted to truckloads of equipment is now an exercise that involves a tour schedule of its own, and those responsible for it plan for months in advance to ensure that whenever the team arrives at a venue or training ground everything is ready for them to get straight down to whatever business is required. The days of Duty Boys are now long gone, and in their place, Baggage Masters have now been appointed. These are full, paid-up members of the back-room staff, not squad members on a rota. The Baggage Master and his staff often have to leave for the next stop before the team and management, and they always have to get to the training ground hours before the first training session in order to set the ground and perimeters up as required. As they also look after the training and playing kit for the players, there are none of problems we used to face with clothing, and players are able to concentrate solely on playing and preparation.

However many players are taken on a tour, there still has to be a way of checking they are all present for whatever is going on. An omnipresent feature of touring is numbering-off, something that takes place about four or five times a day. The easiest way to do this is for the players to shout out their tour numbers sequentially, starting with 1 (obviously) through to the end. This bears strong similarities to a teacher calling a register and it is quick and works well when players cooperate and concentrate.

One might think that no player could possibly get this wrong unless they were being obtuse, but that does not take into account the naturally subversive nature of some players, nor the fact that some players are not that bright. It was amazing how many people missed – or 'missed' – their number because they weren't paying attention or because they just started messing around. 'Oh, was that me?' they would say in mock surprise. Some players called their number out of sequence or in a different language which would sometimes mean the next numbered player did not realise the countdown had got to them.

Other players used to have competitions to see how long they could take to call out without attracting angry shouts of 'Who the fuck is number xx?' So what was already a laborious process often became a frankly time-wasting one which provoked a disproportionate amount of anger from the rest of the squad, especially if the same player was at fault on numerous occasions. One might take the same attitude that some of the miscreants apparently did, namely that this was a trivial issue over which no reasonable person could get annoyed. To which I would reply that, when you have to number off several times a day, you just want it to be rattled off so that you can get on with whatever is to be done. I remember losing it with one player after a long flight following which we had to fit in a training session before going on to an official reception. At his dismissive response to the squad bellowing at him, he said, 'Calm down; what's the problem; it's no big deal!' My retort was along the lines of 'How is it that only you don't seem able to fucking do this? If it's not a big deal, why can't you do it, then? Everyone else can.' In the end, if a player either wouldn't or couldn't get it right it would be brought up in the Tour Court; the sentence was usually severe enough to encourage the player to get it right from that point forward.

Given that we did not have the luxury of a Baggage Master to take care of all the team equipment, we would have to meet well in advance of any departure time, which itself was well in advance of any flight because of the logistical challenge of checking in both our luggage and the team's as set out above. So, for example, if we had a 3 p.m. flight from Heathrow, the countdown to leaving would in effect begin after breakfast. There would be a meeting straight after, to make sure everyone was there, and had everything with them, including (rather obviously) their passport. Shamefully I have to admit that this essential detail once passed me by for a Five Nations game in France. Happily, I was not alone in being ridiculed for this schoolboy error, as Peter Winterbottom had also forgotten his. Fortunately, in those days you could still get a one-year temporary passport from the Post Office if suitable ID was shown, so I was at least able to get a last-minute replacement that day. Wints, incredibly, contrived to have not a single bank card, driving licence or piece of paper that proved who he was. In the end, the management made a frantic phone call to the Home Office and, unluckily for the French, Wints was somehow given a dispensation to travel on that occasion. Post 9/11, it would not have mattered if he'd been the Prime Minister, I don't think he would have been let into the country.

Assuming no idiots had left their passports behind, once we were all assembled, and the coach filled with bags and kit, we would depart for the airport about four hours before flying. On the 2013 Lions tour of Australia the Lions had parts of the various airport lounges roped off for their sole use. Not only did we not have this, we didn't have any lounge passes of any sort. Similarly, there was no going through priority channels at Security or Passport Control. We just went through with everyone else and would make our way through to the departure lounge. There we would sit around, awkwardly, and often bored, while members of the public gawped at us, until it was finally time to board the plane.

Once on board we turned right into Economy Class. Well, except for the Committee who – obviously, given the exhausting schedule that awaited them abroad – flew Club Class. That caused real resentment, not surprisingly, although to be honest, we barely saw them during the whole journey because presumably they disappeared off to the lounge pre-flight, and turned left once on board the plane. Anyway, there was nothing we could do about it – we were amateur, after all, as far as they were concerned. The only concession made to us was that the really tall players, such as Martin Bayfield at 6ft 10in, were given the seats by the exits because there was a little more leg room there. Those seats were given only if they were available, however, not as a matter of course, because that would have been too indulgent. Otherwise, seats were generally allocated alphabetically, so you just sat where you were told. It didn't matter if you were tall, short or wide, whether you were flying to New Zealand or to Dublin, you just got on with it.

The only time things were any different was when the Lions flew back from that successful tour to Australia in 1989, when British Airways decided to upgrade half the party to Club Class. The allocation was totally random: those who got drawn were literally running around whooping, that's how excited they were, which is a bit tragic really when you consider how players travel nowadays. I was lucky enough to benefit, all 5ft 8in of me. This went down particularly badly with those team-mates of mine who were around a foot taller than me and who still had to turn right to go to their seats. 'You don't need it 'cos you're short,' was a polite version of their opinion. 'Sorry guys, tough luck,' I may have replied, just to rub it in. Their response was generous to a man.

The result of all this was that, by the time we had endured all the hanging around before even leaving for the airport, the hanging around at the airport, and the uncomfortable long-haul flight itself, we were usually absolutely drained by the time we arrived at our destination on the other side of the world. I can't sleep on planes as a general rule, so the long flights to Australia and New Zealand were awful experiences. The stand-out example of this remains the journey back to London from Fiji in 1991. I remember timing the trip from when we left our hotel in Suva to when I stepped over the threshold of my house in Nottingham; it had taken precisely 43 hours. We had flown from Fiji to Sydney, sat around for four to five hours at the airport, changed planes, flew to Bali, where we had an eight-hour stop-over. At that stage, we were at least allowed out of the airport, so people did go off to sit around on the beach and while away a bit of time. This was pleasant, but by that stage of a tour we just wanted to get home, so even the beauty of Bali didn't make up for the time it added to the journey. When we got onto the plane for the final long flight back to London, everyone had had enough and tried to endure the flight in whatever way they could. Still, at least I hadn't been suffering from food poisoning, unlike Andy Robinson. He was suffering so badly he had, literally, to go to the final Test match with toilet paper shoved up his rectum, and was not much better by the time he boarded the plane to come home. This would normally have provoked only ridicule from sympathetic team-mates but so bad did he look that, for once, we relented.

The most common mode of transport on all rugby tours – and probably on tours of any nature, for that matter – is by coach. In the past, coaches were a different breed from the sophisticated ones available now to England or the Lions. On the England trip to South Africa in 1984, which predates my years of touring, the seats must have been very uncomfortable because Chris Butcher apparently clambered into the luggage rack above them in order to have a kip between destinations. By the time I started touring, our coaches were probably better than the average, but as a rule they didn't have toilets on board or seat-back video screens, and were still somewhat basic. However, the fact that coaches didn't have all mod-cons is probably one reason why there was so much banter flying around, at least, in certain sections of the coach. It was just a way of passing the time.

The main concern was where to sit. Indeed, the seats that players came to occupy and why they did so would probably provide a behavioural psychologist or a social anthropologist with enough material to fill a book.

First, it soon became apparent that there was a sort of unofficial seating plan. It was almost like a caste system, and certain personality types tended to sit in certain parts of the coach. It was a bit like at school, where those at the front are the 'keen learners', shall we say, and those at the back tend to be 'different', with those in the middle falling somewhere in between. From my subsequent enquiries, it transpires this is the case with many other countries' senior touring teams, and I think junior teams are often the same. There are no allocated seats, yet time and again, people – including me – would sit in more or less the same seat, if not *exactly* the same, from the start of the tour to the end of it, to the extent that sometimes people would actually say, when finding someone else in 'their' place, 'That's my seat,' to which the so-called interloper would reply, 'Oh yeah, sorry', and move. What does that say about human behaviour? That we are all creatures of habit and/or fundamentally territorial?

Secondly, there was a certain tacit assumption that the quieter, more junior or 'sensible' players, such as Rob Andrew, all sat at or near the front of the coach, along with the Committee-men and the management. Similarly, the captain – who, for many of the years I played for England, was Will Carling. At the back sat players who were louder, more senior and/or into serious banter and piss-taking. Will occasionally sat nearer the back, but as he was in a quasi-management position, it was difficult for him to join in with what was going on there. The further down the bus you sat, the more you had to live with the consequences of doing so. Some players actively shrank from sitting there, and if they were new, they soon realised the sort of stick that was flying about, so few would venture too far back of their own volition.

I started playing for England in 1987, and by the early 1990s the squad was fairly settled with an established hierarchy. By 1992-93, the verbal exchanges were so cutting and personal that some players just wouldn't sit back there, because they just thought it wasn't worth it. So while there wasn't exactly a scramble for places, people certainly got on the coach fast to make sure they had some choice as to where they sat and didn't get stuck at the back unless they wanted to. A group of us effectively colonised the back of the coach, helped by the way in which most coaches are configured. There are basically nine seats that form a bit of a unit: five across the back row, and two in front on each side. Those nine seats form a little amphitheatre, especially as the back row itself is often raised up a little bit. Over time I worked my way to the seat right in the middle of the back row, the best place from which to see most of the coach and view what was going on. More importantly, I did not have to literally and metaphorically watch my back.

When I first joined the squad, I think I sat towards the middle of the coach, not being a senior player, but over a couple of seasons I managed to work my way back. Seniority was one way of graduating towards the back rows but so was possessing a sharp mind and tongue. An example of a player who got there faster than would have been normal was the second row, Martin Bayfield, who turned out, against initial expectation, to be a quick and natural wit. He was not demonstrative at first and, as an inexperienced international, took a bit of time to develop, both physically and as a personality. When he joined, Martin was still a policeman with the Bedfordshire force, but was outstanding at parrying whatever what was thrown at him. It's no surprise to me that he's now a successful TV journalist and presenter (as well as, slightly incongruously, Robbie Coltrane's body double as Hagrid in the Harry Potter films).

Perhaps it was because of our physical and psychological reliance on each other that the back of the bus tended to be populated by forwards who unquestionably share a unique bond within a rugby team. As a result, aside from me, Wade Dooley, Mike Teague, sometimes Dean Richards, Peter Winterbottom, John Olver, Mickey Skinner and Paul Ackford were the usual suspects to be found colonising the back row and thereabouts.

What happened on a coach trip of any length was that, at some stage, you knew it would be your turn to be the focus of a concerted verbal attack from all about you. Nobody planned to pick on anyone in particular, and conversation would meander along with people discussing things normally. You'd try hard not to provoke the banter attack, but in truth, anything you said could provoke it, usually inadvertently. And eventually it would be your turn. For example, if you didn't get something quite right, or if you said something that was quite banal and someone picked up on that, then everyone would launch into you for the next 20 minutes. You tried to escape from the sustained ridicule as quickly as possible by deflecting the mocking or changing the subject. But if you tried too hard, this in itself became a reason to extend your ordeal. Usually the best method was to keep quiet and hope it would either die out or somebody else would make a mistake, which would mean the verbal assault would turn on them. The worst thing you could do was react and try to dispute the substance of the derision because this simply gave the mockers more ammunition with which to assail you.

During any attack there was usually one potential saviour, the scrum-half Dewi Morris. Dewi would often join in the lampooning and, while he is by no means a dull man, he did have the habit of being so enthusiastic in his contributions that he invariably ended up saying something dull. Numerous times Dewi unintentionally shifted the focus on to himself, to the extent that you prayed he would join in. On one occasion, on the coach to the training session before a game against Wales, people started singing, which was great. Dewi, whose nickname was Le Singe (the monkey) – I can't remember why he was called this – came back to sing something (you can't take the Welshman out of the Englishman). Quick off the mark, Martin Bayfield christened him Placido Demonkey, which I thought was pretty good, actually. My contribution, Dewi Te Kanawa, evidently wasn't quite as good, because none of the peasants found it funny – well, it obviously required more specialist knowledge.

One bout of scorn lasted a whole weekend, and the unfortunate recipient was Peter Winterbottom. Wints' nickname at the time was 'Serial' (as in serial-killer), for reasons that will be gone into elsewhere. During a normal rendition of 'Under The Boardwalk', the Drifters classic, Bayfield changed one of the lines to make a reference to serial killers. We then started to change other lines as we sang, particularly the chorus. This was all done on the spur of the moment and without even breaking the rhythm of the song. This continued as we got off the bus and into the changing room, by which time everyone was in stitches. I can still remember the final version of the chorus which ended up going like this:

Under the Boardwalk – out of the sun
Under the Boardwalk – there'll be no more fun
Under the Boardwalk – they'll be festering away
Under the Boardwalk – to be dug up some day – under the Boardwalk.

Wade Dooley was a long-time member of the back row club because not only was he large and potentially brutal, he was surprisingly droll; in fact, Wade was responsible for authoring many of the nicknames that stuck to various players. However, like the rest of us, he took his turn in being ridiculed, and on the 1990 England trip to Argentina, he had to endure nearly a whole tour's-worth of stick.

The unlikely genesis for Wade's torment was the fact of me reading a book. Not *The Complete Works of Shakespeare*, which I read on a subsequent tour – and by so doing was accused of showing off. This time, as we were waiting at Heathrow to fly to Argentina, I must have been reading an accessible novel, and as I'm a fast reader anyway, I started working my way through it fairly swiftly. Wade, who had seen me start the book at the airport, asked me a little later, as we were still waiting to board, what page I was on, which I duly told him. Off he wandered, and a short while later, he asked me again. 'Er, ninety-four' (or whatever page it was). As I'd progressed pretty fast, he turned innocently to the others. ''Ere, guess what page Mooro's on?' 'I dunno, what page is he on, Wadey?' 'Ten, eleven?' 'Have you got anything more boring to say?' He'd asked me earlier and had seen how fast I'd read, so he was genuinely surprised and that's all he was trying to convey by asking the others. Of course, none of them had been privy to that exchange, so they just thought it was a big 'What the fuck do I want to know that for?' type of question, and was taken as another example of 'boring, tedious information from Wade that I don't care about'. This then created instant fun-fodder for most of the rest of the tour at his expense. From that point onwards no opportunity was lost to portray whatever he said as boring. His usual nickname of 'Big and Daft' which he cheerfully accepted, was changed, and for the duration of the tour, he became known as 'Boring Bob Grover from Stamford'. (Don't ask about Stamford, it just sounded better.)

His fate was sealed. People would go up to him and ask, 'Say something, Wade,' and then they'd mimic their elbow falling off the table, with their eyes closed, as if they were falling asleep in front of him. Or they'd go up to him, tap him on the shoulder, ask, 'Say something, Wade,' and start snoring or pretend to fall asleep. They'd egg him on to say things. And, when he refused, 'No, go on Wade, go on!' they'd plead. And whenever he said anything, people would then ask him a really inane, boring question, such as, 'And what colour hat was he wearing?' Anything, as long as it was tedious.

On the tour bus Dooley also suffered. Incongruously, there happened to be a small booth at the back, in the right-hand corner of the back row. It was not clear what it was, but it was almost like a small luggage area, with a little window in it. When you sat in it, because it had a seat, it was like sitting in a booth of your very own; very strange. Sometimes, when Wade had had enough of the taunting, he would simply up sticks and go and fit his rather large frame into this strange little booth, which then became known as the Dooley Booth. He would then don his headphones to try and drown out the cacophony of abuse. Wade referred to his headphones as 'Verm Deflectors', in reference to the Vermin, John Olver, who was piss-taker-in-chief. Seemingly safe in his sanctuary, Wade thus tried to ignore us; but before long, it occurred to me that the sight of Wade sitting in the Dooley Booth resembled the winning contestants in *The Generation Game* who had to remember all the items that had gone past them on the conveyor belt in a booth. This analogy found widespread support, and before long, Olver, I and others were announcing, 'And in the Dooley Booth today we have a pair of slippers . . . A sleeping bag . . .' Everybody joined in, listing any item that was vaguely linked to sleep: 'An electric blanket . . . A cuddly toy . . . !' and then on to 'A mug of cocoa . . . A set of earplugs . . . A Richard Clayderman tape . . .' and so on and so on.

As we did this, others hummed the inane tune that used to accompany the passage of the items on the belt, and this proved to be an enduring joke; for us at least. Without fail, every time Wade got into his booth, we'd all start up; and if he didn't, someone else would go in and pretend to be him as a contestant, so he got stick whether he did or didn't; the perfect Catch-22 situation.

It would be easy to get the impression that this 'banter' was no more than disguised bullying, where the weaker players were picked on and taunted, unable to respond because they felt they did not have the standing, confidence or wit to do so. This would be to misunderstand. Like in the Tour Court, everybody got 'done' at some point, including the Court Officials at the end. The verbal stick that flew about was totally indiscriminate, and was more often than not confined to the group who majored in it. The aim of banter is that it does not wound, as it is not then fun; nobody would enjoy or condone seriously upsetting another player. Not only would this be uncivilised, it would, being strictly pragmatic, be contrary to the team ethic and counterproductive.

To be successful, your colleagues need to be on their best form, physically and mentally, because you rely on them during games. That said, there was no room for anyone who was precious, boastful or contemptuous because not only was this not tolerated, it provided a rich source of material with which the diva would be assailed.

The fact is that, unless you are a sociopath, you can only be vicious and personal about people with whom you feel completely safe and at ease. You certainly can't behave in this way towards those you don't like – or are even indifferent to – especially if you know you're going to be in their company for a while. You can only behave as we did when you are secure in the knowledge that others are not going to take it personally. This is proved by the fact that when I first came into the squad the banter was fairly benign, as nobody was that familiar with each other. As we gradually became a more settled and successful side, the verbal sparring got more personal and cutting.

In the end, virtually nothing was off limits, provided it didn't genuinely cause offence or upset. I remember a young Martin Johnson joining the squad. Being a fairly quiet guy, he was taken aback by how savage and cutting the banter was, and consequently he misunderstood what was going on. 'Do they not like each other?' he asked various players about the comments flying around the back half of the coach. I'm not sure he believed them when they reassured him that this was just a sign of affection.

I don't know if professionalism in rugby has changed the dynamics on 'the bus', but if so, I'm sure there are still elements that remain, human nature and teams being what they are. I do know that in the same period that I played, the anthropologists would also have been interested in the workings of both the Australian and New Zealand buses.

The Australians had no strict demarcation by seniority; but like us, players tended to habitually sit in the same seat throughout the entire tour, to the extent that the objection 'You're sitting in my seat' was also heard. When asked what it said about the Australian psyche, Michael Lynagh concluded that it pretty much summed them up as a society: like many, they were creatures of habit, but they were also egalitarian and not too fussed about the small things in life that seem to exercise others.

The Kiwis, on the other hand, were made of different stuff. No surprises there. Their bus reflected to a large extent the manner in which they have always approached rugby. Seniority is respected and reinforced, and newcomers have to know their place and 'work their passage'. Everyone is most definitely not equal on a Kiwi bus. I think it is still the case.

Sean Fitzpatrick explained to me once that players who sat on the back row were the most senior, either in age, or in number of caps. However, the captain could not sit there – he only got as far back as the penultimate row – because he would be party to some of the talk that went on there, which would conflict with his role. That was also the case with us, and was one of the main reasons why Will Carling never sat very far back. The back row's influence, however, went beyond travel: its members organised the rooming list, the Duty Boys' rota, they formed the Social Committee and were in charge – in an era of supposed amateur rugby – of commercial matters. They could also summon any player, Godfather-like, for 'a chat'. This could be light-hearted, but could also involve a warning about some matter.

The position of more junior players more or less corresponded to how long they had been in the squad, but it was also influenced by another factor: at some point on an All Blacks tour, new players had to try and 'take' the back seat, i.e. try and occupy it. This was compulsory, like an initiation rite or rite of passage, though its timing was a matter for the 'attackers'. That word is used deliberately because I gather this attempt was not a half-hearted push and giggle; quite the reverse. It was a full-on assault in which blows were traded without any concession to safety, size or whatever. The attackers had to get there by any means possible but their task was hampered by the fact that back-row members, anticipating the attack, influenced the seating in front of them by posting large 'guards' to protect them, thus making it more difficult for the newcomers. This was not for the faint-hearted, and bus trips obviously provided some good spectator sport.

One trip I was told about took this bellicose philosophy to new heights. It came following what the Kiwis viewed as a disappointing draw in the second Test against Australia in 1988 in Brisbane, having won the first. Before leaving for Gosport for a later midweek game, their coach, Grizz Wyllie, ordered them to report for a meeting. They got a ferocious lashing, but not of the kind they had envisaged. Players were puzzled when Wyllie ordered them to get changed, but to put on their sand shoes (their sneakers), not their rugby boots. They were further bemused when he ordered each of them to give Albert Anderson, one of their second rowers, an A$10 note, and still more so when he ordered them to form a circle around him. Anderson was given a huge jug of beer, which was thereafter constantly replenished, and each player was given a schooner. In turn, they each filed past Anderson who filled each schooner, while the players continued to walk round in a circle. The schooner had to be finished by the time the player got back to Anderson, whereupon it was refilled. This continued for an hour. I'm told the atmosphere was good, because they were chatting away while they were walking round and gradually getting more and more drunk.

This novel piece of man-management psychology led to a particularly spirited attempt to take the back seat on the subsequent coach ride. Normally, people flew in; this time, they just went crazy. And when their hosts greeted them off the bus, they witnessed a variety of burst noses, split lips, bruises, cut eyes, torn clothing and blood splatters, which resembled the aftermath of a street fight. Which, in a way, it was. By the way, the Kiwis won the third Test, and the series.

The only time our own coach journeys reached similar levels of excitement was during the 1991 World Cup, before our notoriously incendiary quarter-final against France. In fact, when I reflect on how that game turned out, that journey was one of the contributory factors, as it raised our adrenalin levels at a time when we were trying to keep them under control. Motorcycle outriders had begun to accompany us in England, but for the first few seasons they were completely useless. They basically consisted of four blokes, who happened to be policemen, on their motorbikes, and they merely rode in front of us but didn't move any traffic out of the way. All this meant that our bus was simply four bikes' worth further back in the traffic; it didn't actually get us anywhere any faster.

We expected much the same on our 15km journey from our hotel, the luxurious Trianon Palace in Versailles, to the Parc des Princes. Normally, we would get stuck in traffic for some or all of the way, because these were the outskirts of Paris, and roads there were always clogged up. However, unbeknown to us, initially, we were not escorted by outriders from the normal Gendarmerie but by officers from the CRS Riot Police. The coach journey to the ground is an important part of match preparation. Often managers will prepare a piece of music or video footage that will reinforce their message for the game or otherwise inspire players in a more general way. If this wasn't done, players used the time to reflect on what was to come, chatting quietly, talking to their neighbours, listening to music or simply gazing out of the windows.

We set off at an unusually rapid pace and shot through the first tunnel without any sign of slowing down. Suddenly, someone came running down from the front of the coach. 'Take a look at this!' he urged. As one we looked ahead to see the outriders basically using their batons to hit any car that was not moving out of the coach's way fast enough. And any that were just too slow to get the message got their door kicked for good measure. A very effective traffic-management policy it was, much admired (and possibly envied) by the various policemen in our squad, and much cheered by all of us, especially the forwards, who thought this was brilliant fun. What should have been an agonisingly slow 40-minute crawl to our destination turned into a 20-minute, adrenalin-fuelled sprint to the stadium. When we got off the bus we had the same kind of feeling you have when you get off a particularly thrilling theme-park ride; not the considered and even-tempered mood recommended by sports psychologists.

Most of the time, travelling, whether by coach or by plane, was not as exciting. In fact, it was an exercise in finding ways to pass the time. Unlike today's sportsman (or general traveller, for that matter) we didn't have the benefit of smartphones, tablets and other gadgets to enable us to pass the time. That being so we had to find other ways of occupying ourselves.

When it came to music, the Walkman had at least been invented (I'm not that old) and some of the coaches also had sound systems which played music to the whole coach. Although these helped to while away some time, both sometimes caused friction. As anyone will attest who has ever sat next to another commuter playing their music loudly, the tinny sound that comes from earphones eventually becomes inordinately annoying, and some players would simply move seats rather than put up with the disturbance.

When it came to a communal sound system, the potential for discord was much greater. Music is, necessarily, a matter of personal taste and rarely will you get four people in a car to agree on what they want to listen to, never mind a whole tour party. If music was played, there would always be several people who did not like the selection and after a while would want to change it. Those who had been enjoying it then objected to it being taken off, particularly so if they didn't like the new music. On one tour, we had to bring in a rule that each player could play their own choice of music for 20 minutes. It was reasoned that, in this way, everyone got their turn, and if a player's music wasn't liked it would only be on for a short time, during which the others would just have to put up with it. Even this egalitarian system didn't work because when I tried to play 20 minutes of opera the protests were so loud that it got taken off – bloody peasants. More often than not, therefore, we simply didn't bother because whatever we did caused upset at some point.

When Game Boys first appeared on tour, it was an opportunity for Jeff Probyn in particular to while away hours on end. Probyn is a geeky sort, always with the latest gadget, so this one was like manna from heaven for him. He would play on his during every trip, and whenever we had any down-time. He didn't turn the volume off, because his many qualities notwithstanding, he delights in winding-up other players. The supremely irritating 'beep beep beep' noise that occurs when the controls on the device were pressed gave Jeff a weapon with which to annoy anyone near, especially as he could claim they were merely incidental to his enjoying the game and it wasn't his fault. In the end he got the message with me because one day, when the beeps were starting to seriously grate with me, like nails down a blackboard, I simply said 'Jeffrey, fuck off and go away.' Off he wandered to annoy his next victim without taking any offence at the remark, and with a little grin on his face, safe in the knowledge that he had achieved his goal.

On one long coach journey, Jeff's mission to annoy hit its zenith with the fly-half Stuart Barnes. Stuart is a studious sort and was sitting in the seat in front of Jeff reading a volume of American poetry. One of the joys of reading poetry is its ability to conjure up moods and thoughts that are highly personal and sometimes quite moving. The possibilities of this happening are severely diminished if your reading is accompanied by a constant 'beep, beep, beep' from the seat behind. Unable to stand the noise any longer, Stuart asked, as politely as he could, 'Can you turn that down a bit?' Jeff apologised and turned the volume down a little, only to gradually increase it over the next few minutes to the same or an even greater level. Stuart then asked again, and again Jeff did the same thing. This pattern continued for the whole journey, leaving Stuart thoroughly unhappy that his potentially pleasant bit of reading had been ruined. However, his mood went from annoyed to apoplectic when Jeff told him, as we got off the coach, that the sound could have been switched off completely. The filth that came out of Barnsey's mouth would certainly have shocked his old tutor at Oxford.

Someone else you didn't cross lightly was Mickey Skinner, the Harlequins flanker. If you ever started a row with Skins, you'd better be prepared for nuclear war, because he's the sort of person who will not let go. I was called Pitbull, but he could be off the scale. If you started a silly little thing, like flicking a bit of bread at dinner or whatever, then you'd get more back than you bargained for. John Olver and Skinner once got into some sort of one-upmanship situation, the final act of which took place at the airport. Somehow, Skinner had managed to get a bucket and to fill it to the brim with water, whereupon he'd gone up to the mezzanine level of the departures hall, while Olver was standing underneath, unaware. He then proceeded to upend the entire contents right onto Olver. I can confirm that a big bucketful of water, dropped from a height, actually smacks down pretty hard. When it hit Olver, it made a huge 'bang' noise and everyone turned round. That's how loud it was. Skinner hit his target spot on, and then the water just splattered absolutely everywhere. This was the final payback for whatever it was they had been in mock dispute over. Fortunately for him, there were no repercussions, but it did enable us to coin the phrase 'being bucketed' that was regularly used thereafter. If you were going to 'get bucketed', it meant you should fear the worst. And as Skinner was an enforcer at one of the Tour Courts, being bucketed by him was not a pleasant prospect.

Indeed, some years later, at a rugby dinner, a member of the public was being an idiot with their mobile, and Skinner told him, 'You've been warned about your mobile phone. Any more and . . .'

And as the guy took no notice, Skinner just picked it up and dunked it in the wine bucket. The guy carried on, oblivious, because he was drunk, so in the end Skinner picked up the wine bucket with all the ice and just tipped it over this guy's head. Well and truly bucketed. And the original ice bucket challenge.

There are no fast ways to travel to far-off places, as we did, simply more comfortable ways of doing so. I am sure that current tourists still find much of the travelling tedious, annoying and exhausting. Yet, while I don't have fond memories of the many flights I took, because I don't like being cooped up in a plane for very long, I do remember many coach journeys in an altogether different way. When people ask me what I miss the most about my playing career, I can honestly say that I miss those moments, whether it was some of the lively Tour Court sessions that were held on buses during my England Students tour of the Far East, or some of the endless banter that went on during England and Lions tours. I miss that camaraderie. In fact, I miss that as much as the actual playing and the winning, because it really was such good fun.

7

'I'd Like a Superior Suite with an Ocean View'

Officially, it became known as 'The Invincibles' Tour'. Unofficially, it was dubbed, by those who knew, 'The Wreckers' Tour'. The 1974 Lions tour to South Africa may have contained some of the game's legends – players such as Willie John McBride, Gareth Edwards and J.P.R. Williams; it may have gone down in rugby history as hugely successful – 21 out of 22 games were won, the Lions won the series and were unbeaten in the Tests. However, some of the managers of the hotels that the team stayed in along the way might remember the tour for slightly different reasons. The team basically had 'wreckers' who used to see how many hotel doors they could break or wrench off their hinges. Mind you, it wasn't always done on purpose and it wasn't always doors; sometimes it was beds, tables, chairs, whatever.

In one hotel after the Lions' victory in the second Test earlier that day, spirits had clearly been set alight and the alcohol flowed. As celebrations spiralled out of control later that night, Welsh forward Tommy David's bed ended up being thrown out of a window. Meanwhile, down on the ground below, chaos reigned, because someone had had the bright idea of setting fire to some empty boxes, causing Bobby Windsor, the hooker, to rip the fire extinguisher from the wall to try to extinguish the blaze. As the hotel manager failed to appear grateful enough that disaster had been averted, he too got a hosing down for good measure. Eventually, at three in the morning, Willie John McBride, the team captain, was summoned down from his room to sort out the situation. He turned up in what was left of the hotel lobby, which had also had the full Lions celebration treatment. He was clad only in his underpants, but clutching his pipe, without which he was rarely seen when he was not playing rugby. The manager was by now incandescent with rage. 'What seems to be the matter?' asked Willie John, very calmly, with his unmistakably Irish accent. Amid his ranting, the manager informed him that things had gone much too far and that the police were now being called. At this, the captain reflected a little, took a few slow puffs of his pipe, and enquired, 'Will there be many of them?'

Before things started to get more serious within the England set-up in the late 1980s, two tours still displayed the full extent of amateurism. As well as the infamous trip to South Africa in 1984, where outrageous behaviour seemed to attract amused reactions rather than sanctions, England went on a 'spreading the game' tour of North America, and because the rugby was relatively unchallenging, they took full advantage of any opportunity to have a virtual playing holiday. The behaviour in the hotels was regularly off the scale, it seems, and the whole tour has always sounded pretty rock and roll to me, only with alcohol in place of drugs. It was on that tour that Maurice Colclough, the 6ft 7in lock, probably made a security guard wish he hadn't threatened him. Colclough, who sadly died a few years ago and far too young, was a huge character, in every sense of the word. Physically massive, he was also a hard man, and an absolute lunatic when he got drunk. One night, in a hotel, the team were so spectacularly out of order that Colclough threw a television out of the window. These were not like today's lightweight flat screens. The hotel security guard duly came rushing up to the room and told him to stop, but when he wouldn't, the guard pulled a gun on him, assuming that Colclough would immediately come to his senses and sober up. Unfortunately, this had the opposite effect. Colclough just punched him and the guy instantly fell to the ground.

Those sorts of antics were a thing of the past by the time I was checking in to any hotel with England or the Lions. Whenever Rory Underwood was on the tour, he would automatically be given the task of sorting out the room allocation, because he genuinely enjoyed doing this. Room-sharing policies differ from one tour to another: junior tours often allow people to room with their mates; with senior rugby, players usually have no choice in the matter. The Australians, apparently, in the spirit of democracy that seemed to characterise their tours, made their own arrangements, whatever the official lists said, and happily swapped if they felt like it. For us, enforced mixing was very much part of the management policy, even though Rory did the actual room lists.

A lot of thought went into who shared with whom, and certain clashes were avoided. On Lions tours, for example, two men competing for the same position would rarely room together, though this did on occasion happen. I never roomed with my fellow-hooker Graham Dawe: it's not that we disliked each other, but it was clear to all that it just wouldn't have been a good idea. Forwards and backs tended to be paired up, which always drew complaints from the backs that they never got their choice of bed as the mean and nasty forward had not given them a choice.

The pairings were changed at each hotel. There are different schools of thought about this, with some arguing that it is better for players to room with their friends. I took the opposite view: having to room with the stipulated player helped to stop cliques from forming. Over the course of a tour, depending on whether it was a tournament or a tour, you would end up sharing with up to half a dozen players, with senior players rooming with junior ones. As a result, it would not be uncommon for a junior player to find himself sharing with a very experienced player whom he might have idolised as a youngster. This could be quite intimidating and difficult at first, but by breaking down barriers in this way and being made to co-exist, everyone got to know each other within a few days, and this was good for team spirit. Nowadays, given that management have detailed psychological profiles of all the players, I would be surprised if 'cohesion engineering' wasn't used to ensure that players shared with the 'right sort' of room-mate.

The upside to constantly changing room-mates was that you got to know many players well. The downside is that you might not always want to. At some stage on a tour you would inevitably find yourself sharing with a player who was either a snorer, a scratcher, was pathologically tidy or untidy, or had some other antisocial habit. I snore occasionally but not badly; the nightmare was if you were paired with someone who did. These players soon became widely known, and the announcement of their new pairing would usually draw unfavourable comment from their fresh victim room-mate. Sometimes there was a policy of rooming snorers together but all that meant was that it was a race as to who got off to sleep first.

I once roomed with Scott Hastings, and I'm not exaggerating one jot when I say that within 30 seconds of his head hitting the pillow, he was snoring so loudly that I assumed he was winding me up. So much so that I called out, 'Scott, Scott, can you stop that!'

When he didn't reply, I was hit with the awful realisation that he was actually asleep. I was left with no choice: off I traipsed, down to the hotel reception.

'Please can I have another room?'

'Why?' asked the bemused night manager.

'Look, I know it's annoying for you, but I want you to come with me.'

'What do you mean?'

'Just come with me.' I made him come up in the lift with me. We got out at my floor, and were *at least* ten doors away when the noise first hit us. And it got louder and louder as we got closer and closer. 'Do I have to explain what the problem is?'

I finally opened the door to the room, for maximum effect, whereupon he tactfully went, 'I understand, Sir,' and found me another room.

My snoring did cause one memorable incident, even if I can't recall a thing about it. On their first ever New Year training camp, England went to Portugal, and I shared with Chris Oti. Chris was the first black man in 80 years to be selected for England, he was a Cambridge blue and talented winger, and he was good company. However, one night the following happened and although I have no recollection of any of it I accept Chris's story completely as he had no reason to make it up. I was snoring so loudly that he tried to speak to me, to tell me to pipe down. No reaction. He then spoke to me again, but in a very loud voice. Still no reaction. He resorted to throwing a pillow at me. The snoring decibels remained the same. In the end, exasperated, he leapt out of bed and started to shake me. Just as he did so, I apparently woke up, and semi-consciously seeing this large figure looming over me I bounded out of bed and karate-chopped him on the neck, leaving him to stagger backwards. Apparently after this, I then went back to bed, as if nothing had happened and promptly fell asleep again. Chris told me years later that the following morning, taking no chances, he removed all the knives from the cutlery drawer of our kitchenette, and while he was at it, all the forks as well, in case I inadvertently did a bit of aggressive sleep-walking.

You soon learned what people's bedtime routines were. Some people went to bed late, or read a book, others wanted to watch the TV, or even had to have it on *in order* to get to sleep. Some could go to sleep when the light was still on, others absolutely not. If you're used to a certain bedtime ritual, it's easy to get irritated when it is interrupted, or when someone has a totally different routine. If you are on holiday with your mates, you will probably put up with that sort of stuff. On tours, you are with people you don't necessarily know, some of whom you don't particularly like – or indeed actively dislike. So the habits of others could easily come to grate very fast, but you just had to be reasonable and put up with it. Any issues surrounding sleep were particularly incendiary, though, because often we were tired and jet-lagged, so not very forgiving if being deprived of rest.

Tidiness and untidiness, on the other hand, were just something you accepted. Some, like Neil Back, would be in the first category. As soon as he arrived in the room, he would unpack absolutely everything, down to the contents of his washbag. Everything would be neatly folded, and the suitcase put away under the bed or in a cupboard, out of sight. Everything was absolutely lined up, and cupboard doors would be kept closed at all times. That's just the way he was. Richard Hill was exactly the same, to the extent that if you left anything lying around, he would tidy that away too, because he couldn't bear anything that was not all neat and ordered. In fact, if I ever roomed with him, I'd leave things lying around, just to annoy him and to see if he said anything – which he never did.

At the other end of the spectrum was Jason Leonard. There was little point in any room having a wardrobe or cupboards with Jason, as he lived out of his suitcase and bags, and just chucked everything on the floor. We once managed to lose two remote controls in the room just because we couldn't find them amid all the debris. It got to the point where even the chamber maid took a stand and refused to clean the room. 'I'm not here to sort, I'm here to clean the room,' she told us before retreating to more salubrious quarters.

Her refusal was understandable, as was that of the maid in Club La Santa in Lanzarote who refused to even enter the living room in the two-man apartment occupied by Peter Winterbottom and Mike Teague. After a particularly large session, the guys had ordered pizzas, after which Wints threw up on the living room table and then went to bed. Not unnaturally, Mike refused to clear it up in the morning, and Wints left it, expecting the maid to clean up when she serviced the unit. When the boys came back from training to find the pool of vomit and the half-eaten pepperoni feast still on the table, Mike point blank demanded Wints clean it up, and Wints, being from Yorkshire, didn't take kindly to the tone and refused. There then followed a stand-off of three days during which neither would back down nor remove the increasingly noxious pile now stuck fast to the table. It eventually got cleared away, but neither would admit he had been the one to yield.

Whenever we arrived at a new hotel, the same process would take place: we knew who our room-mate was because the room list was read out on the coach, and there would invariably be a team meeting in the designated team room, perhaps 20 minutes or half an hour after. We were fined if we were late, usually £1 for every minute, and though this may seem harsh – given we were all amateurs – I didn't disagree with the system because if you let one person be two minutes late, and the next person three, then all of a sudden it's ten, meetings start later and later, and chaos ensues. Not only is this then a complete waste of many people's time, but the casual attitude can easily start to extend into other areas: people can start to think, 'I won't bother turning up on time for this,' be it training, the bus or whatever.

When the team meeting was due to start soon after registration, and there were a lot of us to get through, hotels would dispense with some of the formalities of registration. Nevertheless we still had to get our room keys and that meant there would be a lot of jostling as we tried to get our keys as fast as possible and, crucially, before our team-mates, all of whom were trying to do exactly the same thing. We did this because hotel lifts can be slow at the best of times, but if it's being taken by loads of players going up to their rooms to deposit all their luggage, you could find yourself standing there waiting ages for the lift to finally come back down to reception. By that time the meeting would be about to start and you risked getting fined. Some hotels had 30 or 40 floors, so this was a serious problem, however trivial it might appear to the outsider. In fact, there was one hotel where the lift situation was so appalling that players were constantly being made late and fined as a result. The management had to issue a moratorium and we were actually allowed to use lift-waiting as a legitimate excuse for being late.

People soon learned this useful trick when checking in: they would get their room key as fast as possible; they would run to the lift with all their bags; if it existed, they'd immediately press the 'close door' button, keeping others out who hadn't been as on the ball. Once they reached their floor, just after getting out and before the doors closed again, they would then quickly press every button for the floors below so that the lift had to stop at every floor, thus making all their team-mates wait. It was monumentally childish and very effective, which is why it proved such a popular ploy with a group of competitive and devious players. Everyone knew that their team-mates would do this and try to make them late. I remember very clearly being both on the receiving end of the trick and dishing it out, standing there, while others tried to barge their way in.

'Let us in!'

'No; go away!'

'You horrible little fucker!'

'Not my problem; don't be late!'

The quality of the rooms went from basic to a bit better than that, and very occasionally to very good. One of the commonest problems was that the taller players never fitted the beds. They would often have to put a chair at the end of the bed on which they could rest their feet. Today's players travel with special pillows, and extra-large beds are provided at every stop. Indeed, representatives from the visiting Union will travel to the country in advance, will check every stop, see what's there, and arrange suitable changes to accommodation where necessary. This is not as precious as it sounds. Getting a decent night's sleep is important to everybody if they want to feel fresh the following day. When they are being asked to perform at high levels of fitness and under stress, it is even more important. The significance of this seemingly trivial detail was identified by the ultra-professional Sky cycling team headed by Sir David Brailsford. One of the reasons for the team's stellar success in recent years was the commitment to look at every single area of preparation, from the bikes themselves to every other aspect that could have any bearing on a rider's performance. If anything could be improved, it was, no matter how small. This approach has become colloquially known as the 'aggregation of marginal gains'. To ensure a rider did not have a bad night's sleep because of an unfamiliar and uncomfortable bed, the Sky team have a van that transports the riders' mattresses to each hotel so that this does not happen. A rider might still have a poor night, but not from something that is within the control of his team.

When we toured countries such as New Zealand and South Africa – less so in Australia – we often visited provincial towns that did not always have good hotels. This was nobody's fault because there was insufficient demand for that type of accommodation year round and it would be uneconomic to build one for isolated tours. Eventually, Tour Agreements stipulated that accommodation had to be of a certain 'star' rating, provided that was actually available. Though this sounds reasonable in theory, it was in fact no guarantee of a minimum standard because there is no globally agreed star rating. What one party considers a three-star hotel another might rate higher or lower. Touring teams simply had to rely on the host Union to provide decent hotels and not try to minimise expense. The reasoning was that they would abide by the letter and spirit of the Tour Agreement because they would not want their own team to be treated poorly when it came to a reciprocal tour. This didn't always work.

In the last 25 years, hotels have improved in almost every country. The importance of tourism to many economies and the fact that people can choose from a huge variety of destinations have forced the hospitality business to raise its standards markedly. Furthermore, as there is far greater scrutiny of every part of a tour, it is now the case that teams demand to be told way in advance what hotels are being proposed for their visit. With the internet and review sites, they can find out what hotels are really like, as opposed to what they are told, even if they are not inspected by someone from the Union, though that too is now becoming routine. Though it doesn't happen frequently, I know that some touring teams have refused to accept the proffered base and insisted on being provided with a better alternative.

On single tours, this does not become an issue, but this is not always so during a Rugby World Cup. As with similar tournaments in other sports, it is usual for there to be an official provider of accommodation and as part of the sponsorship agreement the participating teams have to stay in the hotels of that sponsor. If it is a large company with many quality hotels, this is not a problem. However, sometimes the company will have, say, four such hotels and the fifth is of a lower standard. Not unnaturally, the team that is put in the poorer hotel is not happy with this, but there is a limited amount they can do about it. There simply may not be another hotel in the region that is owned by the official provider, and even if the Union is able to pay the cost of a better hotel, they will be prohibited from doing so by obligations in the participation agreement. When the problem comes to a head the team either accepts its lot or risks a row with the tournament organisers and the publicity that inevitably comes with it.

To complicate matters, it is possible for hotels to be of the same technical standard and yet be vastly different in terms of what this means in practice for the players. An example of this was England's stay in Johannesburg during the 1995 World Cup. The South African and England teams both stayed in hotels owned by the Hilton Group, the official provider. The two hotels were similar in standard, but the one the South Africans were allocated was in Sandton, a lively and cosmopolitan part of the city where there were shops, bars and other facilities. Our Hilton was in the Hillbrow district which used to be extremely desirable; however, due to the increase in crime, the housing stock had greatly deteriorated and many wealthier residents had left for the northern suburbs. As a result, there were many under-utilised or abandoned office buildings which had been taken over by squatters, or converted into residential housing units. During the day there were lots of people about, but after the offices closed it was almost empty, save for a few people and gangs. Hillbrow itself was a pre-dominantly black area, and although apartheid had ended, it was nevertheless a place where white people and foreigners were advised not to wander in the evenings. Our two allocated security guards counselled us thus: 'We can't ban you from going out in the evenings, but put it this way – we wouldn't, and we're armed.' So while the Springboks could enjoy their surroundings, we were effectively confined to our hotel. It was a comfortable place with all the usual facilities but it obviously couldn't provide a whole district's entertainment and diversity. Even if we didn't want to buy anything or eat out, it is enjoyable to walk around different cities, take in the atmosphere and see how the local people enjoy themselves. Nothing makes you appreciate this more than not being able to step outside the curtilage of your own building for days on end.

Oddly, three other hostelries that come to mind as high on the list of 'Worst places I have stayed' were on the 1993 British Lions tour of New Zealand. The hotel we stayed in on our visit to Invercargill was akin to the Bates motel featured in *Psycho*, though I have to admit that my memory of it might be tainted by my memories of the appalling weather and of the town itself. No doubt it is different if you live there, but as I don't like Bluff Oysters and am not interested in signs that remind you how many thousands of miles you are away from other places you'd rather be in, there was little that enthused me.

A similar experience was had when we stayed in Whangerei where, on alighting from the team bus, I noticed a sign on the side of the building that said, 'All you can eat $3.99.' It was actually a backpackers' hostel, and an average one at that.

The final place on my list has to go to the place we stayed in Hamilton, though I must stress that when I returned years later, Hamilton had improved beyond recognition. This was, again, little more than a motel but it is memorable for two other reasons. The weather on that leg of the tour was unremittingly awful which, I concede, wasn't their fault. But one day, we came in from training, during which it had rained heavily and incessantly, and our training kit was sodden. The hotel didn't have a laundry room with dryers so we went back to our rooms to get changed, intending to dry our kit on the radiators, only to find they were electric heaters which carried the risk of fire if anything wet was placed on them. In the end we tracked down the few rooms that were being upgraded and had ordinary radiators, and had to try to share those, but with very limited success. It wasn't just the fact that we had to re-use kit that was wet or damp – our boots didn't dry out. Again, this sounds a small matter, but anyone will tell you that this is a disproportionately unpleasant act. Having wet, muddy kit strewn about the rooms not only meant they were messy, the aroma was awful – not so much Eau Sauvage, but Eau de Lions. In short, they stank.

The nadir, in terms of this particular hotel, was reached when, on one of the evenings, the manager decided to entertain us with a Hollywood-lookalike themed night, during which the waiters and waitresses dressed up as their favourite stars. Tragically, not one of them looked anything like the film star they were supposed to resemble. The Charlie Chaplin had a vague resemblance to the great man, but then it's quite easy to paint on a black moustache, grease your hair and wear a black suit. Unfortunately, Marilyn Monroe left a lot to be desired – or rather, she didn't. As for the rest of the stars, it was impossible to even hazard a guess at their identity. In the end, the only response was uncontrollable laughter, which the hotel probably took as a compliment and a sign that we were entering into the spirit of the evening. Really, it was gallows humour on our part: just when you thought things couldn't get any worse.

The captain of a touring team is exempt from the trials of having to room-share because he always has his own room. Will Carling, who was England captain for most of the tours I went on, was no exception. No one minded, because the captain had meetings in the room, and made and received phone calls and faxes – sometimes from highly placed people – that were not for common consumption.

I sometimes thought it was a shame for him that he didn't room with people, because you got to know people really well and in that sense he missed out a lot of camaraderie and bonding with fellow team-mates. As a result, and because of his role as captain, he never became a natural part of any particular player group. It's not as if people didn't want him around, but because he had to have meetings with management or sometimes even go to more official events, no one would ever wait for him before going off to do something. There was no 'Where's Will? We can't go without him, he's normally here.' As we never knew where he was, we would just head out regardless. In fact, I think he enjoyed the one Lions tour he went on, in 1993, precisely because he wasn't captain. He was just one of the boys, with no wider responsibilities, so he could enjoy the tour as a player, and that gave him a different perspective from the one he was used to. He roomed with the then 22-year-old Welsh centre Scott Gibbs on that tour and they got on very well, which one wouldn't necessarily have expected, especially as they were competing for the same position.

Carling's situation was not helped by being appointed captain when he himself was only 22, after only a few caps. This meant that no one had really had time to get to know him, so once he was named, there was even less chance of developing a friendship with other players. As captain, he was involved with team selection, and would approach senior members of the team such as me in order to canvass our view of team-mates in other positions.

Even if you weren't the victim of selection, you wouldn't know if he'd spoken up for your inclusion or exclusion. Consequently, players deliberately avoided saying certain things when he was around, because they never knew who that might get back to. In return, he had to maintain a certain distance between himself and his team, and was therefore rather isolated. It wasn't quite a case of silence descending on the room when he walked in, but, if Will suddenly appeared, there was a slight subconscious thought of 'What do you want? Why are you here?'

Mind you, Carling, who came from an army family, had been packed off to boarding school at the (to my mind) premature age of seven, so had no doubt learnt a few coping mechanisms that allowed him to manage isolation and loneliness. Sedbergh, his boarding school, is so isolated that, one night, I got completely lost when driving back from a dinner in Yorkshire. Suddenly, when I was in the middle of nowhere, and everything around me was pitch black, these big gates loomed up ahead. I stopped the car, angled the headlights towards them, and realised to my astonishment that I was in front of Sedbergh School. That's how far away it felt from civilisation. No chance of escaping from there, I thought. In fact, as a small boy, you'd be terrified of being abandoned there. In any event, it did explain why Carling, who went on briefly to the army after university, was made of stern stuff, and also learnt to manage group dynamics from a young age. With hindsight, I now realise that it can't have been easy for him to come in as captain when so young, and virtually unknown, wanting to be part of a team – rugby is a team sport, after all – yet knowing that he would be excluded from that experience to some extent. Not only that, but somehow he had to gain the trust and respect of senior team members who were going to be led by him, even though he had barely established himself as a player.

Carling wasn't the only one to have his own room, although he was the only player to do so. RFU Committee-members who accompanied us, as well as management and coaching staff, benefited from this perk as well. Mostly, I could see the rationale for this, but there was a memorable occasion where a bit of quick thinking and fast footwork on my part provided me with almost an entire tour's worth of privacy. This was on a tour to Australia and Fiji in 1991. Earlier that year, and four years before the game finally went professional, the IRB had relaxed its rules and allowed players to get paid for communication, not playing. 'Communication for rewards', it was called. Other Unions around the world allowed their players to do deals for non-rugby activities, including sponsorship, speaking engagements and the like. It seemed a good compromise in a still-amateur sport. But the RFU, led by its conservative, amateur Secretary, Dudley Wood, did all they could to prevent England players from benefiting from this rule change. He would even go behind our backs to tell potential sponsors that, whatever we might have told them, they were not allowed to do business with us. Really, he was briefing against the rules and I thought he should have been sacked. Instead, he stayed in his job and enjoyed its benefits for a good while yet.

Not long before the tour was due to depart, Wood came to a team meeting at the Petersham Hotel. It was a bad-tempered meeting, and several players, me included, told him exactly what we thought of him and the RFU. As a result, he refused to come on the tour, which suited us fine. On arrival at the first hotel everyone had, as usual, rushed into reception to try to get their key and leg it up to their room so that they weren't late for the meeting and didn't get fined. For some reason, I got caught at the back of the queue of people trying to check in, which was very unlike me. I was getting increasingly irritated at my stupidity this time round, and was thinking, 'Great, I'm going to have to wait now, I'm going to be late and I'll get fined.' When it was finally my turn, I suddenly saw the name 'D. Wood' on the list of expected guests. Without a second's hesitation, I claimed the key – the hotel clerks had no idea who either of us was – and headed up to his room.

I opened the door: it was a suite. While we the players all had bog-standard twin-bedded rooms, he had a suite. He also had a full bar, whereas if we ever had a minibar in the room, it would be empty – a full bar; brilliant. I remember very clearly going in, jumping on the king-sized bed and then gleefully jumping up and down on it for a good while. I was elated. That's how childish it was, but also how absurd; that this completely undeserving Committee-man should have the best room in the entire touring party. I managed to keep up the subterfuge for about five different stops on the tour. Each time, I knew that a certain D. Wood would be on the room list and each time I'd get in there claiming to be him. No one else thought to do the same and each time my allocated room-mate asked where I was, I would simply say that I'd been moved. Not only did they believe me, they didn't mind because now they had their own room to themselves as well, so they weren't exactly going to pipe up and demand to know who I was now rooming with. Everyone was happy. I very nearly made it to the end of the tour without anyone finding out but I did get rumbled right at the end. Once I'd been found out, I told every-one, expecting to be fined in the Tour Court, but, as it turned out, they all laughed, taking the view that at least one of us had bene-fited and the rooms hadn't gone to waste.

One of the biggest pains about touring – which today's players no longer have to worry about – is the question of laundry. The match kit was looked after, and you'd get a new set of kit for every game. But the training kit and all your other clothes were your responsibility. There was no one to do that for you, as there is nowadays. On my first tour, the England Students tour of Japan and Hong Kong there was no formal Tour Agreement, as there was with the senior team, and any laundry either had to be done by hand, or in the hotel laundry room, if there was one, or else you had to pay.

On senior tours, in the hotels that did have laundry services, paying £5.50 or whatever for a pair of socks was obviously not an option for amateur players, and, anyway, we had to remember to hand the stuff in in time in order to get it back the next day, which would rarely be possible. Where there were paying laundry rooms, we could wash and dry our own clothes, at our expense. However, when there are 34 of you trying to use the laundry, not to mention the other guests, you don't want to hang around there for hours, waiting for your turn. If you were lucky enough to have your room next to it, you'd run in, shove all your stuff in, and tell everyone else to take a running jump. That assumed you'd accumulated enough clothes that needed washing, rather than a few bits and pieces that would hardly make it worth your while. So it was all a juggling act, not knowing what the facilities would be at the next hotel, working out if it was better to wash and dry a few things in your room before you moved on to the next stop on the tour, or coughing up for the hotel's rip-off laundry service if there was one.

There's no doubt though that a freshly cleaned, beautifully ironed shirt delivered back by the hotel's laundry service never failed to please. Especially when they were boxed and folded, with those little cardboard collars – we all loved that. So much so that, one day, this gave John Olver a good idea for a bit of fun. There was a lovely young lad, a prop from Orrell called Martin Hynes. He was a trusting and innocent lad, and new to the squad; an ideal candidate, in other words. We were in the hotel before one of our away Five Nations games, and Martin was unaware that, during the Friday night team meetings, it had become a tradition to play a prank of some sort on someone from the team. Earlier that day,

Martin had seen his room-mate, who happened to be John Olver, with a couple of lovely white shirts, all neatly folded and packed up. They were so pristine, they looked new, whereas in fact they had just been laundered by the hotel. But poor Martin didn't realise this. 'Cor, are they new?' he enquired admiringly.

Sensing an immediate opportunity, Olver replied, 'Yeah, you can order them, they're new. Just go and order some shirts from the hotel, ask them to get you one.'

Martin was duly goggle-eyed with amazement, perhaps wondering, 'If this is the life of a top rugby player, count me in.'

Not wanting to let this opportunity go, John told the manager, Geoff Cooke, about his ruse. Later that day, the whole squad gathered around a big table for a team meeting. Serious matters were discussed. Then Geoff suddenly announced, 'Right, look, I've told you boys before, I'm not happy about certain things that have been going on, like items of petty theft, hotel bath towels and robes, which people steal. You've been given unofficial warnings and I've told you before: this has to stop. This is now an official warning, because it's gone further.'

He paused for effect.

'People have *actually* been trying to order new clothing and charge it to the RFU!' he carried on, deadpan. 'Now I want the people responsible to own up.'

Silence. Those who knew what was going on were trying not to laugh.

Eventually, Geoff went on. 'So, is no one going to say anything?'

Still silence. Everyone was keeping a beautifully straight face.

'Well, if no one owns up, then you'll all be penalised,' went on Geoff, sounding threatening.

At this point, the gentleman that is Simon Halliday, who was in the dark, lost it. 'It's bloody you, Olver, it's you, isn't it?!'

'No, it's not! It's not me,' protested Olver convincingly.

Finally, poor Martin could stand it no longer. 'It's me ...' he mumbled, gingerly raising his hand, before pointing in Olver's direction and adding, accusingly and emphatically, 'but Olver said it would be all right!' At which point everyone just exploded; hook, line and proverbial sinker. Fantastic.

Although I knew all about this tradition, and was often one of those in the know, I completely failed to see coming the Friday prank that was played on me. This was in Ireland in 1993. Once again, we were in the team room on the Friday, discussing the next day's game. 'Okay, so what are the things we have to do to win this game tomorrow? Who are the important players?' asked Cooke, seemingly in all innocence. Now Keith Wood, the Irish hooker, had only got one or two caps at this stage, but he was seen as the new boy wonder: the Irish front row had played against the USA and had done really well, and Wood was now being talked about as the greatest potential hooker, and other such hyperbole. Not unnaturally, this hadn't gone down well with the England front row and me in particular. In fact, just because of this, we shoved them all over the park the next day.

So the talk around the table began, with each player in turn giving his assessment. 'Well,' started the first player, 'obviously Keith Wood is a big talisman for them. New hooker, very mobile.' The next one went on in the same vein: '. . . so and so – and *obviously* Keith Wood, he's got to be ...' and it kept going like this, the fourth person, the fifth, all banging on about Keith Wood. And just as the fifth person said, 'Well, Keith Wood ...' I burst out, furiously, 'Wait a minute!' and then the whole room collapsed laughing. 'You bastards!!' was all I could say.

What Martin Hynes hadn't realised when he'd fallen for John Olver's prank was that, when it came to tours, what was paid for and/or supplied was set out in the Tour Agreement, a document that listed in fine detail everything that we could expect to receive or find while away. This was especially important because we were on daily expenses of around £23, and that would usually include paying for all phone calls (always extortionate in hotels), laundry, general entertainment and incidentals such as food and drink consumed anywhere outside the hotel. In any given squad, there were several who were self-employed, players such as Mike Teague, who was a builder, and Paul Rendall, who was an engineer. They invariably lost money on a tour because their lost earnings were not remotely compensated for by the minimal *per diem* we received. The point of the Tour Agreement – which read like a contract – was that we would at least know what we could expect.

One year, in Australia, the liaison officer that the Australian RFU had supplied – each host Union supplies one or more liaison officers to ease the life of the touring players, organise tickets to shows, or whatever – was a jobsworth sort. In any agreement, there are always words along the lines that 'The host Union shall provide a team room [in each hotel] with a fridge, which shall contain quantities of the following: beer, soft drinks, milk, juice, water.' On this occasion, we'd asked for something else to be added – I can't remember what – and this guy had flatly refused, saying it was not specified in the Tour Agreement and would cost money. 'Okay,' I said, 'Give me the Tour Agreement.' I read the small print and noted what it was they did have to pay for, and one stipulation was that they had to pay for the laundry. So, Dean Richards and I made sure that, from that day onwards, every player laundered every single piece of clothing and kit, whether dirty or not. Within 24 hours, what had been a modest laundry bill became a 'Fucking hell! What's all this?' cry of alarm from the liaison officer. 'Yes,' I said, when challenged. 'Now then, either stop fucking around and give us what we've asked for, or we're going to carry on laundering every single piece of clothing at every stop from now until the end of the tour. That is, to the letter, what it says in the Tour Agreement, so it's up to you, mate.' I remember adding, for good measure, 'It actually says "must supply", therefore technically we could drink anything else we wanted, and you should also supply it.' 'Well that's just silly,' the guy said. Anyway, he duly caved in and we got what we'd wanted in the first place. Lawyers are sometimes useful.

Other nations' Tour Agreements were broadly similar, though it may come as no surprise to discover that the All Blacks, who were much more advanced than us in everything, both on and off the field, went through theirs with a fine-tooth comb at the start of each tour. Indeed, the senior players would always demand to see it, so that they could see what scope there was for exploiting it, whereas I only became familiar with the agreements whenever there was any dispute. To be fair, many of their team also lost money touring, but the Kiwis were much more creative at finding ways both of getting things for free – such as free tickets to shows – and of raising money for the players' kitty. They would print their own tour T-shirt (a novelty back then) which they would then sell during the tour, they would sell their extra tickets from their ticket allocation (in truth, everyone did). As there was a bigger demand when they came over to England than when we went to New Zealand – no surprise there – they could command bigger prices than us.

For many years, Tour Agreements had the quaint stipulation that afternoon tea would be provided for the tour party. This was clearly a throwback to the days when the game was a more genteel affair, because it was hardly an essential. It being thus, the Kiwis decided to negotiate. They estimated how much afternoon tea for 30-plus ravenous men would cost in a London hotel – quite a lot over a tour and then they'd say to the liaison officer, 'We won't have any afternoon teas, but give us a cash sum for the players in return.' Alternatively, they'd ask for more tickets for games (to then sell on). If they met with any resistance, all 30 would appear for afternoon tea and consume as much as they could get away with. After all, they were entitled to 'afternoon tea' and it didn't specify how much. This was followed, immediately in all cases, by another of those, 'Right, are you going to stop fucking around now?' conversations. This tactic worked every time.

The All Blacks were similarly savvy when it came to laundry. If they had to pay for their own, they'd announce, 'We'll do it this way: we could put all the kit in, and if we've got a team wash, we could pay some guy down the local launderette to do a service wash; that would cost x in a hotel, so we'll come to a deal with that.' Again, the liaison officer would end up caving in and putting the difference in cost in the team coffers.

That particular laundry trick was pulled in reverse on one of their tours, by one player, one of their second rowers, who did a deal with a parallel supporters' tour that was following the team round the country. 'I can do your laundry for half the price that you're paying in your hotel,' he told them (presumably, the laundry was free for the players on that particular tour). They agreed, so he would collect their laundry, bring it back to the team hotel, put it through the hotel laundry, give it back, then pocket the money!

The Kiwis also took advantage of the fact that, on any given day, London, unlike Sydney and Auckland, offered scores of shows, plays, concerts, sporting events and other great things to see. Sometimes, a direct plea to the event for free tickets for the All Blacks would reap instant rewards. If not, they exchanged them for not having tea, or cutting back on the laundry, or anything else that they could barter with under the terms of the Tour Agreement. Like I said, they were ahead of the game when it came to getting the best deal – and I mean that as a compliment. They knew the value of their brand, so they were up front about their demands.

I got to know some of the liaison officers provided by the RFU to look after the touring teams in the 1980s and '90s, and all of them said that, although the All Blacks and the Australians were lovely guys, they were kept extremely busy, especially by the former. The Australians had a similarly eagle eye when it came to exploiting their Tour Agreement for their financial benefit. If there was any opportunity for negotiating a payment into the players' fund and in return forgoing one of the services provided, they would grab it. I'm told one player, Tim Horan, a centre who played in their 1991 World Cup-winning team, was a bit of a back-room lawyer, because he would pore over the Tour Agreement in detail. He always made a point of sitting down to afternoon tea, come what may, simply because it was always provided. 'You should come, it's great!' he'd entreat his team-mates, as he sat alone, stubbornly making the most of his rights.

Both the All Blacks and the Wallabies loved touring in the UK but I was surprised when they said that it was hard work. They were a rich target for every team they played against, but they also had many opportunities for socialising, and this meant that those combined yet contrary demands took their toll. When it came to touring in France (which England never toured to, because we always played them during the Five Nations), they had the same view as millions of others who go there: great country, shame it's full of French. Playing there was attritional. In those days, French club rugby was so uber-violent it was ridiculous. Both New Zealand and Australia are not faint-hearted teams, but the French club teams they played against appeared to have been picked basically just to kick them, which ended up rather colouring their memories of the tours.

In the late 1980s and early '90s, the England squad was packed off over New Year for intensive four-day training camps in warmer climes, in an effort to spend some quality time getting fitter. As with touring, being away all together provided a good opportunity for getting to know each other. In our defence, as we all still had day jobs, it was impossible to do this at any other time of the year. We would have odd weekends together, but that amounted to Sundays, because we would all be playing for our clubs on Saturdays, would come down to the Petersham Hotel in the evening, train together on the Sunday, before heading off home, ready to go back to work on the Monday morning. Before internationals, we would not be meeting a week before a game, as they do now; we would meet on the Wednesday before a Saturday game. There was no time for in-depth fitness and strength work; instead, the focus would be on rugby drills.

Just as I came into the England team, the attitude to training and physical preparation had begun to change. Certainly the days of having a pint before a game were already long gone, but there lingered an amateurish approach to physical fitness which changed with the appointment of a leading athletics coach. Tom McNab was engaged by Geoff Cooke to supervise our training programme. He had been Daley Thompson's coach, so had undeniable credibility. He also believed in hard work. That was fine by me, because that was one of the ways by which I fought my way into the team.

What Tom found when he first began to look after us must have shocked him. Our lack of strength and fitness was shown up most glaringly on the very first training day in Loughborough, when shot-putters Mike Winch and Judy Oakes took us for a weights session. What we discovered was that Judy Oakes was stronger than any of us. Even allowing for the fact that Judy was an Olympic athlete, all the big forwards were lifting weights far inferior to what she was managing. Not great, and embarrassing for us all, especially when she tore a strip off some of the players who were messing about at the back and not paying attention to her demonstration of how to do cleans, jerks and squat lifts correctly. Similarly, athletics drills introduced by Tom highlighted a lack of fitness among many of the squad. Some of the old guard, like prop Gareth Chilcott, laughed off their efforts at sprinting and hurdling, as if none of it was to be taken seriously. To be fair, his physique didn't exactly lend itself to either discipline, and watching him was very funny.

At the New Year training camps, the new training regime continued. But although we were worked hard during the day, in the evenings we made up for it, which meant that after the evening meal, we would hit the bar. And I mean, really hit the bar. We shouldn't have done, but I think the management thought, 'Well, they've worked hard during the day, so they're allowed some down-time.' Most of us thought, 'Hell, I'm away from home on New Year's Eve, I've used up precious holiday time, I'm not getting paid for this, so bollocks!' The fact was, for our time, we were fit, even though the levels obviously didn't compare to today's super-fit players. Looking back, given how much we drank, it's remarkable that everyone got up every day and trained really hard. I don't remember ever having a hangover; well, not what I would call a hangover where you can't face doing anything and you feel – or are – sick.

I went to two different training camps: twice to Portugal, and twice to Club La Santa, in Lanzarote. The latter in particular was a well-known training camp for elite athletes from all over the world who would come for some warm-weather winter training; it had outstanding facilities, even though it was also a holiday resort for ordinary members of the public who would end up mingling with the athletes.

At both camps, the athletes would come into the bar in the evening and watch us downing our pints – although the amount we drank had decreased by the time we were going to Lanzarote –

while they sipped their mineral waters. They would look askance at what we were doing, and occasionally would wonder out loud at how we could get up the next day and spend hours smashing into each other on the training pitch. I remember one of the athletes saying to us, 'I just don't know how you can do it. I couldn't do *one* of those days. Actually, leaving aside the drinking, doing those two sessions a day at the times you're doing them is crazy.' 'Well, that's just the way it is,' I replied with a shrug. It's fair to say the athletes were astounded, partly because they were not doing contact sports, and partly because our training regime was the polar opposite of theirs.

Their schedules went something like this: they would start training at around 7.30 a.m. when it was cool – indeed we would watch them from our rooms or while we were enjoying breakfast. What staggered us was that they would spend nearly an hour just warming up. We were mystified. 'Have they done anything yet?' we'd ask. They would then do 30 minutes of flat-out quality training, then a long warm-down, before going in for a rest, lunch, and more rest. And, by rest, they wouldn't be heading off to the bar or a swim in the pool. It meant lying on their bed resting or, for some of them, sleeping. At 6 p.m. they would go back out, when dusk was falling and the heat of the day had abated. They would then have a similar training session to the morning one, involving a lot of warming up and stretching, a short burst of intensive, quality athletic work, followed by a long warm-down.

Meanwhile, our training regime went like this: we would get up at about 8 a.m., have breakfast, while watching the athletes training, have a team meeting, and head out into the sunshine at about 10 a.m, by which time the athletes had ended their first session for the day and were safely back indoors. We would then train hard until lunchtime, doing specific rugby drills, such as line-outs, scrums, patterns of play, tackles and mauls – basically we'd do a lot of violent contact. We would break for lunch around 12 to 12.30 and go back out at 2.00 p.m., just when the temperature was at its peak, and do it all over again.

There was quite a lot of levity during those sessions, particularly in Portugal, before things got more serious. Don Rutherford, our technical director, started filming us for coaching purposes but in the end he lost his temper because everyone kept messing around during the various exercises he'd set up. There was a 'driving' session, where two players were bound together, they turned their backs, and the guy with the ball came from behind and hit them, whereupon they would bend slightly, to show how you took the ball into contact. I was to be one of the two bound players, and Rutherford got his camera all set up to show us how to do this. 'Everyone ready? Right, action!' he shouted. Nigel Redman, the 6ft 4in, 240lb lock, was carrying the ball. Just as he reached us, we parted, so when he went to drive he just fell flat on his face. Mass eruption of giggling all round, while Don Rutherford spluttered 'Will you people stop fucking around!'

During a scrummaging session that was also being filmed, we went down on the scrummage machine, rammed into it, except that someone slipped, and the whole of the front row, me included, landed right on our faces. All you could hear on Rutherford's video was 'Fuck, fuck, fuck!' Even he had to laugh when the out-takes compilation was shown at the end of the camp.

As a result of McNab's appointment, the rugby drills were interspersed with proper athletics drills, such as timed 300-metre runs on proper tracks, longer interval training and plyometrics, exercises designed to increase muscle power and explosiveness. Despite protestations to the contrary, it was clear the timed runs soon got competitive, because when a few people started bringing their spikes, others went scurrying off to try and get some.

Particular sessions such as interval training were very tough, and some players found a way to get out of them. Steve Bainbridge, a 6ft 7in lock, had been a fine decathlete in his younger days. I remember him sitting out one of the sessions with John Hall, a flanker who weighed in at around 17 stone, so someone who wasn't a natural track athlete. 'Oh, we're injured,' they claimed. They were found soon after messing around trying to do the high jump, leaping around on the landing mat like a couple of schoolboys.

Fartlek runs – a form of interval training that involves varying your pace between fast and slow segments during a run – were unpopular with almost everyone. One run we went on in Portugal involved a long circuit through the woods. It was a lovely run, with cedar trees lining the route. As I was very fit, I bounded off, much to the annoyance of some of my team-mates, who thought I was letting the side down by looking so keen. 'Stop! Slow down, slow down! You're making us look bad!' they shouted as I sprinted off. 'Fuck you, that's not my fault!' I responded sympathetically as I shot off. 'Bloody hell,' I could hear them moaning as I strode into the distance. At the end of the first four-day camp, Tom McNab gave out a little trophy to the 'athlete of the camp'. I won it, to inevitable jeering – teacher's pet, and all that. I didn't care.

After the afternoon session, we would then have our evening meal, just as the athletes were emerging for their second session, and then head off to the bar. No wonder the athletes looked on, bemused.

By the time we went to Club La Santa, in Lanzarote, we had a rather less riotous approach to the camps but the training regime remained the same. That's when we started speaking to some of the athletes, who were saying, 'Why are you doing it this way, it's absolutely mad!' and wondering whether maybe they were right. Not that we had a choice, because that was the way the management had decided it would be done. We, in turn, would ask the athletes, 'What are you doing for fifty minutes?' 'Well, that's how long it takes to warm up properly,' and they would explain the importance of stretching, warming up and warming down. No one had ever explained this to us properly, but the fact was, these athletes, such as Steve Backley, the great British javelin thrower, and Merlene Ottey, the Jamaican sprinter and multiple Olympic medallist, both of whom were at the camps in Lanzarote when we were there, spent at least half an hour just stretching, another 15 minutes jogging, warming up their muscles, and almost as long warming down after their short, intense quality training. I have to say, they were very, very flexible. I didn't realise until years afterwards just how important flexibility was – not just in relation to preventing injury but also to performance.

It is actually fairly logical if you stop to think about it – the greater your range of movement, the less you have a chance of injuring yourself, and the more power you have from your muscles because they are utilised to their maximum. If anyone knew this in the England set-up they didn't stress it sufficiently; the only flexibility test we had was a basic reach test. Maybe they figured that, as we were not full-time athletes, they only had limited time to work on our fitness, and as there were enough rugby things to get right, they had to focus on our playing skills. Once back home, given that I and most of my team-mates could only train in the gym in our lunch hour – before wolfing down a sandwich and getting back to our desks soon after – if we'd had to spend as long as the athlete did warming up and warming down, we'd never have held down our jobs.

The Lanzarote camps became very competitive and we were worked very hard. Even when we were not doing standard rugby or athletics drills the squad, about 35 of us, would be divided up into small sub-teams, so that we could play ball-related games against each other, with an element of competition, which made it more fun. A pentathlon-style competition was organised, involving some track and ball-skills events, such as football penalty-taking. One event took place in the Olympic-sized 50-metre pool. My team was lying second, and we were determined to claim first place. In the team currently holding that place was fellow front row team-mate, Victor Ubogu. Now Victor couldn't really swim properly, and certainly not 50 metres, so he sort of dived in and just about got himself to the side, whereupon another person jumped in and swam as his substitute. As soon as we saw this, we went crazy. 'That's unfair, he didn't fucking finish, get him back in the pool!' 'No, he can't swim, that's different.' 'Fuck off, get him back in the pool,' we protested loudly. Nothing doing. When his team came first and starting leaping around in celebration, our team just stood there, petulantly repeating, 'It's not fair! It's not fair!'

All was forgotten that evening because it was New Year's Eve and we were back in the bar. We started playing games, all of which required prior imbibing of alcohol, because any sober bystander would think we were all completely mad. At one point, Steve Backley, who was indeed sober, came up to us. 'Can I join in?' he asked, a bit like a new boy asks to join in a game in the school playground. 'If you want to,' we answered, slightly surprised. He had unfortunately picked the very moment when we were about to start 'the punching game'.

This utterly Neanderthal game simply involved the participants standing around in a circle. Each player in turn then faces to his right and punches the next player on the jaw; that person then does the same thing to the person on *their* right, and so on; quite complicated for some of the forwards. Although this always starts out in a civilised manner, things soon degenerate, and the game never gets very far before all hell breaks out. Steve had the temerity to stand between John Hall, all 17 stone of him, and Dean Richards, his heavyweight equal. I don't know why he thought that would be a good idea. The game started. Bang. Next. Bang. Next. And so on. When it was his turn, John Hall duly hit Steve – lightly, to be fair – on the jaw. It was now Steve's turn to do the same to Dean. When he turned to face the then Leicester Police Constable he had second thoughts, as Dean snarled at him. 'Do I have to?' he asked, to which John replied, 'If you don't, I'll have to hit you again,' and as Steve hesitated, John duly did. Getting the message, Steve turned once more to Dean, who by now had risen up to his full height, which freaked Steve out – not that Steve is a lightweight himself. 'Can I leave?' 'No, you can't.' Bang. In the end, we showed uncharacteristic mercy and allowed him to retire with a modicum of dignity; we're not animals, after all.

Room-sharing at the camps was organised in the same way as it was on tours. You had no choice as to who you shared with. The accommodation was often better than on tours, especially in Club La Santa. We stayed in small semi-detached bungalow-type suites which were like self-catering apartments, with a bedroom and bathroom, a small kitchen (that we didn't use because all meals were provided) and a small living room that looked out onto a small terrace. A small wall separated the terrace of one room from the one next door. This was all very pleasant, especially because the weather was excellent.

The New Year was seen in by an epic piece of cabaret from two members of the front row. John Olver was sharing a room with West Midlands policeman and Moseley prop Mark Linnett, and they formed a lethal combination when it came to 'thinking outside the box'. Unannounced, Olver and Linnett suddenly appeared in the bar wearing little mini yellow Lycra outfits, like sleeveless leotards, and proceeded to perform a dance routine that can't be adequately described. Obviously, given their build, especially Linnett's, this was not a good sight, because they really were bulging out of everywhere. This went way beyond a mere budgie-smuggler. It turned out that in the next door apartment to theirs was Merlene Ottey, and they had spotted her skimpy running outfits drying out on the terrace earlier that evening. So they had hopped over the little wall separating the two terraces, whipped on the mankinis, now stretched to their full Borat-esque potential, and had run over to show us the result. I don't suppose they washed the clothes before returning them, but in any event I suspect Merlene may have been a bit puzzled the next morning when she poured her lithe body back into the first of the outfits. 'Funny, it seems to have gone all saggy overnight,' she must have thought. 'So much for the "delicates" cycle on the machine.'

8

'Don't You Serve Chips with This?'

Today's rugby players follow an eating regime that is planned down to its last mouthful. Forty years ago, when England or the Lions toured, the only planned mouthful was the traditional sucking on half an orange at half time, and eating steak for breakfast, lunch and dinner was perfectly normal, if not encouraged. By the time I first played for England, diets had at last begun to improve.

We still used to eat in the general dining room of the hotels we were staying in, surrounded by hotel guests. The team room was simply the one in which we held team meetings. In contrast, nowadays, there is a very big team room which doubles up as the team dining room. When meals are taken in the hotel dining room, it is probably done more for PR purposes than any notion of convenience. Even then, the team will eat in a cordoned-off part of the restaurant rather than among the general public.

Some of the hotels we stayed in provided breakfasts that had to be ordered from a limited menu. We had no control over how long it would take to get served, and it was not uncommon to end up either having to bolt our food down to make the morning team meeting, giving up on breakfast altogether, or endeavouring to get up earlier the next morning in order to have a fighting chance of being served on time.

In other hotels, breakfast consisted of a large buffet, and we'd be told we could have whatever we wanted. So what would usually happen was this: on the first morning of any trip, we'd start off with good intentions of having what we thought was a healthy, balanced breakfast, inasmuch as we knew what that was. We would aim for sensible-sized portions, and would minimise the saturated fat content, adding some fruit and fibre where possible. We'd all then gradually fall off the healthy-food perch, some at greater speeds than others, and by the end, we'd all have come to the same conclusion: 'Oh, fuck it. I'm having the full breakfast. I don't care if I'm training in an hour's time.' This was especially the case on the first few training camps we went to, where we'd train really hard during the day, drink really hard at night and then fall into bed in the early hours. Some would try to justify themselves, 'Well, I need a lot of energy, I'm training really hard.' Others wouldn't bother and just shovelled down the food.

People had their own rituals and habits for breakfast. John Orwin, who captained England briefly on our tour to Australia in 1988, used to say that all he wanted for breakfast was a fillet steak, even on the morning of a game. We now know that it takes a long time to break down the protein, there are no slow-release carbs, so it's about the worst thing he could have been eating; but, that's what he liked, so that's what he got. I, on the other hand, inadvertently happened upon a reasonably good pre-match meal – a massive bowl of mashed potatoes and some onion gravy, if possible. Delicious and not too bad because of the carbs, though they weren't slow release. I'd hit upon this 'meal' as an impoverished student because it was very cheap and filling. In any event, I was comfortable with that, and it seemed to work, so whenever I could, that's what I would ask for. The Petersham Hotel knew that, and would always serve it up for me but other hotels, in various far-flung places of the world, also did their best to fulfil my strange request.

Even by the time I stopped playing international rugby in 1995, no specific diet was ever compulsory, certainly not at breakfast. In fact, no one was obliged to have that meal, even on match days, which seems absurd now. All that was required was to make it down for the two set meetings after breakfast: the split meeting for forwards or backs, and the team meeting after that. Some players therefore skipped breakfast altogether, preferring to stay in their room, walk outside, or watch TV. They would then have a brunch-type late breakfast after the meetings, while others had what amounted to a second breakfast. We would then all pile on to the coach and go off to the stadium.

For lunch, if it wasn't a match day, we would return to the hotel after training. Time was often tight, because we'd be back out training in the afternoon, with barely enough time to fully digest the meal. Hotels would usually supply a choice of starters and main courses for lunch – typically, there would be one or two meat dishes and a fish and/or vegetarian one – rather than provide a buffet. However, it could be a slow process taking the orders for and cooking well over 30 meals. When you're on holiday, you're not usually on a schedule, so you don't mind waiting 20 minutes for your food. When you're on tour, eating is not a sociable experience, it is a necessity. You just want your food, so that you've got a bit of time to go off and do your own thing before training resumes or afternoon commitments have to be seen to. Sometimes, when delays occurred, we'd be sitting around ravenously waiting for the food to arrive, getting really frustrated at a delay most people wouldn't even register if they were eating socially.

On a few occasions hotels came up with a bright idea. 'Right,' their manager or head of catering would announce either at breakfast or on the team coach that morning, 'to save time, one of us will take your orders early. Here are the menus, so you can tell us what you would like. We'll note it down; then, when you get back for lunch, we'll have the food ready and waiting. Okay?' As with the luggage fiascos at the airport, at first I'd say, 'Don't do it, it'll go wrong,' but I soon realised there was no point in saying this because no one ever believed me. Orders would be duly taken on the bus or before boarding it and when we rushed into lunch the food would start to arrive. However, as soon as the first big steaks came out, loads of hands would go up. 'Yup, that's mine,' 'Yup, that's mine too,' and so on. Thirty steaks. 'Who wanted fish?' 'Nope, not me.' 'Not me either.' 'Well, it says here we've got thirteen fish.' 'Well, it wasn't me,' 'Have you got the names?' someone would ask. 'Er, no.' 'Well, you must have got it wrong, then.'

Food envy, pure and simple. People would see a nice big juicy steak going past and 'forget' they'd ever ordered anything else. Even if they were asked to give their name when they ordered, it still didn't work. 'I never said that,' they'd claim. To be honest, even if they'd been made to provide a signature when ordering, players would probably still have maintained it was forged.

Dinners were usually a much more relaxed affair. Players didn't mind ordering and waiting for their food because they had no other pressing matters to attend to, and dinner often provided a real chance to talk properly to team-mates, and for the banter to fly. Sometimes, to alleviate the tedium of eating hotel food every night, players would duck out of the hotel dinner and would go off to local restaurants, even though they had to pay for those meals themselves.

In the late 1980s, the 'healthy eating' idea started to be introduced. But one of the problems was that it seemed to equate with 'boring eating'. The meals were incredibly bland and unappetising, as if the chefs had been told by the management to drain all the enjoyment out of eating when devising their restrictive menus. So players would eat the food – as a chore – then they'd dash out to McDonald's or its nearest equivalent as soon as they could, either because they were still hungry or because they'd simply not eaten food that tasted of anything.

In addition, no one had really explained to us why certain foods were better than others, nor what the cause and effect was of different diets. Notions such as slow release of energy, insulin spiking and so on were several years away. Now, it's all been turned into a sports science, which I agree with, but when we were touring, the main aim of the management was to try and stop people eating rubbish and to 'eat healthily' (whatever that means), with an emphasis on eating enough carbs to fuel training. We were given examples of what was high in this and that, and what was low, but the information went no further than that. The rest was up to us. To be honest, it was no more sophisticated than what you get in the average women's magazine.

Some of the old guard, who had been established team members when I joined in 1987, made little or no attempt to adapt to a new dietary regime. And even some of those who joined at around the same time as me found it hard to give up junk food. First and foremost among these was Rory Underwood, who happened to have the most astonishingly bad diet you could ever imagine for such an outstanding athlete. Okay, so he didn't drink, because he didn't like the taste of alcohol, but I'm not sure that cancelled out all the rest of the junk that he put into his body. It's fair to say his body was most certainly not his temple. Chips, Coke, pizzas, burgers, ice cream, sweets, he was like a kid, and was the first to admit it.

Tom McNab, the athletics coach brought in to inculcate some better training and lifestyle habits into us, told me a story that surprises him even to this day. He tested us all, using tests that were crude by today's standards, but that nonetheless measured strength, speed and so on. One such test measured a player's explosive power and all it involved was a player holding a 16lb shot in both hands – exactly like the ones used in the shot put – swinging it down between his legs, then hurling it over his head and behind him as far as he could. When Rory's distance was given to Tom his reaction was: 'Are you sure?' Indeed, he had to go and check the distance that Rory had thrown because it was huge. According to McNab, he was quite simply the most explosive athlete he'd ever seen when performing that test, with scores that were higher even than Daley Thompson's. Rory didn't do weights, he wasn't a big, strong guy and his diet was absolutely rubbish. Yet he had explosive strength, raw power and speed that were clearly genetic, as well as lower than average body fat; bastard. The results of that test really annoyed the forwards because, despite being strong men, they just didn't have what Rory had. On the one hand, you could say, 'That just shows diet isn't crucial'; on the other, you could say, 'How much better would he have been if his diet had been better?' Who knows, but Rory made little attempt to find out.

My own daytime diet left a lot to be desired as well: regular cups of coffee at the office, sometimes leaving me hyper; a lunchtime orange juice gulped down with my sandwich at my desk after a gym session; a rubbish snack wolfed down on the way to evening training, followed by a late-night dinner. Most of my team-mates' diets were similar. If you were a policeman, a builder, a doctor or whatever in the 1980s and '90s, you were unlikely to be able to access carefully balanced meals during the day.

On tour, we had to suffer the vagaries of whatever food the hotel chefs rustled up for us. That was usually fairly standard, plain fare, but we were nonetheless given no particular favours relative to other guests staying at the hotel. Nowadays, no Lions team would play in some of the out-of-the-way places we did, playing instead three or four of the provinces and three Tests, whereas our tours were longer, and we would zig-zag around the country playing a wider range of teams.

To avoid dodgy meals, some of today's teams now travel with their own chef. It's not about cooking for prima donnas, the chef simply ensures that players' meals are of a consistent quantity and quality. He knows what players want and need, and food is available when it's required. It also provides some protection from possible food-poisoning, because the chef will oversee food preparation. There was an incident, in the South Africa World Cup in 1995, where four of the All Blacks got bad gastroenteritis just before their final against the host nation. No one pointed the finger directly, but there were dark mutterings in public and louder ones in private about South African nefariousness. It was probably just bad luck but it is also right to say that a few of their players were definitely not firing on all cylinders on the day. It may not have affected the outcome, but if a touring party has its own chef, these sorts of situations are less likely to occur.

Nowadays, ideal eating times are calculated, and all meals are timed around training or games. Similarly, what is eaten and drunk is closely controlled, with the right amount of protein, slow-burning carbs or whatever, and the correct amount of fluids. Nothing is left to chance. Why should it, when these players are paid to be professional? Indeed, even when they are not touring, international players will usually have one if not two meals a day at their club, all fitted in around their training. They will be eating according to their own personalised diet plan, but unlike our bland meals, these will taste good as well, so there is no need for a quick dash to the nearest takeaway.

Furthermore, included in the vast amount of tour luggage are massive boxes full of nutritional supplements and each player will have his own particular cocktail, all checked by the team doctor in order to avoid falling foul of anti-doping regulations. Where we once just used to have water to drink in the dressing room, players are now provided with specially formulated drinks and supplements. The only time some of us ever took anything of that nature was on the '93 Lions tour, when we were offered Creatine powder, a supplement allowed in most sports. Its alleged benefits had to be explained to us by the tour doctor, and it's safe to say we were a sceptical audience. Had I known that its principal benefit was to build muscle mass, I would undoubtedly have asked the unhelpful, but apposite question: what difference would it make to take it for only a few weeks, especially as we weren't doing any programmed weights sessions? In any event, we did as we were told, we took it every day. It might conceivably have done us some good if we'd taken it for longer – and if we hadn't been going out on a number of big drinking sessions, thus nullifying any potential small gains.

When you tour, you get to find out who the players are who have already done a bit of travelling, as they don't go around like the typical Englander abroad. This is particularly obvious when it comes to eating out. Faced with some traditional island food in Fiji there were a couple of half-hearted cries of, 'Is there a McDonald's?' 'No, we're in Fiji, for God's sake!' When I toured Italy with the England Under 23s one player complained that there wasn't any sauce with the pasta. 'Yes, but you didn't ask for sauce. You asked for pasta.'

An England tour to South Africa in 1994 provided us with fare that was more to the traditional rugby player's taste. After a game against Natal in Durban, instead of the usual sit-down function, we were treated to a meal with a difference: we were each given a plate with a huge uncooked steak and were informed that we could go and cook this on a number of braais reserved exclusively for us. This was a welcome departure from the normal post-match dinners: first, because these were very big steaks, and secondly, because all men like to barbecue – it must be to do with the primeval presence of fire. Well, that or the fact that, for some men, it's the closest they ever get to cooking. Whatever the reason, it has to be said that our efforts were mixed, at best. Some players managed to cook their meat perfectly, but others succeeded only in creating vast plumes of smoke and huge flames. Indeed, so alarming were some of our attempts that a South African felt compelled to come over and offer the benefit of his long years of experience. Armed with a spray bottle of water, he strode over, saying, 'For God's sake, no! You don't do it like that!' and proceeded, rightly, to damp down the flames so that the meat wasn't frazzled to a cinder on the outside while staying raw on the inside.

Red meat, particularly in France, Italy or Argentina, tends to be cooked rare, something that several players found inedible. I'd regularly hear comments of 'No, no, that's too rare … I don't want no blood … No blood at all,' before the dish got sent back to the kitchens to be cooked to within an inch of its life. In Argentina, land of meat, we went to a couple of places where there was no menu. Instead, giant silver platters bearing slabs of raw beef would come round and we would then select which cut we each wanted.

One evening, on that 1990 tour, we sampled the delights of their Parilla (barbecue) when we went to a massive restaurant specialising in meat dishes. In the centre featured an Asador, or open fire-pit, on which various pieces of meat were cooked. It was like a caveman's barbecue. The meat was theatrically brought out on long sword-like skewers, each one packed full of sausages, chicken, lamb or beef. It all smelt and looked delicious, and we were starving. What the others didn't realise, but I did, because I'd been warned, was that the restaurant would serve up first one meat, then another, and so on, until we had been given the whole range on offer. The first swordfuls of meat came round, bearing the huge sausages. 'Oh great, I'll have four,' everyone went, before diving in.

'I'll just have one,' I said, knowing what was to come.

'What? Aren't you hungry?'

'No, no, I'm fine,' I replied, not revealing my hand. Next, the chicken came round. Everyone had a couple of pieces each, and I had my single piece. Then the lamb came round, succulent, perfectly cooked. The others were getting full now, but were ploughing on. I was still going strong. Finally, beautiful Argentinian pieces of beef came out, each one approximately the size of half a cow. By this time, everyone was completely stuffed full and could barely face the idea of eating another morsel, except me; I remained relatively fine. However, being rugby players, and many of them forwards to boot, my team-mates weren't about to lose face; plus, the food was free. So, they basically proceeded to force these magnificent steaks down, like Mr Creosote in Monty Python's *Meaning of Life*, while I sat there munching away appreciatively. I'll confess, I did enjoy watching them trying not to gag as they swallowed the food.

Dinners out were not very common, unless they were paid for by the host Union. This was because we were amateur, so not exactly flush with money. Official dinners, held after major games and at the end of each tour or tournament, were an opportunity to let our hair down. Maurice Colclough, the prop who instilled fear and awe not just in his opponents, was responsible for one of the great stories that arose from these official dinners. He had a reputation as a hard and wild man: this was a man who had once jumped naked into the Liffey, in Dublin, an act which the Gardai had somehow failed to find funny. One evening, after a rare win against the French in Paris in 1982, Colclough and his England team-mates were celebrating in style at the post-match banquet. Earlier in the evening, the players had each received a bottle of expensive French aftershave as a gift. Towards the end of the dinner, drinking challenges started to be issued between the two teams. Without anyone noticing, Colclough had somehow managed to empty his aftershave into the ice bucket on the table and to refill the bottle with water, whereupon he made a show of downing the contents of his bottle in front of the others. He then challenged them to do the same. The ill-named prop, Colin Smart, rose to the challenge and promptly gulped down the neat aftershave. He immediately collapsed and had to be taken to hospital to have his stomach pumped. It was a close shave. Still, as Steve Smith, the scum-half, subsequently observed, 'His breath smelt lovely.'

I too had a close shave after the post-match dinner that followed the Lions' successful tour to Australia in 1989. Having won the final Test and, in so doing won the series 2-1, we became – and indeed still are – the only Lions team to lose a first Test and win a series. So the celebrations were going to be good. The dinner got off to a great start because, as we entered the hotel, in Sydney's King's Cross, we were given a rapturous welcome by many of the team's supporters who were staying there or who had gone there specially to show their appreciation as we arrived. That felt very special. After that, things got a bit hazy. I remember that the dinner was mixed – sort of: meaning that the Australians had their partners with them, whereas ours were back in the UK. That made for a different atmosphere from the usual post-match tour dinners. I also remember that Steve Holdstock, a former team-mate at Nottingham who was now playing for Manly in Sydney, was at the dinner, and he introduced me to an Aussie mate of his and his wife. At one stage, after I had already drunk far too much, this big Aussie started making light of the ability of Englishmen to drink, and challenged me to a down-in-one race. No problem, I replied, but could I at least choose the drink? 'Yeah, fine.' 'Right, I'll drink this one,' I decreed, grabbing a bottle of red, 'and you drink that one.' His wife stepped in at once, well aware of the consequences. 'Don't you dare!' 'Come on,' I slurred, making allusions to men and rodents, 'you soft Aussie bastard, drink it!' I then necked my bottle down in one go; I didn't notice the vintage. The other chap had a go at doing the same but collapsed on the floor after barely two-thirds had gone down. Steve told me later that I then grabbed his mate and tried to haul him to his feet to finish the challenge, before his wife intervened and pulled me off him. I did the only responsible thing: I finished off the remaining third. Well, it was a shame to waste it.

Soon after, I made my way out in to the Sydney night, but I have no recollection of what happened next, so the details have been supplied by others and a bit of logical deduction on my part. I must have been aiming for our hotel, which was across the Sydney Harbour Bridge and on the North Shore. Sometime later, *The Times'* rugby correspondent David Hands, together with another journalist, Terry Cooper, and a Committee-man, were driving across the bridge when, as Cooper subsequently told me, they saw a figure that they thought familiar, running towards them against the traffic in the fast lane, doing aeroplane impressions with his arms. As they approached, they were alarmed to see it was me. They stopped their cab and thankfully hauled me into the back seat, thereby in all probability saving my life, for which I repaid them by being violently sick in the cab. To this day, I have no idea how I got to the bridge. It's something I regret, but I suppose it's the idiocy and immaturity of (relative) youth that explains my behaviour. In any event, it was not one of my finer moments.

Mixed dinners as such were not usual, but that particular occasion differed from dinners that took place during the Five Nations tournament. In Sydney, the partners were on the same tables as the players. After Five Nations games, wives and girlfriends came to the early part of the evening, but then went off to another room to have a women-only dinner. This might seem a bit Neanderthal, but they used to say that they really enjoyed them, because it gave them the chance to spend time together and to catch up, while we all got on with talking about the game, rugby and other matters of national importance. Also, to be honest, it's all very well going on about the spirit of the game, and how players drink and socialise together after a game, even though they've been violently opposed on the field, but when women are there sharing the same table, especially if it's just the opposition's partners attending, it's actually very difficult to break down those barriers, because you have to include them in the conversations. As a result, you just don't get to talk to your opposite numbers in quite the same way, and inevitably it changes the dynamics of the evening.

End-of-tour official dinners are routine and usually enjoyable, because it is absolutely normal to hold a celebration to mark the event. Other official dinners or receptions on tour, whether with the Lions or the national team, very soon cease to feel special because they take place at regular intervals. We would arrive somewhere, tired from the journey, and we would almost always have either a welcome reception or a dinner before leaving that particular leg of the tour. In both instances, the dinners were inevitably formal, we knew none of the local dignitaries, but we had to be polite to them even though we might be in a really bad mood because we'd had a bad game that day, or had got dropped or injured. Everywhere we went, the town's top brass would be there, and they were very excited to be welcoming us because for them, especially in the more remote parts of Australia and New Zealand, welcoming an England rugby team was a big event. It was an even bigger event with the Lions, because they only tour every 12 years to each country. Unfortunately – and it's not other people's fault – players always get asked the same questions, and although we did our best, it could get pretty tedious to have to answer them, especially if our mind was not in the right place at the time. 'How is the tour going?' 'Who is the best player/team you've played against?', 'Who is the dirtiest/hardest player?' and so on, are questions that cropped up with unsurprising regularity. In addition, some players were not socially at ease – I myself am not naturally ebullient in unfamiliar company, particularly so in those days – so found such situations a genuine ordeal.

If we were lucky at the dinners, the players would sit together, but often we were mixed up with other guests, and the ensuing evenings could feel endless. I completely understand that for those people, who were generously hosting us, it was a huge deal to attend the dinners. However, if you are not being paid to play, never mind to entertain, I defy anyone to attend them repeatedly and not get to the point where they think, 'I really can't face another evening, because today I'm really pissed off about some- thing and I don't want to be nice to a bunch of people I'm never going to see again.' It may sound churlish, but we were only human. And, being brutally honest, if I had been paid thousands of pounds to tour, I might have felt better disposed towards attending these functions. As it was, by the time the five silver- service courses had been eaten, the toasts and the never-funny speeches banging on about the 'spirit of rugby' been delivered, I was always left thinking, 'I don't want to be here.' Nowadays, of course, players are contractually obliged to attend every function and dinner, so they have no choice in the matter; plus, the media is there, so there is an attendant obligation to be sociable and to behave.

The worst official function I ever went to was at the 1995 World Cup in South Africa. I cannot imagine what the rationale was for this insane decision but they organised an opening banquet-style lunch for all the competing nations at a beautiful winery in Stellenbosch, near Cape Town, just a few days before everyone's first game. That the winery, Klein Constantia, produced some of the best wine in South Africa was utterly irrelevant as far as all the players were concerned because clearly none of us was in drinking mode. Not so the organising committee, who were seated smugly on the top table, making the most of the alcohol on offer.

On the morning of the lunch, we all had to get up at the crack of dawn, from all parts of the country, to fly to Cape Town and then take a bus to the winery. England were based in Durban, a mere 1,000 miles away on the other side of the country. I seem to remember that the plane that collected us from Durban at dawn had picked up the Wales team *before* us, as they were staying even further afield. In any event, we were all exhausted by the time we were greeted by the 'welcome' party, although I could see that the World Cup officials seemed to be adjusting remarkably well to the rigours of travel.

One or two of the players exchanged brief hellos, but since we were all soon to be engaging in battle on the field, it's fair to say there wasn't much mingling. Fortunately, we were all seated on separate tables, so maintaining the charade of a celebratory lunch was not necessary. All the teams spent most of the time glowering at their future opponents, while chewing away on rubber chicken and the sort of formal menu that is fine at a client lunch, but completely wrong for a load of rugby players who were about to play the most important tournament of the rugby calendar.

There was one other notable element to the lunch. Soon after arriving at this massive get-together, we noticed the French. For some inexplicable reason, they had decided to shave their heads for the tournament. Did they hope to scare the opposition? In any event, some of them were suddenly shorn of their distinguishing features. Only one of their players, their sometime captain Marc Cécillon, had opted out. 'Zees is not a good look for me,' he explained with a Gallic shrug. To be fair, he was very good looking, so maybe he thought it would ruin his image. Instead, he had gone in for a token mini-shave on one side of his hair. As for our ludicrous lunch-time party, it appeared to have been organised for the benefit of the Rugby World Cup organising committee. It was no doubt a way of rewarding themselves for all the hard work of getting the tournament staged in South Africa, not long after the end of apartheid. For all the players forced to attend, it served only to get the tournament off to a bad start, and was without doubt a complete and utter waste of time, money and energy.

On the other hand, we usually looked forward to Five Nations dinners, because they were big black-tie affairs at big hotels and were often fun. When games were in France or the other Home Nations, we'd pack our DJs and black tie in addition to all our rugby kit – which made for quite a lot of additional luggage – but that was just part of the excitement of playing away from home.

In London, they took place at the Hilton on Park Lane where we also stayed that night. After the game at Twickenham, we would have about an hour with our families and guests in the Rose Room, under the South Stand. We would then board our coach which would take us up to the Hilton. It was on this journey that any new caps had to fulfil the tradition of singing a song in front of everyone. For some, this was easy, because they could or liked to sing (not necessarily the same thing); for others, it was a rite of passage that they could have done without.

When I first got capped for England, players always sat together and did not have to mix with non-players. Each table would be split roughly 50:50, with players usually seated at the same table as their opposite numbers and any replacements, although captains would sit on the table with members of the host nation's committee. Against the French, even though there was a language barrier, we were initially all mixed up, with French and English players on the same tables. However, after the violence of the 1992 game, when a couple of players got sent off, there was a rethink. The *entente* became less *cordiale* and segregation became *l'ordre du jour*. That said, when the French came to London, we continued to mix the players up at dinner, which implies that the French had more of a problem with us than we did with them. Due to the language difficulty it was harder to communicate with the French, so we always ended up drinking more in order to chill out the atmosphere, because that was all you could do.

After dinner, when the wives and girlfriends had rejoined us, there was dancing until the early hours of the morning for everyone, from the players and the Committee to the backroom staff. They were enjoyable times, and each dinner stood alone as a special occasion, even though it was part of the wider Five Nations tournament. It was at these dinners that new players received their first cap and their England tie: a proud, possibly the proudest, moment in a player's career. After the entertainment had ended, many players then went on to the Captain's Room. This wasn't actually the one he stayed in, but rather a large room in which we could stay until the early hours. Unsurprisingly, it was very popular, not least because the food and drink were free, although the RFU did occasionally have to remind us that ordering crates of champagne and 50 steak sandwiches did not count as allowable refreshments or snacks. You also had to be careful about other players putting drinks on your room bill because this invariably led to being hauled before the management to explain why you shouldn't be made to settle the bill. I only got caught out once like this. After being asked to explain a large champagne bill, which I definitely hadn't ordered or consumed, I found out it was the Bath flanker John Hall who had cleverly stitched me up. He was in the lift going up to his room and among the other lift occupants was my then wife.

In a matter of fact way he said to her, 'I don't know why we've all been stuck on the twenty-fifth floor.'

Innocently, she replied, 'Oh no, not all of us; we're not on that floor.'

'Oh, what room are you in?'

'1814.' Damage done.

When I first started, the Five Nations dinners were relatively small affairs, with about 200 to 250 people attending. That sounds a lot, but by the time you have two teams, partners, and Committee people, the numbers soon add up. By the time I stopped, in 1995, we were up to nearer 500 guests, because sponsors and their clients were now attending as part of the package. Tables were no longer solely for players, they were mixed, with Committee-men and a couple of employees or guests from the major sponsors. What had been a purely rugby occasion and a celebration of the game just played became a nakedly commercial event. This annoyed us because these dinners had been the only chance of getting to know the opposing team off the field, of finding out the truth about rugby in their country, for good and bad. Non-players on the table made it impossible to speak candidly and a losing player was not likely to be in the mood to answer a layperson's questions about the game that day.

Also, from 1991, we were having a lot of trouble with the RFU for wilfully trying to misinterpret the rule changes, drawn up by the IRB and followed by several other leading countries, that allowed us to earn money from off-the-field activities while remaining amateur on it. This in turn resulted, from 1992, with us wilfully misinterpreting what was expected of us at these dinners. So we'd eat the starter, then both teams would decamp to the bar, only returning for the captains' speeches, because it would obviously have been disrespectful not to do so. That was a lot more fun because all the players would go off, mix, have a drink together and a laugh, in a way that was no longer possible now that each table had all sorts of non-rugby people on them.

After this practice occurred a couple of times, a representative from the RFU came and found us in the bar and requested we return to the dinner. Never one to run away from a bit of adversarial discussion, and as the unofficial team spokesperson, I gladly stepped forward to have an exchange of views. The man tried various different grounds on which to object to our behaviour. He shouldn't have tried to argue with a lawyer, because I dismissed all his points forcefully. At first, when I asked why we should return, he tried the etiquette route: 'Well, because it's a formal dinner.'

'Yes, so what? We were going back for the captains' speeches.'

'Yes, but that looks bad.'

'For whom?'

'Well, it looks bad for the Union.'

'Why is that any concern of mine?'

'Well, you're an England player.'

'Yeah, I'm a player; I've played.'

'It looks bad for the other Union, as we are their hosts.'

'Well, their players are all here, so how can that be the case then?'

Next, he tried the PR angle. 'Your absence gives an extremely bad impression.'

'To whom?'

'Well . . . to the others,' he ploughed on.

'Ah, you mean to the RFU sponsors and their guests?'

'Well, yes, partly,' he admitted.

'Do you pay me at all?'

'No.'

'Well, then I don't *have* to be at the dinner, do I? *You* earn money from this, it's part of the package, but it doesn't include *me* being there, because I'm not paid. So, I'm not part of this and I have no obligations.'

As the RFU were toeing the line of strict amateurism, there was nothing they could do in reply to my argument. They didn't like it, but they had to put up with it. His last desperate argument sent me over the edge.

'Look, the Committee are all present and doing their bit, and they and the President think strongly that you should go back to the dinner.'

In the end, I just said, 'No; now fuck off,' and that was the end of the argument. Actually, what I said was worse, but it's not printable. Suffice to say that this stand-off continued for two or three years, until the game went professional in 1995.

To further set this dispute in context, there already existed an antipathy between the England players and the RFU Committee, which was much more powerful than now. Their over-inflated view of their importance was demonstrated by their habit of coming into the team changing room not long before kick-off, ostensibly to wish us luck. That they often smelled of G&T while they patronisingly patted us on the back did not endear them to us at a time when we should have been avoiding all such distractions. The matter eventually came to a head when several of us were openly rude about them when they came in, loudly asking, 'What is that cunt doing in the dressing-room forty minutes before kick-off?'

Strangely, I alone was hauled before Dudley Wood. 'Did you call Micky Steele-Bodger, one of the most senior Committee members, a C?' he asked.

'No.'

'Oh, I was told on good authority that you did.'

'Well, you're wrong, Dudley, I didn't call him a C; I called him a cunt.'

In the meantime, one England player wasn't letting any ill-feeling between the RFU and the team get between him and his domestic dining plans. Gary Pearce, the Northampton tight-head prop, made an announcement at our table during one of the Hilton Hotel dinners that initially made no sense. 'That's it, I've got it; the full set.' When asked to explain, he claimed that, over the years, and a few pieces at a time, he'd been collecting the magnificent cutlery used by the Hilton and he was now pleased to announce that he'd now got a full dining set.

On a similarly perplexing note, when the waiter served our table with profiteroles for pudding, Welsh fly-half (and record points scorer) Neil Jenkins peered at the plate that had been placed in front of him and, with a suspicious look on his face, asked me, 'What's that, then?'

I wasn't entirely sure what he was referring to, so I said, 'What, the profiteroles?'

'Aye. What's that then?'

Again, I wasn't sure if he was taking the piss, so I added hesitantly, 'Well, it's sort of choux pastry with cream inside, dipped in chocolate.'

Still puzzled, he then asked, 'How'd they get that in there, then?' I didn't say any more, as I couldn't tell – and still can't – whether the joke was on him or on me.

Meanwhile, Mickey Skinner was busy on another table, trying out his practical jokes on the opposition. By now, we had seen them all, and we knew what he was up to: he needed fresh victims. More often than not, he chose a pudding, though it could have been any dish from any course. His routine would go like this: he would pick up the pudding, sniff it a couple of times, and screw up his nose. He would then announce that he thought the food was off. He would then repeat this, by which time he had the attention of the players on either side of him. He would sniff the

pudding a final time before holding it in front of one of his neighbours and asking his opinion. 'I think that's off; what do you
think?' When the player bent forward to take a sniff of his own,
Skinner would shove the pudding into his face. Having been
'done', the victim usually took the prank in good heart. This time,
though, Welsh player, Roland Philips, retaliated by simply deposit-
ing his own pudding in Skinner's lap. A full-scale food fight was
narrowly avoided by a shake of hands. What's surprising is how
often this practical joke worked, and how much mirth it created;
I suppose you had to be there, as they say.

One dinner, in Scotland, got similarly out of hand. England
had won at Murrayfield after a really terrible, boring game.
Although we still had one more game to go, the Scots had played
their last Five Nations game and were ready to celebrate the fact.
For some reason, we arrived at the post-game dinner about 20
minutes late. That wasn't very much, by normal standards, but it
was late enough for the Scots to have got stuck in. As a result, the
dinner just turned into an absolute riot, helped by the layout of the
room: there was a top table, with three long tables perpendicular to
it. On the outside two tables sat the many Committee-men, out-
numbering the players who sat on the middle table. This latter
table contained a mix of English and Scottish players. On all the
tables were a large number of miniature bottles of whisky supplied
by one of the sponsors. On the non-player tables, a few had been
opened, but not many. This was in stark contrast to the players'
table, because by the time we arrived, the Scottish team had drunk
all the miniatures available to them. Let's just say they'd made a
good start on the merriment stakes, but as the evening wore on we
worked hard and caught up with the Scots' level of inebriation.

It started with one small flick of the pudding across the table
and rapidly escalated from there. At first, each team targeted the
other but then the inevitable happened. A large spoonful was

launched by one player at his opposite number, the latter ducked and the pudding continued its trajectory until it hit one of the Committee-men square in the middle of the back. Instead of turning round and remonstrating with the thrower, he did not flinch and did not turn round. Unfortunately, this emboldened the players, who began to target various Committee-men, all of whom had evidently collectively decided to take the stiff-upper lip approach: 'Don't let the bastards know they've hit us.'

Two years later, when England were back playing the Scots at Murrayfield, the arrangements had all been changed: the teams were all split up, Committee-men were placed on each table, like teachers sitting in on a school leavers' dinner to stamp out any high jinks. This had the desired effect: a really tense evening, memorable for all the wrong reasons.

9

'Put It All on Number 15'

I believe there's a balance to be struck on tour, even now in this highly professional era, between having too much fun and not being allowed to have any at all. Today's players are required to be at their physical peak, and in order to achieve that, they seem to have every moment of their spare time carefully scheduled. Very little is left to chance. To some extent, that's fine, because they are being paid to deliver results. On the other hand, rugby is a team sport, where performance is not measured by 100ths of a second, as it is in athletics or cycling, for example. The game lasts 80 minutes, during which a lot happens that has nothing to do with the physical condition players are in. It's a dilemma for those in charge: how much do you let players off the leash? There is no definitive answer, given that much depends on the individuals concerned. What I do know is that we were certainly allowed more leeway than today's players.

Our tours had Social Committees, run by a group of players,

usually senior players, whose job it was to organise trips and days out, find out which the best pubs and clubs were, and, sometimes with the management, work out the Duty Boys' rota and the room allocation. The Social Committee would ensure we all mixed and got to know each other, and this undeniably helped tour spirit.

One of the best ways of doing this would be to split the squad up into mini-teams of seven or eight, with each group having a captain. These mini-teams had several purposes: whenever we had various activities against each other, be it quiz nights or practice drills during training sessions, we would split up into these groups. On Lions tours, this was especially important, because nationalities would be mixed up, and consequently barriers broken down. The mini-team captains would also feed back to the management during team meetings about how things were going within their groups.

The All Blacks' Social Committee, as befitted their hierarchical approach, was comprised only of senior players, whose responsibility it also was to maximise their revenue on tour. In contrast, the Australians, democratic as ever, used to allocate the positions on their Social Committee to whoever wanted them – all very relaxed. Whenever the Wallabies stayed in London, they would pitch camp in a hotel in central London's Gloucester Road, conveniently close to the Aussie enclave of Earl's Court, perhaps so that they were always within a stone's throw of some good pubs. It says much about their approach to touring that John Eales, who took over the captaincy from David Campese and became their most successful captain ever, had a habit of getting the tube map out, buying a ticket and just going off. He apparently visited everything and presumably didn't feel the need to prescribe what his team-mates should be doing during their down-time. Apparently, the RFU's liaison officers were kept busy by the Australians forever asking for tickets to the many shows on in

London, which they would try their best to provide. I can't say the requests were reciprocal, because when we toured Australia, let's just say there wasn't – at least not in those days – the wealth of cultural opportunities that there are in London.

I tell a lie. I do remember feeling very excited that tickets were arranged for us to go to the Sydney Opera House during the Lions tour of 1989. Although inside the opera house is not particularly spectacular, outside it is truly stunning, especially when seen close up. I had taken a selection of opera to listen to on my Walkman during the tour, and this always provoked a discussion with my team-mates which usually began with the question, 'Why do you like that crap?' So although I was really looking forward to the evening, I had had to do a lot of persuading of some of my less enthusiastic team-mates. 'Come on, go! You can't know if you'll like it until you give it a try,' I entreated them. Eventually, some agreed to give it a go. When I saw the programme my heart sank: instead of something approachable, like *The Magic Flute* or *La Bohème*, which would have provided a perfect introduction for the uninitiated, it was Massenet's *Werther*, an opera in four acts which, I suspected, might feel like double that by the time the curtain had gone down. Sure enough, it was heavy-going, even for me, and I wasn't surprised that half of our party walked out at the first interval. I stuck it out doggedly, as did John Jeffrey, the taciturn Scottish flanker, who gamely stayed on with me. I couldn't help agreeing with him when, after much singing, our eponymous hero finally shot himself, after which John, with admirable understatement, whispered loudly, 'Thank *fuck* for that!' For him it was definitely a once-in-a-lifetime experience.

Australia had plenty of other culture to offer – sheep-shearing, for example. Unlike England, where it's quite difficult to drive for 20 miles without seeing a village or some form of habitation, in Australia, if you drive for 20 miles outside Sydney's city limits, you're already in the Outback. When England were there in 1988, the host Union arranged for us to be bussed out to a huge cattle and sheep ranch that in reality was not very far away. It came as quite a shock to us to see how vast and empty the terrain was, despite being relatively close to a big city. Still, that shock was as nothing compared to that of the young lad who volunteered to take part in the Q&A at the end of the sheep-shearing demonstration. A big, rangy lad, he was a good wholesome-looking country boy. After demonstrating his undeniable sheep-shearing skills and taking a deserved round of applause for his efforts, he went up to the microphone and hesitantly said, 'Ah look, has anyone got any questions? I don't mind what it is,' assuming that we were going to ask some technical questions about his impressive sheep-shearing technique. Given his audience, that was an elementary mistake because unfortunately for him, the first to stick his hand up was Richard Harding, the Bristol scrum-half. 'Yes. I've got a question,' he boomed out. 'What's your missus like in bed?' The poor lad instantly turned bright crimson; he started to gibber; he looked around helplessly, and in a matter of seconds he went running off the rostrum. Merciless, yes; but, I'm afraid, quite funny at the time.

On another afternoon off, this time in Brisbane, a trip to an amusement park just down the Gold Coast was arranged for our party. Bearing in mind that we had a daily allowance which amounted to nothing very much, it was decided to hand over the entire kitty for the day to a senior player, Peter Winterbottom, and Terry Crystal, the tour doctor, who was adjudged to be a responsible fellow. We all dispersed into small groups and were having a good time when, about halfway through the afternoon, the groups met up, everyone in need of some refreshments.

'Where's Wints?'

'Yeah, where is he?'

It was true that no one had seen him or Terry on any of the rides. After a bit of searching, he and Terry were duly located but denied they had any money.

'Well we haven't got it either,' we retorted. Eventually, under persistent questioning, they finally admitted that yes, they had been given the money, but had spent it all on a helicopter ride round the park – just for the two of them.

'It was a great flight, though,' giggled the doctor.

'You selfish twats,' was the corresponding response.

Notwithstanding this act of embezzlement, I'd had a great time because I'd gone bungee jumping, something I'd never done before. I can't say that up until then I had been terrified of heights, but I wasn't exactly fine with them either. At this amusement park we were jumping over a concrete car park, which psychologically didn't help because, utterly illogically, when I later did another jump above a six-foot-deep river, I felt far safer. The reality was that had the elastic failed, I'd have ended up in a crumpled heap, whatever the surface below. As my turn to ascend the stairs to the diving platform got nearer, I started to get increasingly nervous. So much so that I contemplated ducking out. I didn't because a 14-year-old girl was just ahead of me in the queue to jump. I took one look at her and thought of the ensuing humiliation if I backed out. So I jumped and I have to say, it was great. The really exciting bit is the freefall, which only lasts about three seconds, when the adrenalin really kicks in. As soon as the elastic starts to pull you back and you start to decelerate, you don't get the same high. Since then, I've done a parachute jump and a tandem sky dive in New Zealand – both many years after retirement, I hasten to add, and both fantastic. I'm not sure I would have done either had that first bungee jump not cured my fear of heights.

The previous year, during the World Cup, I had got another

adrenalin high, unplanned this time, when I decided to go out
one afternoon with Dean Richards. He had hired a car while we
were based in Sydney and invited me to accompany him on a tour
of Sydney's sights. Dean, who was with the Leicestershire
Constabulary, was a motorway rapid-response officer. He had
done several advanced-driving courses and he thought it would be
fun to show me what he could do; not that he gave me any choice
in the matter. Before long, he was driving at ridiculous speeds,
weaving in and out of the traffic, cutting corners and showing
me all his tricks. I clung to the dashboard with such force that
my hands almost made imprints in it. 'That might have looked
dangerous, but at no time was I ever *near* to having an accident or
out of control,' he confidently stated when we finally came to a
stop. You could have fooled me.

When the rest of the boys found out he'd hired a car, not just
for a day, but for a whole week, a trio from the party determined
they would become similarly mobile. Steve Bainbridge, Peter
Winterbottom and John Hall decided they were going to hire
motorbikes, in the same spirit of fun. Not surprisingly, the management had a serious sense of humour failure and told them this
was absolutely forbidden. 'Well, they're allowed a car,' they all
moaned. It had to be pointed out that bikes were rather more dangerous than cars.

In the same spirit of not telling your team-mates about something until after you'd done it, during a spare afternoon of the
Lions tour in 1989, we were all taken off to visit Hardys winery,
near Adelaide. We were given a guided tour of the establishment,
which makes some very good wines, then a wine-tasting, followed
by lunch. I sat on one table with a few team-mates, and was
admiring all the plaques hanging up on the wall that highlighted
the many award-winning wines produced by the winery. In slight
contrast the reds we had been given to sample and to accompany

our meal were decent but not stunning. I discreetly flagged down one of the staff members.

'Some of these wines are okay, but could we try some of those?' I asked, gesturing towards some of the plaques.

'Er, well . . .' he stuttered.

'It's okay, we won't tell anyone else,' I added hastily. 'It's just for this table.'

Everyone on the table was delighted to sample some of the prize-winning vintages, and we had a thoroughly enjoyable afternoon. Obviously, for maximum effect, we told everyone what we'd done on the drive back to the hotel. That was part of the fun, after all; plus, we didn't want any secrets to spoil team spirit, did we?

Earlier that tour, team spirit and reliance on others had become evident. We were in subtropical, steamy Cairns and one day went white-water rafting. All good for the adrenalin, but when David Young, the tight-head prop, fell in and got stuck among the swirling waters and rocks, genuine fear kicked in: it turned out he couldn't swim. Despite wearing a life-jacket, within moments it was obvious he was in severe difficulties. Without hesitation, Gareth Chilcott reached out from the boat and, as befits his immense strength as a prop, physically hauled David back to the safety of the craft.

Usually, we weren't seeking adrenalin highs, purposely or not. I would sometimes just get a map of wherever we were and go wandering, taking in the sights, especially if we were in a city such as Sydney, which was great to walk around. For others a favourite way to while away a few spare hours was to play cards. On the 1989 Lions tour in particular, there was a tight-knit group of players who seemed to play cards the entire time. Players such as Gareth Chilcott, Dean Richards and Andy Robinson were always huddled together in a little group playing cribbage or other such games. Unlike footballers, who are known to play for pots worth tens of thousands of pounds, the amounts here were tiny, a few pounds at most. They played for several hours a day and rarely let in any outsiders. The one time I was allowed to join in, I quickly realised I was out of my depth as they were well honed and very good. It's not an exaggeration to say that all three had mastered the art of card-counting and so knew, more or less, which cards were held by which player; it was then just a question of who played them best. Slaughtered round after round, I withdrew – a valuable lesson learned.

Perth provided a great stopover on that tour, and one afternoon we were invited to go sailing in nearby Fremantle, a former venue for the Americas Cup, with its super-smart Royal Perth Yacht Club. I doubt there are many clubs that have a wealthier set of members anywhere in the world, as evidenced by the lavishness of the yachts lined up to take us sailing. A few of us were assigned to each one for the trip. Bob Norster, one of the most effective locks in the world at the time, was in my 'crew'. Before embarking, Bob wanted to take a photo of us on the quayside for posterity. He was a particular man and he had bought himself a brand new camera at the duty-free in Singapore, so he was keen to line up the shot just right. He handed the camera to one of the older club members so that he could take the actual shot and we all stood there beaming. What happened next felt like slow motion, yet it all happened in a flash: the old gentleman, deciding to adjust the focus, dropped the camera on to the quayside stones, while Bob immediately held up his hands in horror, groaning, 'No, no!' We all then watched helplessly as, slowly and inexorably, the expensive camera slid down the steeply sloping quayside, fell over the edge and dropped unceremoniously into the water. The man had gamely scrambled towards the camera on his hands and knees, in a desperate attempt to avert disaster, but nothing could be done.

Bob looked on in horror, as did we, until seconds later our reaction changed to vast and uncontrolled merriment.

Eventually, the boats set off for an afternoon of racing, and on our return, captain Finlay Calder and manager Clive Rowlands thanked our hosts profusely for organising the special race just for us. 'Ah no, mate, we do this every Wednesday!' quipped back one of the members. How the other half lives.

It is important to try to find a balance between letting players entertain themselves – which nowadays often means that they retreat into their own little world with the help of a set of head-phones and gadgets of every description – and arranging outings or entertainment. Forcing them into some cringe-worthy team-building events never works and not all our attempts were successful either. The Lions tour to New Zealand in 1993 was marred, as already mentioned, by poor team spirit, especially among some members of the midweek team, of which I was ini-tially part. The whole tour started to fall apart, so about midway through, the captain, Gavin Hastings, hit upon the clever idea of taking everyone out on a 'fun' evening, in order to do a bit of much-needed bonding.

'Right, we'll have an evening together,' he said, a bit like a dad trying to force his teenage kids to get on.

'Yeah, what is it?'

'Bowling. Ten-pin bowling.'

'Oh great,' some of us replied, sounding like Kevin the Teenager.

Along with Mike Teague and Peter Winterbottom, I decided there was no way we were going bowling, so we hid. Unfortunately, after some searching, Gavin found us, hiding behind a door. Obviously not a very big door, or at least not big enough to hide three forwards.

'Come on, get on the bus,' he ordered, like a school teacher.

'Don't want to go.'

'Get on the bus!'

In the end, we had no choice and sulked all the way there. When it came to his turn to bowl, Wints walked slowly up to his lane and literally dropped his ball. He made no real attempt to roll it and it dribbled into the side gutter, eventually coming to a halt halfway along. Suppressing laughter, I actually had to walk down the lane and give it a shove with my foot so that it could roll down to the end and disappear. 'Fuck it,' said Wints, 'I've done my bit now,' as he sat down and refused to take any further part in the evening.

As the evening grew to a close, a number of prizes were produced. These had been covered up so that their magnificence would not over-stimulate our already inflamed anticipation. We could hardly wait. Kenny Milne was known as 'Village', whose nickname from the Scotland team followed him to the Lions tour, and if readers can't work out why perhaps they should join him. At the designated time he proudly unveiled the second prize: a rugby shirt – on a Lions rugby tour. Genius. 'Oh thanks, I've not got one of those,' the lucky recipient was heard to say, barely able to contain his gratitude, followed by, 'You fucking idiot, Village.' I've erased from my mind what the first prize was, which is probably just as well because it might well have been two rugby shirts.

During the 1991 World Cup, as ever, we were based at the Petersham Hotel, a very comfortable hotel, but whose games room, as mentioned earlier, was not really spacious enough to keep a full England squad entertained. While some players occasionally went off for some quiet fishing, others would go off to a nearby shooting range down in Surrey. This was normally a splendid way of passing the afternoon and caused no problems whatsoever; right up until it did. On one of these escapades, Jeff Probyn decided to treat everyone to an impromptu talk about guns, including his

Marocchi 'over and under' shotgun, though he never adequately explained to anyone how he had passed the suitable holder's test. All was going well, the players were getting very psyched up and competitive about hitting the target, when suddenly John Olver, in a moment of over-enthusiasm, accidentally discharged his rifle and blew the toe off Mike Teague's trainer. Teague immediately started hopping up and down, screaming, saying he'd been shot. To be fair, it looked that way, because the end of his trainer was completely shredded. Deano immediately went into sympathetic copper mode. 'Did you get the bastard?' he asked Olver.

Several players liked golf, and went off for rounds whenever they could. I neither play much nor have much interest in the game, but what I do know is that it was an utterly pointless exercise to play with the England forwards because they couldn't be trusted to record a correct score. On the occasions when I had played with Jeff Probyn, I'd see him hacking around in the rough, and when he eventually sank his putt and was asked for his number of shots, he'd always fire back, 'One more than you.' 'Hold on,' I once said. 'How is that possible? I saw you take five off the fucking tee.'

It was also difficult to tell which hole any of the forwards were actually playing, such was the degree to which they sprayed the ball from fairway to fairway. It wasn't unusual to feel a ball fizzing just past your ear, only to turn round and hear the player who had hit it say 'Sorry – fore!' while collapsed in gales of laughter.

Rugby World Cup preparations are now, rightly, taken so seriously that nothing is left to chance and virtually every moment of the players' time is meticulously scheduled. The first Rugby World Cup, in 1987, was very different, and much of our down-time was left to us to fill. What was scheduled, however, was a short stay in Hamilton Island, in Queensland, as I mentioned earlier. We stayed at this wonderful new resort, and it was great, though perhaps not entirely appropriate if, as was the case, we had our vital quarter-final against Wales a few days later. The fact is, we should never have gone. Yes, we had a lot of fun, but there was so much on offer, including all the water sports facilities, huge pools and a stunning golf course, that we spent most of the time cavorting around. I went scuba diving on the Great Barrier Reef – it was my first time, and I wasn't going to pass up the opportunity. Others spent hours in the surf, or in the pool, diving, doing handstands, everything they should not have been doing, and by the end of the day, their legs were like jelly. And, of course, we were all out in the sun, which in itself is tiring. Even those who just played a round of golf still found themselves getting four or five hours of after-noon sun. Moreover, Steve Bainbridge even managed to wreck a golf cart by driving into a dip and turning it over – which could have had serious consequences for him and the team had he been injured. Basically, we all went mad and paid no attention to any physical harm we might have come to. Not that the management did either. They just thought it was a good idea for us to relax for a few days, after the group games and before the quarter-final. They might almost have added, 'Because you're worth it.' By the time we got down to the serious business of preparing for the game, we had lost two vital days. We then flew almost 1,000 kilo-metres down to Brisbane, played against the Welsh and limped ignominiously out of the inaugural World Cup in one of the worst games I ever played in for England.

The following tournament, in 1991, was jointly hosted by the (then) Five Nations, and England played a quarter-final against the French at the Parc des Princes. It remains one of the most attri-tional games of my career and is one of the stand-out encounters between these two foes of recent years. Our 19-10 win was obtained with a determination and brutality that was unusual, even when taking into account the age-old enmity between these two nations. To give us a break from the rigours of the tournament, the management arranged for us all to stop off in Jersey for a couple of nights. Partly because of where we were staying – a hotel on a quiet island not known for bacchanalian excess – and partly because players' wives and girlfriends came to join us, the 36 hours spent there were somewhat more sedate than the Hamilton Island sojourn. That was also because all we really wanted to do was chill out and recover physically from the game. It was all very leisurely, and was over very fast. Even so, I can't pretend that there was no drinking going on in Jersey, because Peter Winterbottom got very, very pissed. That was unusual for him, because although he was normally a big drinker, he also had a high threshold. By the end of the evening, though, he was staggering around saying to Mike Teague 'Mikey, Mikey, I llllove you . . . I'm going to have fff-five kids . . . and I'm going to cccall them all Mmmmikey.' The next morning, he refused to come out of his bedroom, because he just knew how much stick he was going to get. He was right: everyone was waiting for him to come down, but he wouldn't budge. People were knocking on his door, 'Come on, get down here!' But no, he ordered all his meals in his room and just refused to emerge.

We then went north of the border to prepare for our semi-final against the Scots at Murrayfield. After winning that game 9-6 in an unstylish but effective manner, we were again treated to a 36-hour stop-off, this time at a Midlands spa hotel. This had been arranged by Mr Social Committee himself, Rory Underwood, who had fixed himself up with a free membership for so doing. Once again, partners were invited, and once again, we refrained from excessive ebullience. In between massages and various other sedate activities, we basically chillaxed, to coin a current phrase. Probably too much, because in effect we had now had two such weekends in quick succession. Needlessly, to my mind, especially just before a final, the importance of which it was impossible to understate. I think we lost our focus and edge a little during that stay, and looking back, I don't think we should have had it. We should have remained a tightly focused unit, and returned to our base at the Petersham Hotel to prepare for the final. Hindsight, of course, always comes with 20/20 vision, so who knows if the outcome would have been any different?

In any event, it was obviously felt by the powers that be that those mini-breaks were a positive thing, because when we qualified for the semi-final against the mighty All Blacks in the 1995 World Cup, we were treated to a few days in Sun City, the luxury resort and casino and a sort of South African Las Vegas. Quite why this venue was deemed suitable is a mystery. We were full of confidence after our win against Australia in the quarter-finals, and would have been better off getting a few days' R&R somewhere a bit quieter.

It's true that we had already done a few of the obligatory outings, including a half-day safari to Kruger National Park, so perhaps it was felt that a bigger change of scene would do us good. The safari trip had suffered from the fact that all the animals we saw appeared to be miles away. So much so that Ben Clarke complained that he couldn't really see them. 'Would it be possible,' he suggested, 'to have a lion put in a cage, like a big cage, but near us?' I'm still not sure if he was being serious.

In any event, after that underwhelming experience, we took yet another flight, this time up to Sun City, in the north of the country. I have to say, the resort itself is brilliant. It's like a gigantic amusement park with all the pools, water slides, golf and gambling imaginable. It's awake 24/7, and fun is its *raison d'être*.

As a result, we never stopped. Day and night. Although I was trying to rest a bit in the afternoon, and having regular massages, I too was making the most of the facilities, and going to bed far too late, although what I got up to was as nothing compared to some of my team-mates. But we all just thought, 'Well, I'll just sleep in tomorrow.' Yet it's never the same, because you get out of sync with your body clock, and in effect you become jet-lagged as a result. Our trip was a week before our semi-final, so we reckoned we had plenty of time to recover and to prepare. Plus, we were still training every day, twice a day, and we appeared to be doing that without any problem, so we misguidedly thought the break was doing no harm. It was fine to take us away from the grind of standard hotels in prescribed host cities, but we shouldn't have gone to Sun City. It just had too many distractions.

There were also some keen gamblers among us, which had already been demonstrated a few years before, on the Lions tour in 1989, when we had stayed in the Burswood Hotel and Casino in Perth. Dean Richards and Andy Robinson had wasted no time in locating the gaming tables, and were spending an impressive amount of time trying to make some money. The extent of their determination became evident when they were caught leaving the casino one morning *before* breakfast. They had basically got up especially early so that they could nip over and have a quick flutter before coming in for breakfast.

When it came to Sun City, therefore, Dean and a few others showed similar enthusiasm for the gaming tables, spending a good few hours there in the evenings. Once, he, Jerry Guscott and a third player were at the roulette table and they decided to put a bit of money on the number 15 (weirdly, I can remember that number to this day). Against all odds – because let's face it, that's the point, for a casino – their number came up. Much whooping and jumping of joy followed, with other players crowding round to congratulate them on their good fortune. Consequently they didn't notice that they had forgotten to stop playing and take their money. '*Les jeux sont faits*,' called out the croupier, as he gave another spin of the wheel. Now, normally, that would mean the end of their good fortune, with the ball falling on another number and the ensuing loss of their money. But in a stroke of unbelievable luck, the ball bobbed around for a while before stopping on the same number – again. Suddenly, what had started off as a small punt turned into a windfall worth, I seem to remember, around £6,000. For three amateur rugby players, this was a *lot* of money. Remembering to collect their winnings there and then, there followed a lot of drinking and loud celebrations, as the three euphoric players enjoyed their windfall until late into the night. It was an ideal preparation for the forthcoming game.

10

#drunkendwarftossing
trends on Twitter

Drinking has long been synonymous with playing rugby, more so than with any other nationally played team sport. Alcohol is only part of the social side of rugby; the fraternity and traditional ethos of communality is the other, probably more important, side. However, there is no doubt that by devoting an entire chapter to it, and after telling stories in other chapters in which alcohol plays a central part, it is undeniable that there is abundant justification for this link to be made.

When I first became a member of the England squad, drinking was a regular occurrence. Even the night before a game, some players would have a few pints, and after games many more. Memorably, in 1988 one of the most infamous instances of drink-fuelled player misbehaviour took place. It evolved seamlessly from the previously recounted food fight at the official dinner that followed England's victory over Scotland at Murrayfield.

In those days, the Calcutta Cup was taken along to the official dinner, and passed around among the players. That evening, we all carried on drinking after the dinner had ended, and Dean Richards and Scotland's John Jeffrey thought it would be a good idea to keep filling the cup with champagne and drinking from it. It then got sent round to various players, all of whom simply toasted the first thing that came into their heads. When it got to me, the two miscreants waited for me to bend my head to take a swig; they then hurled the contents all over my head. I was not best pleased. Not because it was a waste of champagne, nor because I got a good soaking, but because I had been dull enough to be duped.

After they had doused me, and without anyone noticing, they both left the hotel giggling furiously and took the trophy out on the town. Though neither ever publicly admitted this, at one point they were alleged to have been drop-kicking the cup to each other along Edinburgh's Princes Street. The first I knew of what had happened was at breakfast the next morning when two lads from my Old Boys' rugby club, the Old Crossleyans, paid a visit to our hotel. They had travelled up for the game and had at one point been in a bar when Richards and Jeffrey had come in with the cup which clearly showed signs of damage. In fact they handed me a copy of a Polaroid photo they had taken in which Dean could be seen sitting on the knee of another Old Crossleyan with what looked like a tea cosy on this head. John was clearly recognisable despite having his back to the camera, and the cup's bottom rim was visibly bent and with small dents in it. I thus had incontrovertible proof of their involvement and of the damage done.

Dean then came into the breakfast room and sidled up to me in a deliberately nonchalant manner.

'Have you heard about the Calcutta Cup?' he casually asked.

'No,' I lied.

'Well,' he continued, 'some people are saying that it got damaged last night.'

I was equally matter of fact when I said, 'Well, did you have anything to do with it?' When he denied this, I added, 'In that case you don't have anything to worry about.'

Apparently satisfied with our exchange, Dean went back to his table, only to return a few minutes later. 'You know the Calcutta Cup? Well, people are saying it got damaged last night.'

'Well, as you told me you had nothing to do with it, it doesn't really matter, does it?' I replied, and he went away again, only to return after a further brief interval.

'They're saying that the people responsible might get banned for a long time . . .' he began.

'Deano, you said you had nothing to do with it, is that right?' When he confirmed that he had not had anything to do with the criminal damage, I concluded the conversation by saying, 'In that case I don't know why you're that bothered, as it has nothing to do with you, does it?' He might as well have started the chat with the immortal words, 'A friend of mine . . .' It was all I could do to keep a straight face during the exchanges, as I had photographic proof to refute his claimed innocence, but to tell him would have been to pass up an opportunity for fun.

As the morning progressed, gossip about the damaged trophy was raging and I knew that if we knew, the rugby journalists would certainly have got wind of it. So, later that morning I rang one of them and used a variation on the 'A friend of mine . . .' line and asked, 'Just say, hypothetically, I had a picture which showed the Calcutta Cup clearly damaged and also the person or persons responsible, how much would it be worth?' He paused and replied, 'It's not my area but I would think at least eight thousand pounds.' In reality, it was probably worth twice that, but I had no intention of releasing it because by that time there were rumours of severe punishments, including the possibility of a long ban, for the culprits. As it turned out, Deano served only a one-match ban, though John suffered more. With hindsight I should have sold the photo and split the proceeds with Dean.

Whether that incident had any effect on me, I don't know. In any event, by 1989, I was so determined to be selected for the Lions squad to tour Australia that I decided not to have a single drink for the six months beforehand – and that included the entire Five Nations campaign of that year. I trained very hard, and not drinking certainly had a positive effect on my fitness; I duly got picked to tour. The downside was that when I did have that first drink in Australia, on one of those 'get-to-know-each-other' evenings, I was bladdered after three or four pints.

Our attitude to alcohol consumption during the years I played changed gradually. We went from being ludicrously amateur in the 1987 World Cup – and therefore happy to drink without too much thought for how it affected us – to an awareness, from about 1989, that a bit more restraint might be warranted. Generally, consumption reduced to a few pints on a Wednesday night (before a Saturday game), though we still drank a lot after. By the time the 1991 World Cup preparations began, we were already drinking less – and less frequently. After that, consumption decreased again, especially after the 1993 Lions tour. There was a realisation that there had been too much booze on that tour, although how much of that was the cause of the poor results or the effects thereof is a moot point. By the time we were training for the 1995 World Cup, we were aware that four teams in the World – Australia, New Zealand, South Africa and France – were in effect semi-professional, and that inevitably made us more serious about our own preparations. There's a simple correlation between boozing and unprofessionalism, and we didn't want to be the only idiots who hadn't made that link.

The 1993 Lions tour probably marked a watershed in terms of alcohol consumption. As previously stated, the midweek team gradually seemed to give up trying and, as the tour progressed, were drinking more or less the whole time. I was initially selected for that team, and had therefore had to sit out the first Test – which we lost. Even before that game, I had already become fed up with the situation, and one Friday afternoon, the day before we were due to play Otago, I headed off with Wade Dooley and Peter Winterbottom to a wine bar near where we were staying. The idea was simply to have a nice lunch and to get away from the toxic atmosphere at the hotel. We ordered a bottle of wine and started drinking. And another, and another, and so on. By the end, we'd drunk nine bottles between the three of us; not bad. We eventually tottered back to the hotel in time for the team meeting that evening. When he saw us, Mike Teague just bellowed with laughter. 'What have you done to Wints? He's completely pissed!' Surprised that our inebriation was that obvious, we sat at the back, hoping not to be noticed. We got away with it and, to be fair, we hadn't set out to get pissed, it was just that we didn't make enough effort not to. Wade and I weren't playing the next day anyway – although I was on the bench, so should definitely have known better than to drink so much – but already by that stage of the tour it seemed that nobody minded what anybody got up to. Wints, on the other hand, was selected to start but, astonishingly, played really well and was even named Man of the Match. Perhaps he should have drunk a bit more. Thankfully, soon after the Otago game, I was selected for the Saturday games and the last two Tests, so avoided any further temptation. Meanwhile, the tour became a semi-permanent booze-up for certain members of that midweek team.

In mitigation, it's true that New Zealand had 24-hour licensing at the time. Considering people joked about how a trip to New

Zealand felt like a trip back to the 1970s, their licensing laws either felt very progressive or very innocent, depending on one's point of view. In some places that were in the back of beyond, the issue didn't arise because the whole town seemed to shut down by 9 p.m., so there was nowhere to go even if we'd wanted to. In the larger cities, such as Christchurch and Auckland, we always managed to find 24-hour bars, with the result that after games, people would stay out until far too late and nothing was ever said. I should point out that Britain still had its archaic licensing laws at the time, so it's perhaps not surprising that we made the most of the opportunity.

For a bit of a laugh, after having a few drinks one evening, a group of us once went on to a strip/something extra club in Auckland called the Firestone Club, only to find one of our squad already ensconced, all on his own, bang in the middle of the front row. 'Oh, hi,' we said, slightly surprised. Rather than look particularly perturbed at being found, he said, by way of explanation, 'Look, I've agreed with my wife that if I just have a hand-job, that's not being unfaithful.' My initial thought was: how admirably mature to sit down with your spouse before setting off, with she perhaps declaring, 'You're going away with the boys for eight weeks, and I completely agree: a hand-job doesn't count as cheating.' I then thought: hang on, I cannot conceive of *any* situation or context in which I could have begun to have that sort of conversation. I mean, when do you start? Over Sunday lunch? After driving back from the in-laws? Whatever works, I guess.

At the end of that miserable tour, with nothing to hold us back, we all went absolutely berserk. I remember drinking three jugfuls of tequila and lime. This is an absolutely insane amount, because probably about two pints of that was neat tequila. In my defence, it was drunk over a period of a few hours, and the thing was, I do remember doing so, which means I can't have been paralytically drunk. I'm sure I was pretty pissed, but I was not violently sick or rendered unconscious, so somehow my body managed to cope with vast quantities of spirits. Nor was I alone in getting very drunk, because the vast majority of the squad was doing the same. Presumably, that's how relieved they all were that the tour was finally at an end.

Irresponsible drinking wasn't confined to teams from these shores. Bob Templeton, the former Aussie coach, now sadly deceased, told me that the night before the 1991 World Cup final some of the Australian players who were not picked for the match-day squad went for a night out. They included David Knox who was Michael Lynagh's understudy. Instead of having a few consolation pints, Knox staggered into the team hotel in the wee small hours. He was seen by Templeton who only used to need four hours' sleep a night and was still up at that time.

First thing in the morning, Tempo woke Knox and said, 'Listen, mate, Noddy's [Lynagh's nickname] crooked; you're playing today.' Knox, who was white and trying not to shake, then spent the rest of the morning dousing himself with water to try and freshen up, but couldn't hide the fact that he was sweating and green at the gills. By now, the rest of the party had been told of the wheeze and delighted in seeing Knox's agony as the morning wore on. They kept up the charade until just before the final team meeting when Knox was released from his agony. 'That'll serve you right, you little bastard,' were Tempo's parting words.

Australia was good for bars and clubs, even if they had stricter licensing laws than New Zealand. When in Brisbane with England in 1988, we had discovered various clubs in town. One such, the Underground Club, remains one of the best I've ever been to. It wasn't a particularly spectacular place, there was no dress code, it had a very mixed crowd; perhaps because of that, and a stellar playlist, it had great energy while being very welcoming and laid back. Every time I went to Brisbane in subsequent years, I always went back.

Another place, the Ship Inn hotel, had been granted a special 24-hour licence as a result of Brisbane holding the World Expo earlier that year. So, when we played there that year, several of us would go over there after training or games. It was a great place, because it was one of the few places in town that stayed open, even after most of the nightclubs had closed. They had a resident pianist, an English guy who played and sang pretty well. We soon got chatting to him because we were fascinated by what had brought him to this particular place. He told us that he'd travelled across America and around the world, playing his way to finance his travels. He would tell bars and clubs that they didn't need to pay him, because he could survive on the generous tips he received everywhere he went. He also revealed the best bit about his nomadic life: playing the piano and singing was the biggest woman-magnet imaginable. The women *loved* it, he said, smiling from ear to ear. 'I've had more sex on this tour than anywhere else. It's been absolutely fantastic!' he said with evident delight, but without boasting. 'Yeah, right,' everyone was thinking. He also happened to be a thoroughly decent bloke and good looking as well. Not that we were envious – git!

As an add-on to that tour we went to Fiji and it was there that I discovered Kava, not to be confused with the Spanish fizz, Cava. Kava is a drink made from the pulped leaves of the eponymous plant and it is consumed throughout the Pacific Ocean cultures. It's also a drink with sedative and anaesthetic properties, though it is supposed not to impede mental clarity. It has also been known to induce liver failure. None of this did I know at the time. All I do know is that the moment the drink touched my lips, they went numb, and as it slipped down my throat, so did my tongue, my mouth and my throat. I also realised that it had the same sort of feeling as that induced by smoking dope; and yes, I admit, I have inhaled.

John Olver was at the centre of another incident in Fiji. We were staying in a beautiful hotel on the seafront on the main island. It was all particularly idyllic, especially as this was the hotel where I had impersonated Dudley Wood to bag myself his suite. It was also there that the team to play the forthcoming Test against Australia was announced. Being selected, I headed off for a quiet dinner in a nearby hotel with Colin Herridge, who was the secretary of Harlequins. By the time we went off, those who hadn't been selected had begun to drink the bar dry in the traditional way of those left out of Test teams. It was going to be a lively night.

By the time we returned, things were in full swing, but I decided to go to bed. Some hours later, and well past midnight, a few of the guys spotted an opportunity for more fun. Outside, a small stage had been built on which had performed, earlier that evening, a local Fijian band who had delighted their audience with traditional islander songs such as 'Y Viva España'. The band had temporarily gone off and had left their instruments on stage. This was too tempting for the rock stars manqué that were John Olver, Nigel Redman and a couple of others. Up they leapt, Olver immediately grabbing the microphone, while the others started to play air guitar with the instruments. 'Hello, Wembleee!' shouted Olver in the ever-original way of a born rock god addressing his adoring fans. Instead of hearing their reply, he suddenly spotted Geoff Cooke, the manager, striding purposefully across the grass towards their band, looking grim-faced. Terminating his performance there and then, Olver dived off into the adjoining bushes, quickly followed by his band-mates. All except Nigel Redman who was too pissed and therefore too slow to work out what was happening. 'Fair play to you, Geoff,' he shouted cheerfully at the fast-approaching figure. 'Still up with the boys at this time of night.'

Fair play to Geoff indeed: he swiftly issued the mother of all bollockings.

A couple of years later, I went on the fun but ill-conceived tour to Argentina. This was the first tour undertaken by any British sporting team since the end of the Falklands War, something we were a bit nervous about. As it turned out, only once, at a game in Tucumán, did the crowd display any animosity towards us, burning a Union Jack. At another game, I did get a pair of scissors thrown at me, but I'm fairly sure that was the crowd's way of showing their dislike of me specifically, rather than of my country.

We soon realised that the locals had a very Latin culture when it came to socialising. They ate late, never before 10 p.m., after which they would move on to clubs and bars at about 1 or 2 a.m. Given we would start our post-match celebrations not long after the final whistle, we were therefore packing in the equivalent of a working day's worth of drinking on a regular basis. It's not surprising our results suffered.

We managed to endear ourselves to the locals, none of whom seemed to have any urge to drink themselves into oblivion, when we piled off the coach one evening in Buenos Aires, on our way to the perplexingly named New York, New York club. Already well loosened up, we lined up to get off the vehicle. First off was John Buckton, our centre. He staggered off, promptly fell into the gutter and threw up. Very classy. And in full view of the cool-looking beautiful people who were queuing to get into the club.

A further example of how the Latin nations just don't have the same approach to alcohol as us was demonstrated in South Africa, shortly after England and France had had to play the third place play-off game in the World Cup. This game was excruciating for me: I was exhausted after Jonah Lomu had almost single-handedly demolished our defence, and the game took place in Pretoria, at altitude, the first game for us that was not at sea level. England's tired legs and tired minds meant that, after eight straight losses against us, the French beat us 19-9 in what was a shockingly poor game for us. Our opponents, on the other hand, were elated, and were jumping around all over the place. There's no doubt they had developed a bit of a fixation about us in recent years, because on a couple of occasions, they had just imploded. What's that oxymoron again about French Resistance?

Afterwards, dejected, we repaired to a bar to drown our sorrows. The bar happened to be divided into two halves. In addition, as its particular selling point, it sold shots of alcohol in little glass containers that were, in effect, test tubes. You could buy a rack of them, which would be presented to you just as they would in a science lab. We started ordering the racks of test tubes and downing the shots. After about an hour, the alcohol had started to dull the pain of our loss, and we had come round a little bit. Then the French team suddenly walked in to the other half of the bar. Naturally, they were overjoyed because a fair number of them had never actually been on a winning side against us, so this was a big deal. On seeing them, we just thought, 'Oh, fucking hell, can it get any worse?' and turned away to carry on drinking.

To their credit, despite their happiness, the French did not gloat, but thought '*Et bien*, we're not going to let ze Eengleesh spoil our night.' One or two of their players, such as Philippe Sella, who knew some of ours, even came over and said hello. Jeff Probyn did the same to some of them. They started to have a beer together and go in for a bit of *entente cordiale*. Before long, someone called out in their direction, '*Eh, monsieur, boisson?*' gesturing towards our racks of test tubes. After they nodded their agreement, a rack of shots was duly sent over. And downed. One was then sent back to us. Backwards and forwards these racks went for a while. Then players started to walk round to the other side of the bar, and although the French couldn't speak much English, and we couldn't speak much French, we didn't need to. By the end of the night, about four years of hatred was drunk away and this is between two teams that had torn into each other in both the 1991 World Cup quarter-final in Paris – a savage affair, by universal agreement – and the 1992 Five Nations game when two of their number had got sent off, such had been their brutality. But all this enmity just disappeared in the space of one evening.

Before long, as is the tradition in rugby, jackets and buttons had been ripped, sleeves and pockets torn off, and ties cut in half. Some of that was due to the language barrier: we couldn't really talk, we all reasoned, so let's just have fun. I do remember that my tie was the first to go. Someone just cut it in half, and that was that. Next thing, someone threw some booze over someone else, and soon, sticky, gooey liquid was dripping all over the place. Everyone was completely trashed physically and sartorially, but everyone was really happy.

We all enjoyed each other's company until closing time. We then piled on to our respective coaches which set off down the dual carriageway to the hotels we were staying in. The coaches kept overtaking each other, in a further spirit of jollity. At one point, when the French were going past us, they all turned round to face backwards in their seats, and started pretending to row, which I thought was really funny and inventive. And it showed that they weren't so wasted that they couldn't come up with some really original – and some might say surprising – French humour.

There is often a lot of rubbish talked about the spirit of rugby, which can irk fans of other sports, notably football. Some of it is indeed rubbish but this was a very fine example of how that spirit can and does exist, even in the most difficult of circumstances. The fact was, here were two teams which had, and continue to have, a significant amount of bad blood between them. They found themselves in the same bar, had a lot to drink but didn't argue and didn't fight. In fact, they became friends, if only for one evening, and had a great time together.

During that same tournament, I was the victim of an incident which, were it to occur today, would have guaranteed me front-page headlines. It is a good example of what can go wrong in bars, completely unintentionally. Some of us had gone to a bar and, fairly soon, we noticed a guy nearby, making the internationally recognised 'dick-head' gesture, while shouting out 'You' aggressively in my direction. He was obviously enraged by me for some reason. Well, he was Scottish, so fair enough. Except that he wouldn't stop, even though I was doing my best to ignore his taunts. Eventually, I approached one of the security chaps and said, 'Look, I'm sorry, but could you get rid of this guy, because there's no need for him to be like that. We haven't done anything, but he's just causing trouble.' I saw the security team walk up to the guy and begin to escort him out, seemingly without resistance. I thought, 'Right, that's sorted now,' and turned back round to my group. The next thing I knew, this guy had obviously broken away from the security man because he'd run up to me and 'thwack': he absolutely smacked me from behind, hitting me hard on the side of my head. He could have broken my jaw.

All hell broke loose: I immediately jumped up and tried to hit him back, but others around me were quick off the mark as well and were reining me in, while the bouncer went mad and leaped on this guy and dragged him out before ejecting him forthwith from the bar. 'It's okay, these things happen,' I told him. But I felt it only fair to add, 'Mind you, that shouldn't really have happened, because you were supposed to be keeping hold of him. Anyway, leave it now, it's fine.' They were lucky because the guy could have had a knife; and the unfriendly Scot was lucky because the guards wanted to give him a good hiding.

The incident never came to light but had it taken place today, people would have been filming it in its entirety and posting it on YouTube before you could utter that other oxymoron, 'Scottish Amicable'. The media would also have got wind of it and the headline writers would have had a field day, issuing predictable variants on the 'Pitbull brawls in bar' for the next day's papers. In the meantime, my professional career could have been ended or disrupted – not to mention my reputation irrevocably damaged. I could have tried to say in my defence that people needed to understand the context, blah blah, but the fact is, the public is not interested in these situations. And nor are certain sections of our media.

During the 2011 Rugby World Cup, in New Zealand, the England players got caught out on a couple of occasions in a way that would not have happened before social media existed. Yet nowadays, there is not much room for manoeuvre when a player is confronted with a three-minute video of dwarf-tossing in a state of undress, being the worse for wear, or jumping off the backs of ferries. Even something entirely innocent can go wrong and be misconstrued. One night before a Test abroad, I had gone to bed at a reasonable hour but just couldn't get to sleep. At about two in the morning, I had reached the stage of being angry about my failure to drop off, so I decided to get up and go for a short walk outside. As I got back to the hotel about ten minutes later, the management and a few members of the public were still in the hotel bar. One of them spotted me and called me over, whereupon I explained why I was awake. One of them suggested that a small drink might help, and I let him buy me a half. I drank it, left, and that was the end of that.

If a player did that today, it is very possible that the event would have been recorded, downloaded onto the internet and disseminated worldwide by dawn. Need I say what the social media jury would then make of the incident?

We didn't have the internet, we didn't have camera phones, mobile phones, or instant worldwide dissemination of photos and information. Moreover, the media that did follow us came by and large from the sports pages of the newspapers. These rugby writers were not interested in gossip. They also knew that their livelihood relied on maintaining a decent long-term relationship with players and management. Otherwise, their chances of getting a rugby-related story from us were hugely damaged, in which case, bang went their daily columns. If a journalist wanted to speak to a player or the coach, he just went up to them, either as they came off the field, or informally afterwards, in the bar, in the hotel, or wherever they happened to be. Many were never approached, because they weren't newsworthy. Unsurprisingly, I often was. But I didn't mind, and I often quite enjoyed it, even though it might not have looked that way. I also made a point of never getting particularly friendly with any journalist, because I was aware that, at some point, their job would require them to criticise me. And if I was friends with them, I would feel particularly let down.

Inevitably, players also learnt the hard way what they should and shouldn't say; as did the journalists. I remember the *Daily Mail*'s Peter Jackson once upset Will Carling because of something he'd written. And we all stopped talking to Jackson for about a week. This was not something I necessarily agreed with, but I knew I had to show solidarity with Will.

During this period, I remember walking past Jackson in a restaurant and he said, 'Oh, I suppose you're not speaking to me,' slightly forlornly.

'Look,' I replied, 'I've got no problem speaking to you, personally, because I know it's your job. However, you wouldn't expect me to break a team thing, would you?'

Eventually, the ban was rescinded and that's when he admitted to me that the whole incident had personally got to him a lot. It probably affected his job, too. Meanwhile, although some of his fellow journalists were outwardly sympathetic, secretly they might have been a little bit pleased that there was now one person less who could get a story from under their nose.

Although the non-rugby journalists started to appear in the 1991 World Cup, it is now a given that they are there in significant numbers on every tour and for every tournament. The players try to be careful, as do the management, but they are never fully immune from an unfortunate incident which often gets blown up out of all proportion in sections of the British media. I also think that, within reason, management should stand by its players, and front it out. 'Yes, this happened, but actually, they're extremely fit, they've been working extremely hard, and we said they could go out and have fun. It was good for team bonding [or whatever excuse they choose to give]. You know nothing of their fitness levels, so who are you to say they can't do this? We authorised it, so you'll just have to live with it.' That would silence the critics, because by definition none of them is an insider and therefore none of them truly knows the facts.

I realise I was lucky that, in my day, the press were not all over us like a rash. But I can't apologise for that. There's no point in current players saying 'It's all right for you, because in your day ...' because we're not in my day now, and it's up to them to handle what goes on today. This, to some extent, is why the All Blacks have a Twitter and social media ban on their players. They also refuse to allow cameras in their dressing room. For them, it's all about protecting the players from unnecessary intrusion, as well as preserving that vital All Blacks mystique. And very effective that policy is too.

On the other hand, if the management is too elusive, at least in the case of England, the media start to complain. Some of the questions might be stupid, but journalists feel obliged to ask them.

It's their job to file copy every day, which is actually harder than some people think, and it's the job of the England coach to answer their questions without sounding disparaging. If you actually feed journalists – and I now count myself among them – a few helpful snippets, they will be very grateful. If the management comes across as hostile – even if it doesn't mean to be – they will trot out and possibly twist some old story, it won't help the management, and it won't help the team either. More importantly, the management should not expect any favours if an individual or the team gets into a situation where they would like the media to take a sympathetic line, or at least not to go for the jugular. They may not like the media's job, they may not think it's of any worth, they may think their questions are banal. However, that is the reality.

For the players, they too have to be aware of their relationship with the press, and many of them do get themselves media training in order to be able to handle themselves well with journalists. It is in their contract to make themselves available for the press for a certain number of times during each tour or tournament, so if it's their turn on the rota of who is put up for interview, it's in their interest to do the best they can. It's quite difficult to keep answering 'no comment', when a microphone is placed under your nose, without sounding hostile. Yet it is now part of their job to come across well, to strike the right balance of sounding interesting and not too 'coached' or bland.

In 1991 everyone in the England squad was given a camcorder at the start of the World Cup, so that we could film each other. Nowadays, such is the media's dominant role in sport, that would be asking for trouble, although once again, had YouTube existed then, we would clearly have been a lot more careful with what we filmed. At the time, though, we were like kids with a new toy, really excited, filming absolutely everyone and anyone. We'd be on the team coach, and we'd all be filming . . . everyone else filming.

Bizarre. And very tedious. Anyway, the novelty soon wore off because those early camcorders were like outside broadcast cameras: bulky, heavy, and a complete pain to haul around. I did about two days' worth of filming. Then, along with almost everyone, I just thought 'Fuck this, I can't be bothered,' and stopped my Scorsese impersonation. Rory Underwood was about the only one who continued, but that's just Rory. There was a bit of a technology-geek lurking inside him.

Similarly, mobile phones. When we went out to the 1995 World Cup, BT gave us each not only a new phone (many of us didn't even own a phone by then anyway) but a new, easy-to-remember phone number. This was the epitome of techno-fun for many of us. Except that we soon realised two things: firstly, our small daily allowance didn't cover extortionate international mobile calls, so although it beat having to queue for a pay phone, it cost an arm and a leg to make the briefest call; secondly, hardly anyone back home owned a mobile at that stage, and text messaging was still unusual. So the idea of texting your partner or calling your kids when you were out and about was completely unlikely. And using the phone for taking a photo to share with the folks back home? That option was unimaginable. The result was that these devices were soon consigned to the bottom of our cases (although I happen to know that a few of the squad did hold on to their memorable numbers, so I suppose there was some benefit to that PR effort).

Communicating with home was a lot harder, but this safeguarded players from unwanted publicity. However, I do remember always trying to ensure I had a load of change so that I could call my then wife. In Australia, because of the time difference, I would regularly find myself – as would my team-mates – queuing at 11 o'clock at night for the public phone in the hotel lobby. Sometimes, the guy before me would be taking a long time, so I'd be hopping from one foot to the other, more or less telling him to hurry the fuck up. At least I didn't have kids, so my calls were relatively brief. Only now that I do have children do I realise how difficult it must have been for those among my team-mates who tried to stay in touch with theirs during the weeks when they were away. And one can't expect a child to stay up until 11 p.m. to talk to their dad the other side of the world, or delay going off to school until the team meeting is over. The fact was that the time difference often made speaking to family very awkward.

It also affects players if things at home are not going smoothly, something which is not always factored in. At least with Skype one can see the other person, and that helps communication immensely. In 1995, in South Africa, my wife and I were going through a separation. Trying to speak to her sporadically on the phone was absolutely terrible. I would try to call at a pre-agreed time, or thereabouts. Attempting to call her on a payphone with a line of people waiting behind me was always tricky, but doing so on the room phone was not much better, because there was no guarantee I would be alone at the time that I'd agreed to call. When we were in the process of separating, these logistics became a complete nightmare.

When I toured, even newspapers were either non-existent or 24 hours old, at best. In other words, next to useless. This had its benefits, because half the time we did not know what was being written about us. These days the problem has gone the other way: there is now a surfeit of information available to players, to the extent that it must be extremely difficult for them, if not impossible, to filter out and concentrate on what they are paid to do: play rugby.

How would I have coped with the situation if I were playing today? Would I have managed to keep myself entertained without being permanently plugged in to some electronic device? Would I ever have taken the time to read a book, or get to know my team-mates other than superficially? Would I have found myself in hot water (as I sometimes do today) thanks to social media and ended up getting sent home from a tour in supposed disgrace? All I can say is, I'm just pleased I never had to find out.

11

'What Did You Say Your Name Was Again?'

Something happens when a group of blokes – or a group of women, for that matter – go away for a period of time together. When, in addition, they are away on a sports tour and are representing their country, they are inevitably immersed in a high-intensity environment. Due to the sporting pressures on the field (or pitch, or wherever), the enjoyment of it is also, to some extent, pressured because it somehow has to be fitted in among the training and competing. Relationships between fellow members of the team also become more intense because they are spending more time together than they ever normally would and they rely on each other for company and for sporting success. Team-mates, in effect, become the most important people in their life for the duration of the tour and, as a result, the bond that develops between them is unique.

One result of that bond is that players feel very relaxed in each other's company and soon learn to get on with those with whom they do not have any great affinity. One way in which this easy relationship among team-mates expresses itself is via the assignment of nicknames. In rugby, this is a phenomenon which seems to be more prevalent among players from the Home Nations than those from other countries.

Nicknames can't be 'invented' on purpose, and indeed never were. Moreover, the reasons why one player would end up with one nickname, rather than another, is the stuff of mystery. Indeed, nicknames are strange: they come from positive and negative associations and you can never know which ones will stick, so there is never any point in trying to 'force' a nickname onto someone.

The least inventive ones I ever came across were the ones attributed to the All Blacks during the 1991 World Cup. Perhaps in an attempt to 'big up' the whole event, after the success of the inaugural one in 1987, the organisers tried to personalise the programmes and to inject a bit of humour into what are normally fairly identikit and boring player profiles. I remember looking through the Kiwi ones and, given the players in their squad, I was expecting some original, if not amusing nicknames. Instead, they were all along the lines of Fitzy, Browny, Dowdy, Brookey, Jonesy and so on and so on – clearly a lot of thought had gone into these monikers. Anyone opening the England team programme would have been presented with Pitbull, Strangely Brown, Big and Daft, Serial; just as a random selection.

First things first: my nickname had originally been Cato, named after Inspector Clouseau's Chinese manservant, who is hired to improve his boss's martial arts skills by attacking him at random moments. I can't remember who thought it up, but I was anointed with this nickname during the England Students tour of Romania. I was happy with the reference, even though I'm half Malaysian not Chinese; but it's fine, I know that in the eyes of Westerners, we all look the same.

My Pitbull nickname came along later, courtesy of PC Dooley. Wade, who was immensely popular and respected, was the mastermind behind several of the better nicknames, which is why he didn't mind any of the monikers that he then got stuck with over the years, Big and Daft being one of the more enduring – and possibly endearing.

Wade also nicknamed Jason Leonard 'Golden', some years before Beckham came along. 'Golden' had arisen because Don Rutherford, our then technical director, seemed to revere everything Jason did. One day, during a team meeting, we were watching a tape of one of our games and Don kept pointing out to us, with apparent awe, how well Jason had done. 'This is an example here: look what Jason has seen ... Look what Jason has done here ...' On and on he went till in the end, after the umpteenth piece of praise, Wade just burst out, 'Oh, Mr Fucking Goldenbollocks again!' and we all collapsed laughing, to Rutherford's complete bemusement.

Paul Rendall's nickname, 'Judge', arose because he was always given – and hugely enjoyed – the role of judge in the Tour Court sessions. This nickname conferred on him a certain gravitas, unlike Rob Andrew's, which was 'Squeaky'. Some say this was supposed to relate to the fact that he was squeaky clean, others that it related to ... well, I'm afraid I just can't reveal, but it did involve women. Dean Richards's nickname was a little more prosaic: 'Warren', as in 'Warren ugly bastard'. Jeff Probyn was nicknamed 'Fibbin'. This had nothing to do with being economical with the truth, but arose simply because on one tour, there was a rubbish typo in the tour programme and he was listed as Jeffrey Fibbin – which is quite a departure from his name. So for no other reason than that, and to tease him, we suddenly began to call him 'Fibbin', which he cheerfully accepted.

Someone who was not so enamoured with their nickname – or at least the one he was given at club level – was Rory Underwood. Rory's mother is of Chinese-Malaysian origin, so his club, Leicester, named one of their moves 'The Chink' after him. It was meant in a caring and loving way, as Edna Everage would say. But Rory begged to differ.

'I don't like it, it's not nice.'

'Oh, all right, then, we won't use that,' his club-mates said, and began coming up with other names for this move, eventually settling on '68'.

'Sixty-eight? What's that?' Rory asked, perplexed.

'Sixty-eight? Chicken Chow Mein and rice,' came the reply. Well, he did ask.

A player who always embraced his origins and was happy to take any subsequent piss-take was Simon Halliday. He also seemed to acquire nicknames with the speed that Brangelina acquire children. He must have had a good half dozen over the years I played with him. Hallers was educated at Downside (an august Catholic boarding school), followed by St Benet's Hall, Oxford, a small, male-only college that still operates alongside a community of Benedictine monks. His father was a commander in the army, and Hallers now works in the City. By anyone's reckoning, he is a very proper gent, is Hallers, but he was also very much one of the boys, and always up for being on the receiving end of some stick. Whatever Halliday's nicknames, they all centred on his innate poshness, and he did nothing to dissuade us from using them. Over the course of his international career, his nicknames included 'Farquhar', simply because it sounded like the epitome of a public-school name; 'Cravat', which he never wore but might well have done; 'The Commander,' as a result of his father's army rank; and 'Strangely Brown'. The last of these was one of the many colourful and fictitious pupils' names read out by Rowan Atkinson in a sketch I once saw where he plays a public school master taking the register.

Peter Winterbottom was not always so amused by the nicknames he acquired. Originally nicknamed 'Strawman', on account of his very fair hair, this was, by common consent, neither funny nor original. When I came into the team, the Strawman was simply known as 'Wints' until I just happened to see a documentary on BBC2 about serial killers and what their characteristics were: they tended to live on their own, keep themselves to themselves, and weren't married. One evening, a group of us were discussing this documentary when someone made the connection that Wints also fitted this profile perfectly, because he was single, he lived alone, and wasn't the most gregarious of team-mates. In a flash, he was rechristened 'Serial', a name that he initially laughed at, but in time he found irritating, though I can't think why.

Of course the worst thing you can do, when given a nickname, is show you don't like it, because that's guaranteed to ensure it will then get used more and more. With Wints, you had to watch him, because when he got really angry, just before the outburst, there would be a small twitch of his jaw, as he clenched and unclenched it. It was just a little twitch, but if you saw it . . . well, it was just best to stop what you were saying or doing.

That season, nobody passed up the chance to make an allusion to a supposedly nefarious deed that Serial had allegedly carried out. He was asked about various murders that were reported in the papers, and much besides. This reached its zenith in the hotel in which we stayed before a game against Wales. Following the training session before which the performance of the amended version of 'Under The Boardwalk' (see p. 130) had taken place, we checked in to our hotel. As a way of publicising an event being held there that evening, the hotel had placed a group of life-size mannequins in the foyer. Never one to pass up an opportunity to wind someone up, John Olver grabbed one, put it over his shoulder and marched into the bar. 'Hey, Wints,' he announced in front of everyone, 'I've got one you killed earlier; where do you want me to bury it?' You had to be there, but the sustained howls of laughter that, literally, lasted for a good ten minutes, reduced many to tears – until Wints' jaw was seen to twitch and we knew this was possibly a jest too far.

To be fair, Wints was usually very phlegmatic, and he just got on with things. Which meant, for example, that, although he was single at the time, it didn't bother him when wives and girlfriends were invited to spend 36 hours with their partners on two separate occasions during the 1991 World Cup. The issue of spending time with other halves is a vexed one, and one which applies not just to rugby, but to football, cricket and any other sport where teams tour abroad for any length of time. My own opinion is that, unless you are going away for prolonged periods, like the cricketers do, there should be no need to have partners around, even briefly. Certainly, just days before the World Cup final, in 1991, our partners should not have been anywhere near us. Instead of which, they were invited to join us on our mini-break at the spa hotel in the Midlands. This was doubly inappropriate because they had already been treated to a similar stay only a week or so before, after we'd won our quarter-final game against the French in Paris, when they were all flown over to Jersey for a couple of nights.

At the time, I thought the Jersey trip was fine, because it had been short and the game in Paris had been so brutal that it had been no bad thing to recuperate in the gentle surroundings of a nice hotel. The post-Murrayfield stop-off was definitely unwise and I believe it affected our focus in the run-up to the final, albeit it in a minor way.

There seem to be two schools of thought on this whole mine-field of a subject. There are those who say, 'Oh, it helps the players to have their partners there, because it helps them to feel more comfortable, as if they're at home.' There are then those, such as me, who have the following view: you're not *meant* to be comfortable and it's not a family tour. If you're the sort of person who is so homesick that being away for five or six weeks of your *life* actually affects your play, then I'm sorry but I don't believe you should even be selected. These big tournaments, such as football or rugby World Cups – or Olympic Games, for that matter – occur once every four years. For many players, they will experience them only once in their entire life and they have trained and sacrificed huge amounts in order to be selected, to an extent that few people will ever understand. This is why I don't honestly believe that, in many cases, it's the players who are demanding they see their partners. They want to remain completely focused on what they have trained so long and hard for. I am convinced, in reality, that the pressure to have partners there, if only briefly, comes from the women themselves. Perhaps because they see it as a way of being involved with this big event that has taken over their lives, as well as that of their partners. Perhaps because they also see it as a way of being thanked for putting up with the pressures they undoubtedly come under when their husband or boyfriend is being a miserable and selfish obsessive for months on end. However, with Skype and other means of communication, nowadays it's very possible to stay in close touch, not only with partners but with children, in a way that was not possible in the past. It should not therefore be necessary for couples to be reunited for a few days or – God forbid – the entire tournament.

I had this view in 1991 and I still hold it today: wives and girlfriends have no need to be at rugby tours or tournaments. A couple of nights are fine, depending on the timing of the trip, but nothing more. If they want to come out, watch the games and stay at a separate venue that too is fine. What is not, is for them to stay in the same hotel because it detracts from the total commitment and focus required during highly intense and competitive tournaments or tours. This view got me into trouble with my first wife, when the RFU sent round a questionnaire to the players in 1990-91, in advance of the World Cup. The idea, I presume, was to assess our mindset and our commitment to different elements of our lives. One question read: 'On a scale of 1 to 5, state the importance of rugby in your life.' Remember that we were amateurs then and had careers outside the sport. Anyway, I put 5; rugby was definitely the most important thing in my life. Somehow, this questionnaire fell into my wife's hands. 'You might at least have had the fucking decency to lie! I mean, it wouldn't have mattered if you had, would it?' Well, maybe, but why not tell the truth?

My all-consuming commitment to rugby at the expense of trying to maintain a relationship was one of the reasons why, in 1995, my then wife and I were in the process of separating, just as the World Cup in South Africa got under way. As with the previous tournament, the RFU had offered to fly the partners over for a brief visit after we knocked Australia out at the quarter-final stage. Most of them duly came out, watched a game, stayed for the Saturday and Sunday nights and then flew home. It was a long way to come out for such a short period of time, which was why I left it up to my wife to decide if she wanted to make the journey. As it turned out, she did, and it was a mistake, for all sorts of reasons that are irrelevant for the purposes of this book. But not surprisingly, it was awful for her, and it certainly did nothing for my peace of mind.

The other problem that arises when partners are put into the already fraught atmosphere of a tournament is that cliques often occur because some of the women don't get on. I have been told by several well-placed sources that this apparently happened on the now-infamous 2006 football World Cup in Germany when the presence of wives and girlfriends turned into a media circus, with newspapers claiming that factions were formed, allegedly between the Scousers and the Mancunians. The tabloid press at that tournament spawned the acronym WAGs so successfully that it has gone on to become a fully fledged word in the *OED*. It is a good illustration of how irrelevant and possibly harmful the partner's presence was and it led to a rethink for future tournaments.

There is no doubt though that if a player knows his partner does not get on with another, this puts him in a difficult position relative to his team-mate. Does he side with her or with his team-mate, on whom he depends for the good functioning of the team? It's a no-win situation and therefore never one which should arise during a tournament. Disagreements between partners are extraneous factors that should have nothing to do with a player, yet they inevitably do, especially if they are all away together.

Fortunately, when I was playing, time with our partners was always limited to a couple of nights but I know that arguments or disagreements between them did occur. Occasionally, I would be told about a particular incident and it would always be of the 'and she said this, then she said that' variety. I would respond in the same way: 'I don't care. I don't want to know. It's got nothing to do with me.' Sometimes, I would add for good measure: 'Anyway, I don't like either of them!' which always put an end to the discussion.

The fact was that, in those days, a lot of rugby players' partners were strong characters. And when you have strong characters, you have the potential for things to become combustible, which they were anyway because partners would always come out at a crucial stage of a huge tournament. Many partners had significant jobs. Rob Andrew's wife was a pharmacist. My then wife, was (and still is) a doctor. Sharon Dooley was, like her husband, a PC. Susie Ackford, Paul's wife, was a very successful City head-hunter. So they were all (and are) sharp, intelligent, fiercely independent women, who were strong characters, which didn't always make for a serene atmosphere when they got together. And no, the final reason why I didn't see the point in partners joining us on tour was not because my team-mates and I were intent on being unfaithful. Again, if readers are able to cast their minds back to the amateur days when I was playing, to misquote Caroline Aherne's Mrs Merton, a woman would never be asked, 'And what exactly attracted you to millionaire Mr Rugby Player?' As a result, surprising though it may seem, we didn't have rugby groupies; that is, women who followed us around in the way they seem to follow today's players or other sportsmen, notably footballers or tennis players. Plus, rugby is not, and certainly wasn't then, a big enough sport in countries like Australia, where it is the fourth sport, so our tours there did not attract much attention outside the specialist media.

That said, on the notorious 1984 England tour to South Africa, when the old-style England appeared to be on a four-week beer bender, the team was treated to one of several evenings out. The urban myth of every boys' tour, sporting, stag or otherwise, is that a bus full of nurses turns up at wherever the party happens to be drinking. I don't know if there is a women's equivalent, and if there is, what it might be – possibly a truckload of firemen? Whatever – this bus is a myth for most, save for the one time it did actually turn up to the hotel where the team was staying in Durban. As the team went in to a function laid on to welcome them, a large group of very attractive young nurses appeared. Who said rugby players never scored?

Personally, my lack of action on tours was not down to any moral superiority, although I was in a relationship for several of the years in which I was an international and simply wasn't look- ing for anything beyond that. But even if I had been, it came down to the fact that some – well, several – of my team-mates were more blessed in the looks department than me. To be quite brutal, if a girl had a choice between me, with my various teeth missing (as I had in those days) and, say, Jeremy Guscott (or whoever), realistically, she was not likely to pick me. She just wasn't. I had never been like some of my pals from university who would confidently go, 'Ah, she fancies me,' when a girl looked their way. They would automatically make that assumption. In my case, a girl would have to come up and hit me with a shovel and say, 'No, please, really, I do,' because my default assumption was simply to think, 'Why are you bothering?' And now that I was surrounded by the Carlings of this world, that assumption remained. Consequently, it was not that I didn't have any success, it was that I never courted it. If you don't try, you can't fail.

When it came to my team-mates, some were single, and some were more pre-disposed than me to playing away. In the case of the latter, they had to calculate what the risk was of their partner getting to hear of their indiscretion. Back then, with no camera phones, social media or scandal journalists around – the journalists who were there were from the sporting press – the risks were fairly small. In addition, the women themselves weren't bothered about selling their stories to the papers back in Britain. That is clearly not the case today, as many kiss-and-tell stories clearly prove.

As a result, today's players are, or should be, much more aware of the potential for gossip, and the good and bad it can do to them. Players therefore have to weigh up whether a woman might possibly go to the papers or put their relationship, however casual, out on Twitter before they decide to take things any further. None of these considerations was ever on our minds whenever and wherever we met women, and for that I and, I am sure, many of my team-mates are extremely thankful. Mind you, perhaps we should just have done what the French did and have their mistresses go to the games, which I'm told they regularly did. By all accounts, this was accepted and no one batted an eyelid.

My team-mates weren't saints, but neither were they monks; the truth lay somewhere in between. One of the reasons was that, first of all, you had to meet a woman who was happy to have a one-night stand, and not that many were – or not with us, anyway. Equally important was the fact that we shared rooms. So you also had to find a woman who didn't mind your room-mate being around or coming back half way through any action. Strangely, not many were up for that. You could always try and get a room to yourself, but that depended on one being available at short notice and you not getting seen by one of your team-mates, as they would invariably tell the whole tour party.

On our tour of Argentina in 1990, Chris Oti and Victor Ubogu, jointly the coolest dudes on tour (not much competition, to be fair), came back to the hotel in a highly excitable state. 'We've found this great bar; it's full of great-looking women and they're really friendly.' We couldn't pass up an opportunity like this and a group outing was duly fixed for the following evening. We walked into quite a small room and there was a small bar situated in the corner, like one of those home bars some people liked to construct in their homes circa 1973. There were a few men in the room and about 20 admittedly gorgeous women. Each one was seated at a table and sipping a drink.

'Victor, this is a brothel, you idiot!' I exclaimed.

'No it's not, they're really friendly!' he protested.

'Yes, precisely.'

Victor conceded the point after a brief conversation with a couple of the girls, during which they offered him something called the 'bang bang special'.

In some hotels, our physio would do the treatments in his room. Consequently, he would be given a larger room so that he would have enough room to set up his treatment bed. This must have been a bit of a pain for him because he always had people in

245

there. In other hotels, the physio had a separate room for treatment and that room, conveniently, was free at night. When that happened, a player would go off there with his newfound 'girlfriend' as fast as he could persuade her to get down to business; it was very much a case of first come, first served.

In any event, the physio's room did come in handy for me when one of my fellow forwards once came back to our room at a ridiculous hour in the morning with a woman and told me to get out.

'Come on, I've got this girl . . .'

'No! Look, I won't watch, I'll just go to sleep.'

'No, no, no, she won't do it if you're in there.'

'No! It's nearly four o'clock.'

'No, come on, come on.'

'Look, use the physio's room.'

In the end, he went away only to return five minutes later. 'I can't find the key to the physio's room so come on now,' he announced. 'You're going.' Faced with my ongoing refusal, he dragged all the bed covers off me and said, 'OUT . . .'

Up I got and began to wander around the hotel. My initial thought was to bang on manager Geoff Cooke's door and tell him I had nowhere to sleep. I thought he might not be too pleased, not just with being woken, but also with the reason for the disturbance, so I thought better of it. I padded down to reception but no one was there. However, I saw the key to the physio's room and, luckily, I found the room was empty, so I slept on the physio's bench for the remaining few hours before breakfast.

The same player also saw action on a different Australian tour when a very good-looking, thirty-something divorcee took a shine to him and flew all over the country, following him on each leg of the tour. At the final stop, she again turned up, and naturally both were intent on making every spare second of their 'relationship' count. This meant that his room-mate had to clear out of the room for several hours that evening, so he walked into the bar and announced, 'X has got that woman up there.' Meanwhile, the woman turned out to be into bondage, and I suppose it would have been rude for Mr X not play along. Eventually, his room-mate, along with a few others, decided he'd had enough of waiting. 'Right, I've had enough of this – let's go up there, so we can watch.' Up they went. Meanwhile, back in the room, the woman was tied up and spreadeagled. She then heard a load of guys trying to break down the door, so not surprisingly she panicked.

'Untie me, untie me!' she pleaded.

'I'm trying, for God's sake, but stop struggling, the knots are getting tighter,' replied the player, fumbling at the increasingly tight knots. 'I can't fucking-well untie you! Stop moving! You're making it worse!' He had literally just untied the last knot when the door gave way, his team-mates burst into the room, and the woman dived under the bedclothes. The player, meanwhile, was helpless with laughter.

Not all my own room-mates demanded privacy, including one in particular who shall remain nameless because he was married at the time. In total, I must have roomed with him three or four times. Each time, he'd been super-fast about getting to the room before me. And each time, when I walked in, he'd already be on the phone, saying, '. . . and what services does she offer? . . . And she'd better be good looking.' I can only assume he must have pounced on the Yellow Pages equivalent as soon as he'd got into the room so that he could immediately get on the phone to the local escort agency.

Equally brazenly, he once brought a woman back to the room. I was in bed trying to get to sleep, but I could hear her saying, 'I know there's someone else in the room.'

'It's okay, he's asleep,' he tried to reassure her.

'No, no, I don't think we should do this,' she said.

'No, look, it's fine, he's asleep.' I carried on feigning sleep, and she agreed to get it on with my room-mate, so they clambered into bed and got going. All was going to plan, then at one point I turned over, caught his eye in the dimly lit room, and he started to giggle. Not surprisingly, his companion noticed.

'What are you laughing at?' she asked.

'No, nothing,' he replied, trying to simulate a state of bliss that might account for his happiness. Things hotted up, she got caught up in the action once more, she started to scratch his back, and he responded with suitable groans of pleasure, as if he was enjoying the pain. It was all getting very steamy, when suddenly I couldn't hold it in any longer: I burst out laughing. I couldn't stop. She immediately turned towards me in a fury.

'You said he was asleep!' she screamed, before starting to hit my room-mate. I'm afraid to say we were both helpless with laughter by this stage. Meanwhile, she gathered up her clothes and stormed off into the night, never to be seen again. Not our finest response, I grant you.

One woman who was definitely keen on rugby players was a very nice woman we met in the hotel bar in Paihia, a beach resort in the north of New Zealand's North Island. At one stage in the evening, long after I had gone to bed, she asked a group of guys if they'd be up for a session. I must stress that the offer very much came from her. Sensing that this sort of opportunity didn't exactly present itself every day, they all duly followed her back to one of the rooms. There were seven of them, just like the dwarves in *Snow White*. I'm told a good time was had by all, at the end of which one of the guys said to her, 'I bet that's the most you've ever had at one time.'

'Ah no, mate,' she replied, 'I had nine of the Brisbane Broncos!'

It was only when I was told the story that I understood why one of the Lions players had been running down the team corridor at four in the morning, banging on the players' doors, shouting, 'We need three more for the record!' As a postscript to the story, it is worth mentioning that the young woman was back in the hotel bar the following night, socialising with the squad as if nothing had happened. Had she been a man, and the roles reversed, there would be no comments or judgements made, save for most men thinking, 'You lucky bastard.' Indeed, a man would probably have been holding court about the escapade. My opinion is: good for her – no double standards.

My own forays into such activity were fewer and further between but the 1989 Lions tour to Australia did produce two memorable moments. I was single at the time but, as I have already explained, although that might have been a necessary condition for some action, it was certainly not a sufficient one. Nevertheless in a Brisbane bar one night I got on famously with a girl and she agreed to come back to the hotel with me. She might have been 'going ugly early' but that made no difference to me. My room-mate was out, which was good, as the girl immediately noticed that the room had two beds. I thought he would be out till the early hours, as that had been the case hitherto, so the girl and I decided to have a shower together, as a preliminary to the main event. We were in the shower, having fun, when in walked my room-mate holding a kettle.

'Oh, hello, Brian,' he said, cheerfully while he started to fill it up in the sink.

'Fuck off!' I replied, in disbelief.

'Oh, hello, you,' he politely said to the girl, as if this was the most natural thing in the world to be calmly filling a kettle while two naked people got it on in the shower. To be fair to her, she was pretty friendly back, and, rather than running off, screaming 'Oh, my God,' she responded with an equally cheerful 'Oh, hello!'

My room-mate carried on calmly filling the kettle while chatting to us.

'FUCK OFF!' I had to say before long, not to put too fine a point on it, since he clearly didn't get the message.

'No, it's okay, I don't mind.'

'Yeah, but . . . BUT!!'

'Okay, well, I'm going to go to bed,' he announced nonchalantly.

'What are we going to do now?' I asked the woman.

'Well,' she said, 'I guess we'll just have to be quiet then,' after which she stayed the night. She also whispered at one point during sex, 'Listen, if you put it up my arse, you'll have to be gentle – I don't want to scream.'

My lucky streak, if you can call two occasions lucky, continued when I was in The Rocks pub in Sydney one evening and met up with two girls who had read Law in the year below me at Nottingham. As a result, I sort of knew them and, as is the way when one is abroad and meets a vague acquaintance, I chatted to them for far longer than I ever had done back home. The one thing we had in common suddenly became a unique bond and before the evening was out we had all got blind drunk. They were renting a flat in Manly and I ended up in a taxi with both of them going back to their place. It was the only time two women have ever, well, not exactly fought over me, but both expressed a vague interest simultaneously. To be honest I had no idea what to do as I hadn't the courage to suggest we all took part, and any choice might have caused offence. Fortunately the conundrum solved itself as one of the girls was sick in the taxi on the way home and more or less passed out. In any event, the next morning, I woke up in the other girl's room and suddenly said, 'What time is it?' 'Seven-thirty,' the girl said, bleary-eyed. 'Shit, I've got a team meeting in an hour!' Like in a scene from a movie, I literally got dressed as I ran out the door – gallant, I know – and ran all the way down to the Manly ferry, getting back to the hotel just in time to try and stroll through the door of the meeting room as if nothing had happened. I didn't look as fresh as a daisy but nobody guessed what had happened – not surprising really with my track record.

Appendix A

Rugby Song lyrics

Words to 'Four And Twenty Virgins'

> Four and twenty virgins came down from Inverness,
> And when the ball was over there were four and twenty
> > less.
> Singing, 'Balls to you father, backs against the wall,
> If you don't get shagged on Saturday night you'll never get
> > shagged at all.'
>
> Little Tommy, he was there, but he was only eight,
> He could not woo the women so he had to masturbate.
> Singing, 'Balls to your father, backs against the wall ...'
>
> Farmer Giles he was there, his scythe was in his hand,
> And every time he swung around, he circumcised the band.
> Screaming, 'Balls to your father ...'
>
> The Bride was in the parlour explaining to the groom,
> That the vagina not the rectum is the entrance to the womb.
> Singing, 'Balls to your father ...'
>
> There was shagging in the hallways, shagging on the stairs,
> You could not hear the music for the swish of pubic hair.

Singing, 'Balls to your father ...'

The village policeman he was there, a credit to the force
They caught him in the stable block tossing off a horse.
Singing, 'Balls to your partner ...'

The village cripple, he was there, he wasn't up to much,
So they laid the bugger on his back and fucked him with
    his crutch.
Singing, 'Balls to your father ...'

The village idiot he was there, sitting on a pole,
Pulling his foreskin over his head and whistling through
    the hole.
Singing, 'Balls to your father ...'

And when the ball was over, everyone confessed,
They'd all enjoyed the dancing but the shagging was a
    mess.
Singing, 'Balls to you father, backs against the wall,
If you don't get shagged on Saturday night you'll never get
    shagged at all.'

Verses to 'The Sexual Life Of The Camel'

These are the traditional verses:

    The sexual life of the ostrich is hard to understand,
    At the height of the mating season,
    It buries its head in the sand.
    And if another ostrich finds it,
    Standing there with its ass in the air,

Does it have the urge to grind,
Or doesn't it bloody-well care?
  Chorus
Singin' bum titty titty, bum titty titty titty, titty bum
Bum titty, bum titty, yea.
Bum titty titty, bum titty titty bum titty bum
The assholes are here to stay

In the process of civilisation,
From anthropoid ape down to man,
It is generally held that the navy,
Has buggered whatever it can.
Yet recent extensive researches,
By Darwin and Huxley and Hall,
Have conclusively proven that the hedgehog,
Cannot be buggered at all.
  Chorus

We therefore believe our conclusion,
Is incontrovertibly shown,
That comparative safety on shipboard,
Is enjoyed by the hedgehog alone.
  Chorus

Why haven't they done it at Spithead,
As they have at Harvard and Yale,
And also at Oxford and Cambridge,
By shaving the spines off the tail?
  Chorus

The sexual life of the bullfrog
Is hard to comprehend.

254

Appendix A

At the height of the mating season
He tries to bugger his friend.
But his friend's posterior orifice
Is clogged up with mud and with slime,
Which accounts for the eyes of the bullfrog,
And why he goes 'bleargh' all the time.
  Chorus

These are some additional non-traditional verses:

I went to the church on Sunday,
The vicar asked me to pick a hymn,
So I turned to the congregation and said,
'I'll have him and him and him.'
  Chorus

I wanted to sell my motorcar,
So I took it to Brocklehurst,
The salesman offered me his bottom price,
But I said, 'No, let's sell the car first.'
  Chorus

My name is Basil,
My boyfriend's name is Bond,
When we go out together
We're known as Basildon Bond.
  Chorus

'If I Were The Marrying Kind'

CHORUS:
If I were the marrying kind,

Which thank the Lord I'm not sir,
The kind of man that I would be . . .

. . . WOULD BE A RUGBY FULLBACK.
I'd find touch, she'd find touch,
We'd both find touch together,
We'd be all right in the middle of the night,
Finding touch together.

. . . WOULD BE A RUGBY HOOKER.
I'd strike hard, she'd strike hard,
We'd both strike hard together,
We'd be all right in the middle of the night,
Striking hard together.

. . . WOULD BE AN INSIDE CENTRE.
I'd pass it out, she'd pass it out,
We'd both pass it out together,
We'd be all right in the middle of the night,
Passing it out together.

. . . WOULD BE A RUGBY REFEREE.
I'd fuck up, she'd fuck up,
We'd both fuck up together,
We'd be all right in the middle of the night,
Fucking up together.

. . . WOULD BE A RUGBY PROP.
I'd support a hooker, she'd support a hooker,
We'd both support a hooker together,
We'd be all right in the middle of the night,
Supporting a hooker together.

... WOULD BE A RUGBY FLY-HALF.
I'd whip it out, she'd whip it out,
We'd both whip it out together,
We'd be all right in the middle of the night,
Whipping it out together.

... WOULD BE A RUGBY SCRUM-HALF.
I'd put it in, she'd put it in,
We'd both put it in together,
We'd be all right in the middle of the night,
Putting it in together.

... WOULD BE A RUGBY SECOND ROW.
I'd push hard, she'd push hard,
We'd both push hard together,
We'd be all right in the middle of the night,
Pushing hard together.

... WOULD BE A RUGBY NUMBER EIGHT MAN.
I'd sniff ass, she'd sniff ass,
We'd both sniff ass together,
We'd be all right in the middle of the night,
Sniffing ass together.

... WOULD BE A RUGBY WING-FORWARD.
I'd come early, she'd come early,
We'd both come early together,
We'd be all right in the middle of the night,
Cumming early together.

... WOULD BE A RUGBY WING.
I'd go hard, she'd go hard,

We'd both go hard together,
We'd be all right in the middle of the night,
Going hard together.

'I Love My Wife'

I love my wife;
I love her truly;
I love the hole
She pisses through.
I love her tits-tittly-tits-tittly-tits
And her nut brown arse hole.
I would eat her shit,
Chomp, chomp, gobble, gobble
With a rusty spoon,
With a rusty spoon.

'I Used To Work In Chicago'

CHORUS:
I used to work in Chicago
In a department store.
I used to work in Chicago
I did but I don't any more.

A woman came in and asked for a dress,
I asked her what dress she adored,
A jumper she said, so jump her I did,
I don't work there any more.
    Chorus

A woman came in and asked for a card,

I asked her what card she adored,
A poker she said, so poke her I did,
I don't work there any more.
 Chorus

A woman came in and asked for a dog,
I asked her what dog she adored,
A cocker she said, so cock her I did,
I don't work there any more.
 Chorus

A woman came in and asked for some shoes,
I asked her what shoes she adored,
A slipper she said, so slip her I did,
I don't work there any more.
 Chorus

A woman came in and asked for a cake,
I asked her what cake she adored,
A layer she said, so lay her I did,
I don't work there any more.
 Chorus

A woman came in and asked for a ball,
I asked her what ball she adored,
A rubber she said, so rub her I did,
I don't work there any more.
 Chorus

A woman came in and asked for some booze,
I asked her what booze she adored,
Liquor she said, so lick her I did,

I don't work there any more.
    Chorus

A woman came in and asked for hardware,
I asked her what hardware she adored,
A screw she said, so screw her I did,
I don't work there any more.
    Chorus

A woman came in and asked for a girdle,
I asked her what girdle she adored,
'Rubber!' she said, and rub her I did,
I don't work there any more.
    Chorus

A woman came in and asked for a pet,
I asked her what pet she adored,
'A pussy!' she said, I took the hint,
I don't work there any more.
    Chorus

A woman came in and asked for a hat,
I asked her what hat she adored,
'Felt!' she said, so felt her I did,
I don't work there any more.
    Chorus

A woman came in and asked for a ticket,
I asked her what ticket she adored,
'Bangor!' she said, so bang her I did,
I don't work there any more.
    Chorus

A woman came in and asked for a dairy,
I asked her what dairy she adored,
'Cream!' she said, so cream her I did,
I don't work there any more.
    Chorus

'Let Me Call You Sweetheart'

(to the tune of 'Let Me Call You Sweetheart')

Let me call you sweetheart,
I'm in love with you.
Let me stick my nasal organ up your flue,
A bit of your clitoris
Is much better than a screw,
So let me call you sweetheart,
I'm in love with you.

'Masturbation'

(to the tune of 'Funiculi Funicular')

Last night, I contemplated masturbation,
It did me good, I knew it would.
Tonight, I will repeat the operation
'Tis my desire, to pull my wire.

You should have seen me on the short strokes,
It felt so grand, to use my hand.
You should have seen me on the long strokes,
It felt so neat, to use my feet.

Slam it, ram it, throw it on the floor,
Lick it, flick it, slam in the door.
Some people think that sexual intercourse is grand
But for personal satisfaction I would rather use my hand.

'Sit On My Face'

(to the tune of 'Red River Valley')

Oh sit on my face and tell me that you love me.
I'll sit on your face and say I love you truly.
I love to hear you oralise,
When you're between my thighs,
You blow me away.

Sit on my face and let my lips embrace you.
I'll sit on your face until you answer truly.
Life will be fine when we're both 69,
And we can sit on our faces in all kinds of places,
And wait till we're all blown away.

Appendix A

'The Good Ship Venus' – the full version

CHORUS:
There was frigging on the rigging;
Wanking on the planking,
Tossing on the crossing,
There was fuck all else to do.

T'was on the good ship Venus,
By God you should have seen us,
The figurehead was a whore in bed
And the mast the captain's penis.
   Chorus

The captain of this lugger,
He was a dirty bugger,
He wasn't fit to shove shit
From one place to another.
   Chorus

The captain's wife was Mabel.
Whenever she was able,
She'd fornicate the second mate
Upon the galley table.
   Chorus

The ship's cook's name was Freeman,
My God was he a demon,
He fed the crew on menstrual stew
And hymens fried in semen.
   Chorus

The captain had a daughter,
Who fell into the water,
We heard her squeal and knew an eel
Had found her sexual quarter.
    Chorus

The first mate's name was Carter,
By God he was a farter,
When the high winds would cease
They'd use Carter to start her.
    Chorus

The second mate's name was Andy,
His balls were long and bandy,
We filled his arse with molten brass
For wanking in the brandy.
    Chorus

The cabin boy was Kipper,
A dirty little nipper,
He stuffed his arse with broken glass
To circumcise the skipper.
    Chorus

The captain's name was Morgan,
By Christ he was a gorgon!
Ten times a day sweet tunes he'd play.
On his productive organ.
    Chorus

The captain's daughter Mabel,
They laid her on a table!
And all the crew would come and screw
As oft as they were able.
Chorus

T'was on a Chinese station,
We caused a great sensation.
We sunk a junk in a sea of spunk
By mutual masturbation.
Chorus

The captain's daughter Mary,
Had never lost her cherry.
The men grew bold and offered gold
And now there's no more Virgin Mary.
Chorus

The ship's dog's name was Rover,
The whole crew had him over,
We ground that faithful hound
From Singapore to Dover.
Chorus

The engineer was McTavish
And young girls he did ravish,
His missing dick's at Istanbul
He was a trifle lavish.
Chorus

So now we end this serial,
Through sheer lack of material.
I wish you luck and freedom from
Diseases venereal.
    Chorus

'*Fisherman, Fisherman, Home From The Sea*'

CHORUS:
Singing ho tiddly ho
Shit or bust!
Never let your bollocks dangle in the dust!

'Good morning Mister Fisherman.'
'Good morning, Sir,' said he.
'Have you a lobster you can sell to me?'
    Chorus

'Yes, Sir,' said the Fisherman.
'I have two;
The biggest of the bastards I'll sell to you.'
    Chorus

I took the lobster home
And I couldn't find a dish;
So I used the pot where the missus has a piss.
    Chorus

In the middle of the night
The wife got out of bed;
She piddled in the pot on the lobster's head.
    Chorus

The missus gave a giggle
Then she gave a grunt;
A dirty big lobster hanging from her cunt.
 Chorus

The wife grabbed the shovel
And I grabbed the broom;
We chased that lobster round the room.
 Chorus

We hit it on the head,
We hit in on the side;
We hit it till the bloody lobster died.
 Chorus

The moral of this story
The moral, it is this:
Always have a look-see before you have a piss.
 Chorus

'*The Wild Rover*'

(to the tune of 'Wild Rover')

CHORUS:
And it's no nay never, no nay never no more
Will I play the wild rover, no never, no more.

I've been a wild rover for many a year
And I spent all my money on whisky and beer
But now I'm returning with gold in great store
And I swear I will play the wild rover no more.
 Chorus

I went to an ale-house I used to frequent
And I told the landlady my money was spent
I asked her for credit, she answered me, 'Nay
It's custom like yours I can get any day.'
    Chorus

I took from my pocket sovereigns so bright
That the landlady's eyes opened wide with delight,
She said she had whisky and beer of the best
And the words that she spoke were only in jest.
    Chorus

I'll go to my parents, confess what I've done
And ask them to pardon their prodigal son,
And when they forgive me as oft-times as before
Then I swear I will play the wild rover no more.
    Chorus

Appendix B

What makes a great tour?

If I had unfettered discretion over its destination and composition, this is how I would put together a great tour:

1. Go to a warm country – nothing dampens the spirit, literally, than endless rain.

2. Make sure the playing schedule is reasonable, both regarding the level of opposition and the amount of travel. You won't enjoy getting thrashed or thrashing, and travel is irritating when you have to go unnecessarily long distances.

3. The first rule on selecting a tour party: No cunts; however talented.

4. Put together a tour handbook for everyone. It should have all the logistical details, flights, times, hotels, contact details and so on, but also tour rules. I would also add tour songs and games, plus their rules (see Chapter 2).

5. Have some form of dress, even if it's just a tie or a top that is specific to that tour. If you can afford full formal and informal dress then do so. The items will be mementos of

the tour when it ends, and players will look back fondly to this or that piece of tour regalia. Doing this also means that at least you will give some uniformity to the tour party.

6. Make players share rooms and change room-mates at each stop. Players might prefer single rooms but that allows some to hide away and others to be inadvertently forgotten. Changing room-mates regularly ensures players get to know others who are not their friends. It's not unusual for players who, before the tour, thought they did not like a particular team-mate, only to see another side of that person on tour and to become friends. This helps the tour on and off the field. Even if particular players don't get on, it teaches them tolerance, and that is always needed on longer tours and those which take place under pressure.

7. Do not just leave a group of players to their own devices. If so, they will gather into familiar groups because they will naturally feel more comfortable. This makes players who do not have many club or international team-mates feel isolated, and even when they are around these other groups, they will always feel peripheral. To counter that, the most successful methods I've experienced are:

    a. Divide the squad into mini-teams.
    b. Make sure you have one senior player in each group who acts as a leader and a conduit for comments which the leaders then take to what should be regular meetings with management. Players sometimes have good points to make but don't feel able, for a variety of reasons, to voice them. By creating mini-teams, this allows all players to feel they have some input into what happens to

them on tour. It is also an effective way of disarming possible problems that arise if concerns are not heard and addressed.

c. Ensure there are players from different positions in each group, and mix the personalities; the latter is particularly important.

d. Organise training exercises that pit the teams against each other to create team spirit.

e. Though players can now happily sit and read Kindles or play endless games on their devices, arrange regular non-specific sporting competitions. Shooting, golf, whatever, it doesn't matter what the activity is; what matters is the competitive element and the ensuing bonding.

f. Set up regular events, such as general knowledge, sporting, movie or music quizzes; poker tables; even games like charades, Articulate and Trivial Pursuit. The competitive nature of players will be revealed and one or two surprising statisticians and general knowledge titans will emerge. This is not juvenile; it stops players being isolated or forming their own cabals. Most of all, it is bloody good fun.

g. Have a Tour Court – they are very amusing and a good way of subliminally reinforcing discipline. See Chapter 3 for how to do this.

8. Try to plan trips that make players see a bit of the country or area they are touring to. This may sound simplistic, but all too often players see only airports, hotels, motorways and small areas of a town or city near to their hotel.

9. Ban all digital devices from meals and meetings, no matter how much protest this provokes. Players have enough time

to call, text and Skype their mates outside these times; they should be communal occasions.

10. Last – and a bit contentious – for international or high pro-file teams on tour or at tournaments, I would ban Facebook and Twitter. It is only for a limited amount of time, and the advantages of supporter interaction are outweighed by the trouble and stress caused by stray remarks, abusive posts/tweets and so on.

Appendix C

My Top Tour XV

The following team is picked solely on the basis of the respective players' qualities as a tourist; it has nothing to do with their rugby talent. It is also picked with balance in mind, as I wouldn't want to tour with 15 maniacs; well, not unless I wanted to bear the ever-present risk of arrest, injury or scandal. Inevitably, it is England-centric because I toured more often with England players and know them better. No player was considered if he didn't have the requisite sense of humour, whether overt or covert, or the ability to take and give in equal measure – for me a defining characteristic of what makes a good tourist.

Some of the names might surprise readers and won't be familiar, but they are worth looking up because they are extraordinary men, even if they didn't hit the heights of international stardom.

There are literally scores of other players who could have made the team and who were brilliant tourists. I rewrote the team numerous times but could pick only 15 men; so, to those who did not make the line-up, I apologise for their omission.

15: Marcus Rose – A non-drinker with a fantastically rounded mind and dry wit, and a super orator.

14: Mark Bailey – Listed his hobbies in the England Students tour to Japan as: Medieval Suffolk villages, and Del Shannon. A former Cambridge don and now High Master of St Paul's School. The best character witness ever to take the stand, he had the rare ability to make testimony fun, plausible but eventually damning.

13: Brendan Mullin – An Irish scholar and an exceptionally bright and interesting man; little more needs to be said. Also the man who gave me the considerable comfort that my failure to finish James Joyce's *Ulysses* was not down to my dullness but because it is, in fact, 'total bollocks'.

12: Fran Clough – A perpetually combative character who wouldn't shrink from what needed to be said. The nemesis of Mark Bailey, he once hammered on the toilet cubicle which Bailey was occupying, saying, 'How fucking long are you going to be in there? What are you doing, committing your thoughts to paper?'

11: Rory Underwood – Teetotal and an immensely likeable man who would do all the quiet organising work in the background and be happy to do so; a rare but essential breed.

10: Micky Quinn – Another non-drinker, and thank God he was because God knows what he would have been like when inebriated. Possessed of an almost preternatural sense of infectious optimism and fun, Quinny would make the dark times less dark and keep them short.

9: Robert Jones – Rooming with Rob was never, for one second, anything other than remarkable – that's all I want to/can say.

1: Jason Leonard – The untidiest room-mate I ever encountered but another man with a contagiously bright outlook – oh, and he could probably outdrink most of the players on the planet.

2: Me – An uneven, cynical and sometimes over-intense character – I get in because it's my touring team, and nobody can do
anything about it.

3: Stuart Evans – A quiet and simple lad, and that is no criticism,
who would often see things as they were and not as they were
dressed up to be. Few comments came from Stuart but they were
usually good when they did. When asked what he thought about
the scenery on a coach trip in Brazil, his pithy reply was, 'I don't
know; I can't see it for all these fucking mountains.'

4: Wade Dooley – You have to have someone who is happy to take
a lot of stick without getting upset about it, and Wade did just
that. However, he was also unexpectedly sharp in retort and was
the author of most of the good nicknames that stuck to England
players of his time. Plus, you have to have someone who could
keep up with Jason Leonard's drinking.

5: Martin Bayfield – A natural wit with the right touch of self-
deprecation; a great raconteur and a counter to the lingering
menace of his former team and police colleague in the second
row – a sort of community touring officer.

6: Finlay Calder – We needed a conscience and someone who
would say the hard things that sometimes need to be said on tour.
Finlay is the most direct and upright man I know and, as an aside,
he is my only Scottish friend.

7: Peter Winterbottom – A hard man in every sense: player,
drinker, banter-merchant, and enormously loyal team-mate.

8: Dean Richards – An evil Weights and Measures officer in Tour
Courts, possessing of an unusual sense of humour and an almost
photographic memory when it comes to playing cards.

Acknowledgements

To all the players who made my rugby career fulfilling and fun and, actually, even those who didn't.